W0259636

PARTITION

PARTITION
THE LONG SHADOW

Edited by

Urvashi Butalia

HEINRICH
BÖLL
STIFTUNG
INDIA

PENGUIN
VIKING
An imprint of Penguin Random House

ZUBAAN
128 B, 1st Floor, Shahpur Jat, New Delhi 110 004, India
in collaboration with

VIKING

USA | Canada | UK | Ireland | Australia
New Zealand | India | South Africa | China | Singapore

Viking is part of the Penguin Random House group of companies whose addresses can be found at global.penguinrandomhouse.com

Published by Penguin Random House India Pvt. Ltd
4th Floor, Capital Tower 1, MG Road,
Gurugram 122 002, Haryana, India

Penguin
Random House
India

First published in Viking by Zubaan and Penguin Books India 2015

Published in collaboration with the Heinrich Boll Foundation, Delhi

10 9 8 7 6 5 4 3 2

ISBN 9789383074778

Typeset in 11/13 Garamond by Jojy Philip, New Delhi
Printed at Replika Press Pvt. Ltd, India

www.penguin.co.in

This is a legitimate digitally printed version of the book and therefore might not have certain extra finishing on the cover.

Contents

Partition: The Long Shadow

An Introduction

URVASHI BUTALIA

Every year on the 15th of May Palestinian communities across the world come together in their respective countries to observe al Nakba, or the day of the catastrophe, which marks a long, ongoing history of homelessness, refugeeism, violence and often despair. In 2011, I happened to be in Israel on this day – that was the year when the marking of al Nakba in Israel's neighbouring countries (Jordan, Lebanon, Egypt) once again became contentious. In Israel, the border forces reacted with tear gas and shooting. Accompanied by two Palestinian friends, I managed to make my way across from Tel Aviv into Ramallah – just a stone's throw and a somewhat intractable border wall away – and found myself, first, in the thick of tear gas attacks and shouting and anger on the streets and then, deeper inside the town, in the marketplace where people sat around an improvised stage, singing, talking, remembering the day, in 1948, on which they became strangers in their own land – remembering, almost mourning, a day which one might think was best forgotten.

I realized then how contentious acts of remembering and forgetting can be, and how, sometimes, State power can be called into the service of suppressing memory. For the Palestinians, the necessity of remembering was a way of keeping alive a history that stretched its long arm into their present, and indeed into the future of their children. And yet, the imperative to remember was not universal among Palestinians either, for many felt this was a history best left behind, a history from which it was time to move on. For the Israelis, the necessity of forgetting that very same history made it incumbent that they do their best, indeed use their power, to suppress and not allow the surfacing of that memory, even if it meant using tear gas shells and guns. But here too, there were Israelis who sympathized with, and supported the need for remembrance because without it, there would be no real moving on. Depending on where you are placed and which perspective you approach them from, acts of remembering and forgetting can mean very different things.

Something like that applies to Partition too. Broadly speaking, for Indians, remembering Partition means recalling the dark side of Independence, a moment of loss, a moment when the country was divided and that which was lost was immeasurable – for it was not only homelands, and families, and material things but much more that could not be articulated, sometimes not even named. In a moving essay in this volume, Prajna Parasher describes how after Partition, her grandmother would constantly mutter and babble, an incomprehensible stream of almost-words. It was only much later that Prajna, a second-generation child after Partition, recognized that what she was hearing and not comprehending was a sort of madness and bewilderment on the part of an aging person trying – and failing – to make sense of nations and borders.

This is perhaps why, nearly seven decades on, we have still not found a way of memorializing Partition, acknowledging what people lived through. Not only does it look different from either 'side' – for Pakistanis, the same moment is one where a nation, an identity was gained – but, over the years, its memories have become more complex, acquired more nuance and layers, and been seen differently, depending on the particular circumstances of the moment of remembering. Further, as the numbers of those who retain direct, experiential memories diminish, as their stories recede, ways of remembering also change, the filters through which such memories are passed on – whether in and through literature, or music, or art and so much more – now begin to shape *how* they are passed on. With distance, the power and poignancy of the direct story are often muted, and what tends to acquire more importance is the business of living with the consequences of that history. And in many ways this is in the fitness of things, for generations who will not have the direct experience of having lived through violence, loot, rape, arson, can only know that history through the multiple ways in which it is handed down to us.

The exploration of memory is also not something that is or can be finite. One cannot begin to open up memory and reach a point where the exercise is done and can be laid to rest. Every historical moment that offers us the possibility of looking at it through the prism of memory demonstrates that the more you search, the more there is that opens up. Onion-like, each layer peeled away reveals another beneath, the core itself being made up of layers within layers. When the initial works that opened up Partition histories, particularly those that drew on first-person accounts, appeared, they tended to focus on the untold stories of Partition victims and survivors, mainly Muslims, Hindus and Sikhs. It was only later that other studies, such as those of Sindhis, or minorities, or Muslims who stayed behind in India, or stories of continued displacement, of caste and class and studies with other perspectives, began to open up (and it should come as no surprise that much of this exploratory and pioneering work of excavating forgotten histories was done by women historians, sociologists and writers). Today there is talk of second generation experiences and the impact of Partition, and the focus on migration and violence has broadened to include so much more.

This volume, initially conceived as a set of lectures to mark the 60th anniversary of Partition, and later expanded to take in new works as well, reflects some of these new explorations. It turns its attention to the 'peripheries' – Ladakh, Kashmir, Assam – in its exploration of the long-term consequences of Partition. Similarly, it explores art and literature, and new forms of narrative such as the graphic story; it looks at the experience of 'resettlement', forcible eviction and the massacre of Dalits and poor refugees in Marichjhapi: it examines Gandhi's ideas of violence and non-violent action. It examines the involvement of communists, of Sindhis, and the meaning, for Partition refugees and survivors, of notions of home, belonging, territoriality. And time and again it poses the question: how do we move forward and not only carry this history with us, but also transcend it? Is this even possible?

Each writer here comes to his or her own exploration of Partition through a political engagement, an academic or activist interest, a deep concern with how to move forward. None of the writers has a direct history of Partition, although a number belong to Partition refugee families. One way or another, the connectedness of a history recently lived, variously represented, and profoundly present in its consequences, remains.

We open the volume with an evocative essay, part family history and part geo-political history of a region that has not seen much writing, particularly in the context of Partition, and which is seen as somehow having been inured to the kinds of divisions sown by the retreating footprint of colonialism. Siddiq Wahid, a Ladakhi Muslim with deep roots in the region, but also someone who has lived outside, traces the trajectory of Ladakh, now a part of the state of Jammu and Kashmir and once part of the wider Tibeto-Himalayan region, with extensive links and connections within the region. He shows how identities and borders form and change through geographical consolidation, military operations, territorial expansion, religion, colonial conquest, and political game-play – describing, as he puts it, an extended historical moment when 'the histories of entities in the region began to converge and economies began to expand, changing societies abruptly and radically (p. 2).' Much of Ladakh's ethnic, linguistic and cultural closeness to Tibetan civilization, he shows, began to undergo radical change after the annexation of Tibet by China in 1950.

Zoning in on his family history, Wahid asks: how did this kind of state formation impinge upon the lives of the inhabitants and their relationships with each other? From a free roaming extended family spread over much of the region, once the Chinese borders were sealed in 1957, the Khwaja-Radhu clan became subjects of the erstwhile Dogra state of Jammu and Kashmir. The emergence of hardened boundaries as a result of the creation of modern 20th century states in China, India and Pakistan, and new questions of identity and belonging began to have social and perhaps more importantly psychological effects on the lives of the inhabitants of frontiers-turned-borderlands.

Many of the questions raised in Siddiq Wahid's essay find resonance in Rita Kothari's reflections on beginnings and endings. Growing up in a Sindhi refugee household, Kothari found that in many ways for the Sindhis, the experience of migration, the loss of home and in some ways identity, seemed to have been done and dusted. It seemed to her then, that Partition was not only incidental but irrelevant, and that the Sindhi community's decision to put it behind them was not so much a suppression of memory as a pragmatic, mercantile decision to get on with life and rebuild everything anew. It was not until much later, when she began work on the pastoralist communities of Banni in Kutch that she began to understand how 'inconclusive the Partition event had been and how its ramifications exist even seven decades after (p. 11).'

For the Banni pastoralists, Kothari found, movement was the only constant in their nomadic life guided by the seasons and the search for pasture; borders were meaningless. This changed after the 1965 Kutch award that transformed forever these nomadic, temporarily settled lives. In Kothari's words, 'People and cattle had to restrict their movement, they had both become Indian citizens without realizing it' (p. 42). The fixing of borders therefore constrains people, turns them into settled, sedentary beings, which they may not necessarily be. In Kothari's words: 'When situated in the context of Partition and its preoccupations, readjustment of spatial maps and their alignment with mental geographies opens up a relatively under-researched aspect. The tragic effect that Partition had upon the people of Banni was not manifest in movement, but the fact that *movements had to be arrested*.' (p. 44, emphasis in original). For Kothari, it was this that made her question the temporal marker of 1947 'as the nucleus around which Partition is understood and theorized.' (ibid)

Continuing the discussion on Sindh, and the concreteness or otherwise of a 'home', Kavita Panjabi reflects on the longing, among many refugees, to return to the homeland, and its co-existence with a sense of fear at what they may or may not find there. Her own first journey to Sindh led her to discover 'a different narrative of Partition' and therefore, to confront a new set of questions. What then, she asks, is the meaning of the longing nursed in so many hearts for the homeland left behind? What, in the now, can a sense of 'a homeland' mean when the home being imagined no longer exists, when there is no actual territorial possession? In many ways this is the flip side of the shifting homeland of the Banni pastoralists, for whom territory had no real meaning, but movement did. For Panjabi's father, who carries within him both the desire, and the fear, of return, his identity was defined as much by the experience of growing up in Sindh as it was by the sense of being Indian, almost a sort of tearing apart schizophrenia. Must all those dislocated by Partition, then, Panjabi asks, lead such schizophrenic lives?

It is one thing, however, to nurture the longing and hold the memory, for those who have lived through that time. What of Panjabi herself and others of her generation? Why is it that they too continue to hold on to and nurture the sense of loss, particularly as 'the loss is but a memory borrowed from our parents and grandparents?' (p. 51) An imagined homeland without territoriality, an inherited memory without direct knowledge, what do these mean for us today? Panjabi poses a question that lies at the heart of almost every essay in this volume: what does it mean to hold on to a sense of loss when the people doing so have wronged as much as they have been wronged? Can such loss ever be redeemed honestly, by confronting one's own culpability, and if so, how? Politically engaged in friendship initiatives across the border, Panjabi concludes by looking ahead: is there a way, she wonders, that this mutual loss, a shared history of trauma and dispossession, can be turned into a movement towards reparation, perhaps even reconciliation? Should not such reparation involve the joint task of examining our past, looking at our role in it, and holding our States accountable? Bound together in mutual culpability and mutual suffering, can we not turn the focus away from mutual enmity, and begin to look at mutual forgiveness, turning the experience of belonging to different homelands into something other than to territorial ownership, a claiming and belonging without possession? These are important questions that post Partition generations have posed again and again.

Possession, claiming, belonging – these ideas also resonate in Sanjib Baruah's essay on Assam, as he asks: who belongs, and how, and how does belonging look when seen from the point of view of the citizen, and from the point of view of the State. The colonial policy of attracting settlers to Assam's 'wastelands', Baruah shows, was not only continued but accelerated after Partition, especially because of the pressure on India to recognize its responsibilities towards those who had found themselves on the 'wrong' side of the border. The long shadow of 1947 stretched into 1971, a moment that added to the tension around this emotionally charged and polarizing issue of cross-border migration, leading to street protests, civil disorder and violence. The subsequent imposition of restrictions on areas where migrants could settle resulted in considerable political turmoil – and the demographic transformation these policies led to is evident in the consequences it has had for Assamese politics, and for militancy in the region.

A little-known history until the eighties, this legacy of Partition came into the public arena when the six-year-long Assam agitation threw the foreigner question into the limelight. The insecurity generated by movement leaders' claim that as many as 4.5-5 million people in the state (roughly a third of its population) could be foreigners, erupted into terrible violence and slaughter (as in Nellie where over 2,000 people, mostly Muslims, were killed). Political attempts to 'settle' the issue based themselves on how the State chose to define citizenship – what Baruah calls the 'rudimentary definitions of citizenship' – as opposed to how people understood it. A process that could have been many years in the making was now defined, for example, by cutoff dates that changed lives from one day to the next. The question of who is and who is not a real – read legal – citizen remains a contentious one to this day, and also one, as Baruah points out, that needs a solution based, rather like Panjabi's call for us to work together across borders, on a deep partnership, rather than animosity or opposition.

Another forgotten history is that of the Marichjhapi Massacre which, as Jhuma Sen shows, continues to live on in the minds of its survivors – although for those responsible for creating this history and perpetrating the atrocity, it is one best forgotten. Once again here, memory work becomes a political project, deeply influenced by class interests and power. Jhuma Sen points to twin, and often unequal, sides of certain kinds of remembering and forgetting so while the marginalized subject at the receiving insists on preserving the memory of trauma till some kind of closure, or some form of justice is found, their more privileged counterparts actively persist in the erasure of that memory while remembering to articulate their own as the only one worth preserving. Clearly power and privilege are also a part of memory-making and unmaking. Sen locates the history of the Marichjhapi Massacre, as it lives in the minds of its survivors and those who have chosen to remember it, in the wider context of partition, migration, issues of caste ecology, and discriminatory, casteist, refugee policies.

Sometimes, however, forgotten histories surface afresh. This happened with Marichjhapi with the recent debacles of the West Bengal Left Front government in Nandigram and Singur where the setting up of Tata's small car manufacturing factories resulted in the mass displacement of farmers and small landowners. This conflation of corporate and state power tragically held up an almost-mirror to the forcible eviction of East Pakistani origin refugees by the Left Front government in 1979 from the island of Marichjhapi. While not disputing that the process of state formation is one that generates refugees, Sen draws our attention to the fact that refugees are not an undifferentiated mass, and class and caste stratify them, influencing not only modes of migration, but also processes of subsequent resettlement after, and the rights and facilities that receiving states provide. So while migration on the east was relatively easy for the more privileged, and they found it possible to integrate in India, for the untouchables, the depressed classes, the poor, it was a different case entirely.

While Assam was the 'wasteland' where settlers had to be encouraged, the fate of Kashmir, which has been the subject of much historical discussion, was altogether different. Here, Andrew Whitehead traces once again a little known history, that of the communists who were, at the time, an important presence in the state. The movement against autocracy in Kashmir was what gave the impetus to communist activity, and communists played a key role in the shaping of Sheikh Abdullah's campaign against princely rule. They were involved too in organizing a popular armed force – in which many women participated – mainly to repulse the pro Pakistan irregular forces. At a time when the Communist Party had no real history of armed activity, and in an atmosphere of considerable conservatism, both of these were unusual firsts. Located firmly within the mainstream – they did not set up a separate party – communists were also instrumental in the drafting of the New Kashmir Manifesto. The headiness of being involved, the preparedness to do battle, the willingness to work with the 'mainstream' are what defined communist activity in Kashmir in the lead up to Partition. A change in the Party line was to end all this, and with the steady erosion of Kashmir's autonomy and Delhi's persistent interference and rigging of elections, paved the way for the insurgency of 1989 – the ghost of Partition once again casting its long shadow.

Is there a moment when the question of whether or not histories such as that of Partition can be represented at all gives way to a different one: *how* can such histories be represented? This is the question Sukeshi Kamra poses in her essay. Drawing on Marianne Hirsch's term postmemory (www.postmemory.net), or the ways in which subsequent generations who have no direct experience of traumatic or catastrophic histories remember them by means of images, cultural expressions, stories, behaviours, Kamra points to the importance of this question for India and Pakistan. With time, Partition is now a reality mediated by its representations, and we need to engage not only with the question of why representing Partition is an imperative, but also how we can and must do this. Her critique of the early studies that began the process of opening up Partition studies points to what she sees as lament and nostalgia. These, she feels, have become our only points of engagement with this history, which has meant that important questions, such as intergenerational trauma and memory, have begun to recede from view.

Tarun Saint takes this discussion further by looking at a recently published collection of graphic stories about Partition, *This Side, That Side,* in an attempt to answer the basic question: how can we find a mode of representation that adequately bears witness to the 1947 Partition and its traumatic after-effects? Drawing a line from the fictional and non-fictional narratives of the first generation of writers – some of whom were direct witnesses and survivors of violence – he looks at the newer generations whose focus is more on the long-term consequences. In common with other writers in this volume – for example Kavita Panjabi, Siddiq Wahid – for Tarun Saint the fact that the 'restorying' of Partition in the volume in question involves work across borders, and a sharing of ideas and their execution by people who have sometimes not even met but have just communicated via the internet, offers hope for 'the possibility of dialogue across borders.' The collaborative dimension, in which all three countries come together to make sense of the event offers a multiplicity of perspectives that enrich the dialogue.

If fiction, narrative non-fiction, oral testimony and music, all offer ways of understanding the many- layered realities of Partition, so does the visual. In an visual essay that draws on his grandmother, Amiya Sen's memoir *Aranyalipi* (The Forest Chronicle), Vishwajyoti Ghosh looks at the experience of refugee life in the forests of Dandakaranya and in refugee centres in Delhi, where he grew up. A mainly epistolary narrative, this graphic story turns its attention to the reality of displacement (and here echoes the work of Jhuma Sen in this volume, which also addresses the same region), and its dehumanizing effects, choosing to deploy the perspective of a woman social worker assigned to assist the refugees. Memories of Ghosh's own childhood spent, in part, among refugee children, punctuate this account, and in it, Ghosh pays homage to his grandmother and the many women who worked in refugee camps, providing succour, support, often monetary help, to the displaced and the destitute. The work of providing care is something that women, especially, took on in large numbers post Partition and for many, an initial humanitarian response to a ground situation, led to lifetime commitments and careers in what came to be called 'social work'.

Prajna Paramita Parasher writes the story of her father, S.L. Parasher, an artist and an administrator, who held charge of the largest refugee camp in north India, in Ambala. Agreeing with the truth that conventional history is written by the winners, she asks, what of the stories of everyday awareness, 'individual in each person, yet always just below connection, like suddenly recognizing an unexpected old friend (p. 204).' As they crowd in on us, especially in the context of Partition, and surface memories that have so far stayed in the background, we see afresh what is before us, through the prism of what it left out. She speaks of her grandmother and her memory of her as a somewhat shadowy presence, to be avoided. 'In my child's mind', she says, 'it never occurred to me to try and imagine what her experience must have been…torn away from what she recognized and most of what she must have loved. To be made into a refugee must be the hardest on the old, who can't really imagine creating a new life and whose sense of themselves and whatever their lives might mean has been left behind in the road.' Years later, when the same 'child' begins to recover memories of her father, the artist, she finds that by standing in front of his works and seeing through the artist's pencil, 'some brief image of what is lost in this terrible past, we are changing, by only a little, the shape of the present.' (p. 204)

Memory and recall are important questions that now inform our study of Partition. Another aspect that has seen little problematizing so far, and that has been taken as more or less said, is the distinction between violence and non-violence, particularly as seen and articulated by Gandhi. In a complex and nuanced essay, Jyotirmaya Sharma complicates this question by examining Gandhi's writings on non-violence in light of the very violent death by assassination of Swami Shraddhananda. Jyotirmaya Sharma argues that post-Partition narratives have often sought to divide 'our understanding of history into a world divided between men of light and men of darkness,' whereas the reality is, in fact, much more complex. The non-violence of Gandhi is often pitted against the Hindu nationalist espousal of violence but this, Sharma suggests, is not a useful way to look at the ways ideas were being formed and discussed in this period. Rather, it may be more useful to think of this moment as 'a heady mixture of European modernity, orientalism, ideas of reform and restatement of society and religion forming the foundational basis for much of what masquerades as the decisive versions of nationalism.' (p. 239)

In the concluding essay Alok Sarin, Sarah Ghani and Sanjeev Jain bring us up to date by looking, as many other writers in this volume do, at the long-term consequences of social dislocation and trauma on the psyche. While the large-scale breakdown of civic life in the run-up to and in the aftermath of Partition can, in part, be seen as the general shifting of populations in the post-World War II reorganization of 'national boundaries' in Europe, its effects on the newly decolonized regions in Asia and Africa were vastly different. These emerging states, they suggest, did not have the adequate administrative or medical infrastructure to cope with this unprecedented transmigration, attended as it was by violence, looting and sexual assault. Nor does the trauma stop at one generation, for in the absence of psychiatric and counselling services for the survivors, many traumatic memories lingered and were passed on to the next generation. The discovery of the impact of such trauma in relation to Partition became clear to them in their professional work, leading also to the realization that the silences relating to this were not only personal but also professional. The authors pose an important question: 'Is this an aspect of the rather inadequately informed "colonial" mindset that has characterized psychiatric thinking? The inner life of the individual, which is often the subject of scrutiny in contemporary psychology, was not considered relevant to the specific person under colonial rule.' (p. 256)

Taken together, this collection of essays draws our attention to a small fraction of the many unexplored histories of this major moment in our recent past. The recovery of memory, the 'settling' (if that is ever possible) of questions of closure and justice, the sense that a history of trauma and loss, of guilt and culpability, can now be put behind, and people's lives can move on – clearly a period of nearly seven decades is in no way enough to deal with this. The long shadow that Partition cast, touched not only those who lived through it, and those who died because of it, but also the generations that came after. This volume, for reasons that are only too well known to people in the South Asian region, is only able to address some aspects of the Indian experience – other histories being barred to researchers because of the politics of hatred and enmity that our three countries exercise against each other. Perhaps the real moving on will come when we are able to work on these histories together – across countries, across class, across caste and across gender.

CHAPTER 1

Converging Histories and Societal Change

The Case of Ladakh

SIDDIQ WAHID

Ladakh is at the very edge of South Asia. To its north lies Eastern Turkestan (or Xinjiang) and to the east the Northern Plains (or Changthang) of the Tibetan Plateau, connecting it to the wellspring of its culture in Lhasa. Isolated for a century because of imperial rivalries in what became known as the Great Game, Ladakh was not a hub of anti-colonial activism, nor was its population familiar with the discourse on the partition of the subcontinent. So when I was asked to speak on the attitude and effects of partition on various parts of South Asia in a speakers' series, I requested—and received—some guidelines for it.[1] In that context, I would like to begin by sharing a little of the context that influenced the tenor of this paper. The organisers' guidelines were instructive: 'You may want to bring in a bit of the history of Ladakh to make the context clear.' Translation: *Most readers will not know anything about Ladakh.* The second suggestion was, 'Please do not make it too academic.' Translation: *Please don't bore the readers with information that they do not need or care about.*

Given Ladakh's location in space and its lack of demographic salience, these suggestions were not unexpected or, indeed, unfair.[2] But they made the assignment both more difficult and more attractive to me. They forced me to think about how the story of the partitions (the use of the plural here is deliberate and the reasons for it will become clear as we move forward) of Ladakh can contribute to an understanding of our present-day historical conditions. The guidelines also pushed me to focus on the *universals* in Ladakh's historical, social and cultural experience, and, by extension, in the world of the Tibeto-Himalaya. Finally, they compelled a discussion on what links abstract history with our practical present. Combined, the past and the present speak to the important and relevant question of where we might be headed—to our future.

The Ladakh region, comprising the two districts of Leh and Kargil, is by far the largest territorial expanse in the state of Jammu and Kashmir (J&K).[3] Until recently, the participation of Ladakhis in discussions about their land was often prefaced with an apologia about their demographic size. Meanwhile both state and central government officials gave way to the temptation to politically manipulate this small population for their own interests.The revolutions in mediums of communication, geographic mobility and identity awareness have changed this—and continue to change—to make Ladakh's participation in its own future meaningful, keenly debated and widely argued since the 1990s.

The historical process that allowed this active participation can be traced to the mid-19th century, when the histories of the entities in the region began to converge and economies began to expand, changing societies abruptly and radically. To describe these events and their impact in the short space of an essay is daunting, but that is precisely what this chapter demands. To enhance the chances of articulacy in such a compressed space, a brief summation of the perspectives from which I address my hypotheses, and some basic assumptions that frame them and the intended structure of my essay would not be unwarranted.

My perspective is that of a person with multiple sociopolitical identities: first, as a member of a Ladakhi family with roots in Kashmir who have identified with their former origin for the better part of 300 years; yet also as an individual who is puzzled by what appears to be at times a fascination among Ladakhis with our own quaintness. This is a complicated statement, so allow me a quick digression to illustrate what I mean.

The thought that we could be fascinated by our own quaintness was brought home to me in the early 1990s by a Ladakhi compatriot who arrived in Washington, D.C., for a visit as a guest of the Smithsonian Institution. I was living in the United States at that time, so went to visit him. During our meetings in Ladakh, my friend was noticeable for wearing the best and latest available in down jackets and other winter wear. But when I met him at the top of the steps of one of Washington's ultra-modern Metro stations, he glided out of the subterranean escalator wearing a traditional Ladakhi gown, the *gos*, looking decidedly out of place. This assertion of his difference in a foreign land illustrated a sense of romantic nostalgia about who we are, but it also set me wondering as to whether it was not an imagined purism that is experientially false and so a weakened argument for the 'preservation' of an essential reality about 'Ladakhi-ness'. When done for political gain, is it not just old fashioned cynicism? It began a dialogue within me on this trend to isolationism and eventually the belief that idiosyncrasy weakens rather than strengthens any struggle for survival, even for a unique and fragile cultural entity, in this case Ladakh, which is part of the Tibeto-Himalaya.[4]

Second, I write as a citizen of the state of J&K, who wonders how we have come to be so miserably fragmented. True, we are a multiply diverse state, but diversity need not translate into divergence. It makes one wonder about the circumstances that allow us to live in an interdependent coexistence for centuries with Kashmir and Kashgar; Lhasa and Yarkand; and, more recently since the mid-19th century, Jammu and Hoshiarpur. Third, I speak as one who lives in modern India but severely questions whether India really is 'shining', 'rising' or 'emerging' as an economy, democracy or great power respectively as many social scientists and commentators are wont to argue. And fourth, I write as a part of South Asia who militates against what has been called the 'narcissus of small differences' that has so fractured and divided our larger regional milieu in the last six decades.

The implied assumption, indeed bias, of all of these locations of perspective is that my argument tends towards an expanded canvas of coexistence that accepts the phenomenon of historical convergence or, in economic terms, globalisation, but argues that it cannot be pursued by legitimising homogenisation in a manner that assumes hegemony as a given, at a *pace* that is presumed to be universally acceptable and with a *definition* that is a centralised parochialism.[5] Homogenisation, which seems to be a fact of modern life, in other words, does not imply hegemony. Put otherwise, the missionaries of political democracy and economic globalisation need to be less zealous about their gospels and engage in an equitable dialogue with those whose experience of homogeneity is less familiar and for whom its effects are traumatic. In this context, the missionaries of democracy must inure themselves to accommodating plurality of political ideas just as much as the missionaries of identity politics. Both these 'missionaries', as we have tragically experienced, are equally prepared to shed blood for their causes.

All this is, I know, a mouthful. It is difficult, if not impossible, to link the experience of tiny Ladakh to arguments of convergence theories of history in the short space at our disposal. But for better or for worse, I attempt it because we are compelled to think on these things if we are to make sense of where we are in history today.

This chapter begins with an outline of the history of Ladakh and its geopolitical setting in the context of the Tibeto-Himalaya. When did the Ladakh–Baltistan region come to be within the ambit of Tibetan civilisation? How was this accomplished over a period of 1,200 years? Following this, I concentrate on the effects of the last 150 years of Ladakh's history through the prism of the experiences of one family. I conclude with a discussion of the state of Ladakh's culture in the context of the march of history and, more specifically, Inner Eurasian history, over the last 500 years, ending with the partition of the subcontinent.

LADAKH AND THE INNER EURASIAN MILIEU

It is important for us to remember that in premodern times Ladakh was almost exclusively a part of the world of the Tibeto-Himalaya within the Inner Eurasian complex of civilisations.[6] This Eurasian landmass lies between the Altai Mountains in the east to the Urals in the west; the Siberian steppe in the north to the southern slopes of the Himalayan range in the south. To demonstrate a unity between the entities within this landmass, the languages of this region have at times been clubbed together into one language family, and termed the

Uralic-Altaic. Indeed, one of the first and most persistent European Tibetanists travelled from Hungary to Ladakh in an attempt to demonstrate that Tibetan and Hungarian were related languages.[7] The technicality of whether such a relationship or a grouping of languages holds water apart, my point here is to argue that there has been a gradual churning that has brought this vast region together since the 6th century CE. What follows is the briefest of summaries of this convergence.

The first phase begins in the middle of the 7th century CE with the introduction of Buddhism into Tibet.[8] Soon after this, the Yarlung Valley of Central Tibet witnessed a consolidation of political power under Srongsten Gampo (618–641 CE). He and his descendants adopted Buddhism as the state religion and gradually, over the next 200 years, the population of the Central Tibetan region also became adherents of this religion, which, by then, had been flourishing for about a thousand years. By the middle of the 9th century, the Tibetans had spread as far west as what is today Baltistan in Pakistan and in the east to the western parts of China. Coincidentally, a Tibetan military empire had also exploded on to the scene, not unlike the Mongol one almost 600 years later, and tangled with the advancing Arab armies in present-day Gilgit, a Himalayan province on the Pakistan side of the Line of Control that divides J&K today.

It was at this time, around the mid-9th century, that Ladakh also began to become Tibetanised in language, culture, politics and religion; a good 250 years after Buddhism was introduced to Central Tibet. The impetus was in all probability a royal migration to Ladakh that occurred as a result of palace quarrels in Central Tibet, where Ralpachen (r. 838–42) was king. In the eyes of the aristocracy, he favoured Buddhism at the cost of their powers and had 'capitulated' to it. This was symbolised by his acknowledgement of his indebtedness to Buddhism, which he demonstrated by tying ribbons from his plaited hair to carpets on either side of him; on these carpets sat the monks of the new religion. This act was interpreted by the aristocracy as a capitulation to a 'foreign' power. The old aristocracy, of course, had a vested interest in the political power that came with adhering to the earlier political and religious orders of Tibet.

As a result of this, Ralpachen lost his throne and his life in a palace revolt, ushering in a period of confusion during which one part of the royal family emigrated from Central Tibet to the western reaches of the empire.[9] One of the assassinated king's sons eventually settled in Ngari Khorsum, the empire's western outpost, and from there expanded further west to what is now known as Ladakh, establishing a new dynasty known to us as Lha Chen.

By the end of the 9th century, the Tibetan military empire had more or less abated. However, its assimilative interpretation of Buddhism was only just beginning to spread to the regions around it and proved to be a potent force in itself. Between the 10th and the 16th centuries, Tibetan cultural influence had spread to Mongolia in the north to western China in the east to the edge of Europe in the west. At the same time, its influence had spread southwards as well, to places that we know today as Baltistan, Ladakh, Nepal, Sikkim, Bhutan, Assam and Arunachal Pradesh along the southern slopes of the Himalaya. Political influence in these regions—some sovereign states and others suzerains—stayed on until much later, into the late modern period, even up to the mid-20th century. In Central Tibet, in the mid-17th century, there came into existence an ecclesiastic form of government, headed by the abbot, called the Dalai Lama, of its most powerful monastic coalition the Gelugpa or Yellow Hat.[10]

A few centuries before this, and four centuries after the Tibetan empire, there was another expansion in the interiors of Eurasia that connects with Tibetan history. It was a second phase in the consolidation of the Inner Eurasian landmass and took place at the start of the 13th century out of Mongolia. If the Tibetan expansion occurred through a combination of intellectual synthesis through a cementing adaptation of Buddhism and military expansion, the Mongol explosion was a purely military one. Starting in the first quarter of the 13th century, and within a span of less than 75 years, Chinggiz Khan (also spelled Genghis Khan) and his descendants, through a combination of military skill on horseback and sheer terror, conquered the entire lands between Russia in the west to China in the east to Iran in the south.[11] By the time they were done, the Mongols had established an astonishing empire, the likes of which had not been seen until then or since. It welcomed Marco Polo in the court at Beijing under the Mongol-Chinese rule we know as the Yuan dynasty, and established the Ilkhanid dynasty in the region of present-day Iran. Nor did the Mongol empire stop there in time and space; it was an indirect descendant of the Mongols when Babur, through Tamerlane, established the Mughal Empire in South Asia. The Inner Eurasian lands, therefore, came to directly influence three major 'outer Eurasian' civilisations in Yuan China, Mughal India and Ilkhanid Iran.

It may be relevant to mention here that so deep was the Mongol influence that it even effected western sociopolitical theory in the idea of 'Oriental despotism', although it has been well discredited since (Weber 1965). The Mongol-conquered lands, it was argued, influenced tsarist Russia to such an extent that they learnt their authoritarian and repressive measures from the less rational Oriental mind. Tibet, however, was spared outright Mongol conquest and instead became the only other civilisation, apart from the Chinese, to make inroads into integrating into this empire. This happened decisively in the late 16th century when the ruler of the western Mongols, Altan Khan (1543–83), converted to Buddhism and in response promised political patronage to the abbot of the Gelugpa, or Yellow Hat, order of Tibetan Buddhism.[12]

To return to the subject of this essay, the Ladakh–Baltistan stretch of the Tibeto-Himalaya, as we have just seen, was introduced to the ethnic, linguistic and cultural world of Tibetan civilisation in the mid-9th century, when descendants of the then Tibetan monarch emigrated westwards.[13] It was an extension of the Tibetan power centre at Ngari Khorsum and from there the dynasty formed smaller principalities in the regions now known as Lahul, Spiti, Skardu and Zangskar. In the 11th century, an extraordinary flowering of Tibetan Buddhism took place in this western bastion of the religion. This is evidenced in the works of art still extant in Alchi, Sumdo and many other monasteries and even shrines in the western Himalaya, including in Ladakh, Lahul and Spiti, the latter two in the Indian state of Himachal Pradesh.[14]

This, then, was the milieu to which Ladakh belonged until well into the modern age. It was a Tibetan identity through the adoption of its language, arts, literature, culture and religion. The dynasty that established itself came to be known as Lha Chen, which had its origins in the Tibetan kingdom and to which it was linked for the next six centuries. Its proximity to Kashmir and the presence of Buddhism there gradually resulted in Ladakh becoming a separate power centre, although still intimately linked to Tibet in religion and culture. The sway of the kings of Ladakh spread as far east as Kulu (Petech 1977), although a detailed history of this is still awaited. In the mid-16th century, in an assertion of Ladakh's autonomy from Lhasa, the Lha Chen dynasty recast itself to be known as the Namgyals, and remained in power until the middle of the 19th century, when the dynasty was dissolved after the Dogra conquest.

By the last quarter of the 19th century, the East India Company was firmly established in South Asia and the colonial project of expanding from this base was well under way. The East India Company was innovative in its relations. It colonised areas that it could, and where it could not, it established relationships of dominance. But this was not entirely without problems, as resistance from native rulers at times resulted in innovative arrangements and at other times in wars. Simultaneously involved in this region were other 19th-century empires, also asserting themselves. The forces that converged in the north and west of South Asia came to be characterised, increasingly famously, as the Great Game. Kashgar in Xinjiang, just to the north of Leh in Ladakh, became an important geographical space for this imperial rivalry as a robust spy game was being played out between Russia, Britain and Qing China.

One of the East India Company's strongest rivals in north India was the Sikh kingdom of Ranjit Singh. Amongst his vassals was a very able military commander Gulab Singh, who was actively carving out a kingdom for himself around Jammu during the early part of the century. Gulab Singh was part military adventurer, part strategist and part statesman, not unlike Ranjit Singh himself.[15] The Sikhs were engaged in a war with the British who, simultaneously, were busy in a series of wars with the Afghans directly to the north of Punjab. In the thick of this rivalry, Gulab Singh displayed great foresight in dispatching one of his military commanders to Baltistan and Ladakh for a series of campaigns in the 1830s. But in 1842, the commander, Zorawar Singh, had firmly annexed both these Tibetan plateau provinces to Gulab Singh's fledgling feudatory.[16] Ranjit Singh, meanwhile, had died and his successors lost the war against the British who sued them and, as part of the spoils of war, received the valley of Kashmir. They, in turn, sold it to Gulab Singh and allowed him to form his own kingdom, which became, in 1846, an independent, sovereign state, and styled itself Jammu and Kashmir, inclusive of the Ladakh *wazarat*.

The historical, cultural and economic connectedness between Ladakh and Kashmir was, of course, of much earlier, indeed, ancient provenance. Apart from being the source of the famous pashmina wool, it was to Kashmir that the earliest scholars of Tibet came, presumably via Ladakh, to give Tibetans their first alphabet. Similarly, in the 13th century, it was artisans from Kashmir who travelled to Ladakh to paint murals for its temples; and in the following century, it was Rinchena Bhota, a man who seems to have originated from Ladakh, who gave back to the Kashmiris an independent monarchy under the banner of Islam. Much later, in the 17th century, Buddhist Ladakh sought and received an alliance with Mughal Kashmir against a Tibetan-Mongol army that marched against Ladakh.

The Dogra conquest, however, was different. It brought about, for the first time, a greater political confluence between the Tibetan plateau and South Asia on its western frontiers, one that has lasted until the present. As part of Jammu and Kashmir since 1846, the Gilgit–Baltistan–Ladakh expanse too became enmeshed in the dispute over the state after 1947. One of the by-products of this conflicted dispute was that the Cease Fire Line (CFL), which was transformed into the Line of Control (LoC) in 1972, cut off Gilgit and Baltistan from Ladakh for the first time in history, turning this westernmost outpost of Tibetan language and culture into two smaller, isolated enclaves.

The 1950 occupation of Tibet by the People's Republic of China had the added effect of cutting off the tiny Buddhist community of Ladakh from the source of its religion. The acuity of the severance is even starker if we consider the fact that, in a remarkable example of cultural connectedness even in modern times, Ladakh continued to pay tribute to the office of the Dalai Lama until as late as 1942, when the last tribute (or *lo phyag*) mission would its way across the

Changthang (or 'northern plains') of the Tibetan plateau from Leh to Lhasa.[17] It took three months to travel one way across this route.[18]

CHANGE LIVED: LOCAL AND GLOBAL

The beginning of the 16th century saw a deep change and a vibrant churning all over the world. The European discovery of sea routes and the growing use of gunpowder in military campaigns ushered in an age of colonisation. The Spanish, Portuguese, French and British were in the European vanguard of this revolutionary change in the political and economic history of the world. But such expansions were not maritime forays from Europe alone. There were other expansions, land-based expansions of older empires, such as the Safavid in Iran, the Ottoman in Eurasia, the Mughal in South Asia and the Ming in China, all of which consolidated their powers and formed lasting empires of their own.[19]

An example of this is the Mughal empire, an offshoot of the last Turkic-Mongol pan-Eurasian empire of Tamerlane. After establishing themselves in north India in the early part of the 16th century, they expanded by forming colonies. Among them was Kashmir, which they conquered in 1586 after wresting power from the local dynasty. Closer to the subject of this paper, but largely unnoticed by mainstream historians until recently, Tibet too began to expand its frontiers not long afterwards. By the middle of the 17th century, the religious and political power centres in Lhasa had united under the Gelugpa order of Tibetan Buddhism. It was, therefore, during the rule of the Great Fifth Dalai Lama (1617–82) that the Tibetan expansion took place. But simultaneously, there were a series of Tibeto-Himalayan political consolidations independent of Tibet. So Bhutan, in 1629, became an independent nation and continues to be so today. Sikkim also formed itself into a sovereign state, lasting as such until 1975. Ladakh had, of course, had been an independent kingdom much earlier; indeed, in its case a consolidated ecclesiastic government in Tibet sought to bring it within its sphere of power, but, as was briefly mentioned earlier, this was successfully resisted by the local king with the help of the Mughal governor of Kashmir between 1682 and 1685.

Similar state consolidations were taking place elsewhere as well. By 1750, Nepal had united itself under the Shah rulers, whose rule lasted more or less without interruption until 2008, when the monarchy was forced to abdicate. Just to the north of Kashmir, a clutch of small city-states and larger state-entities were being formed in western and eastern Turkestan (today's five '-stans' and Xinjiang respectively) under the suspicious eyes of the Russian, British and Chinese empires.[20] A comparative historical and political study of the formation and functioning of these states would add much to our understanding of the modern state formation in Eastern lands well before they became conceptually familiar with the Westphalian model.

In this context, the state of Jammu and Kashmir of the Dogras was a newcomer in 1846. But this newest state was also one of the most intriguing of the Himalayan and Central Asian one in that it was wildly plural and diverse in ethnicity, language, religion and culture, with its rulers attempting, against great odds, to form a modern nation-state.[21]

How did this kind of state formation impinge on the lives of the inhabitants and their relationships with each other? To understand that, at some point, one must abandon the story of empires, their rise and fall. Nor is the story to be found solely in the nostalgic remains of museums of disappeared cultures or civilisations. It becomes meaningful and vivid in the lived experience of ordinary everyday people who either ignore historical change, are traumatised by them or, what is most often true, cope with the complexities of their lives by taking the middle road.[22]

For the next part of our discussion, I would like to take you through the story of one such lived experience, of a family that is today somewhere between being traumatised by the rapidity with which its world has been transformed and attempting to assimilate what has happened in the last century. The Khwaja–Radhu clan, on its male side, originally emigrated from Kashmir in the early to mid-18th century.[23] The descendants of the emigrant patriarch, who belonged to the South Asian Chishti order of Sufism, settled in Leh and its vicinity, married Buddhist women whom they converted to Islam, became landed gentry, and soon thereafter ventured out to trade along two important Inner Eurasian routes: one from Leh to Lhasa in Central Tibet and the other from Leh to Yarkand in Xinjiang. Sometime early in the 19th century, trade had prospered enough so that one branch of the family established a permanent base in Lhasa. Soon after this, another branch of the family settled in Yarkand, almost directly to the north of Leh, where they also acquired land and engaged in the traditional trade of Inner Eurasia. Several members of the family married Buddhist Tibetans in Central Tibet, Uighurs in Yarkand and, in at least one or two cases, Chinese Muslim women, while integrating well with the local culture. By the early 20th century, the family consisted of 'about a hundred members [with]… various branches of the house in Lhasa, Shigatse, Gartok, Yarkand and Srinagar…. Three hundred years ago the family migrated from Kashmir to Ladak [*sic*]' (Hedin 1909–13: 55).[24]

Sometime in the late first half of the 19th century, the Khwajas, as they came to be known, were entrusted with carrying the tribute from Ladakh to the office of the Dalai Lama at the Potala. It presented a unique circumstance for a Muslim family to be carrying the tribute for a Buddhist community to a compatriotic ecclesiastic government. At the same time, this allowed the trade of the Khwaja–Radhu clan to prosper at a faster pace. The family's branch in Leh also established relations with the local British authorities in Kashmir and male members of the family were appointed *aksakal* in Yarkand and Leh. The word *aksakal* (literally translated, it means 'white beard') implied a village or town elder who would adjudicate among its inhabitants. The actual task of this official, after British innovation, became to keep a record of all non-local activity in the area and inform the British authorities, which meant the 'resident' where the British sway held or the 'consul general' where it was more ambiguous.[25] The aim, of course, was to keep an eye on British imperial rivals in the Great Game that was still playing out.

Although the Khwaja–Radhus did not know at the time, the world with which they had grown familiar with had already been unravelling since around 200 years after their forebears had migrated from Kashmir. The 'forward policy' of the expanding British empire had brought many travellers, missionaries, adventurers, agents and wannabe agents of the East India Company to all parts of the Himalaya, including Ladakh. Their reports and books fuelled an already robust rivalry between the powers of the age. A direct result of this was the slow but increased monitoring of the frontiers on both sides of imperially imagined borders. It had the effect of curbing the natives' traditional social relations and the interdependent economic ties between, for example, nomadic and sedentary populations. But it was only just beginning, for the Great Game started in earnest in the early part of the 20th century.

For Ladakh, the lifelines of its trade had been with Yarkand, Kashgar and Khotan in eastern Turkestan to the north, Kashmir to the west and south, and Tibet to the east. But this was changing. At the turn of the 19th and 20th centuries, China had already seen a series of indigenous modernist rebellions against the imperial throne. The year 1912 saw these culminating in the overthrow of the almost 300-year-old Qing dynasty (1644–1912) and the establishment of a republican government. After consolidating its powers at the centre, the republican government of China, like the Qing dynasty before it, set about incorporating the borderlands of the Chinese empire, among them Xinjiang and Tibet, into its fold. At the same time, by the 1920s, British India was moving aggressively to protect its imperial interests in South Asia, and a direct consequence of this was a certain sealing of the borders in the Tibeto-Himalaya frontier lands.

The Khwaja–Radhus had begun to sense this turnaround, although it was not consciously articulated. Its Lhasa branch concluded that the old trade routes were getting expensive and time-consuming, so they shifted their trade along a directly southern route through Kalimpong to Calcutta and beyond. They also began to trade in daily commodities such as silks and brocades from Benares (today's Varanasi) and, in the late 1930s, even opened and operated a movie theatre in Lhasa that brought the early Indian movie industry into Tibet. On the western end of their operations, they began to wind up their connections with Yarkand in the early 1940s. Here, the conditions in the early period were less benign than the ones in the east. The nationalist government of China was on a drive to Sinicise their Central Asian possessions, resulting in mass expulsions of non-Uighur and non-Han inhabitants, for which identity the Ladakhis qualified. This caused the Yarkand branch of the Khwaja family to make a hurried exit from Xinjiang, leaving property and, in one instance, an Uighur spouse behind.

The last *lo phyag*, or tribute mission, led by a Khwaja, took place in 1942. In many ways it represented the beginning of the end of the free-roaming traditional trading life of this extended family. With the British departure from India in 1947, that life ended. The ensuing turmoil because of the partition of India closed the Lhasa branch's southern route through Calcutta. Although there were sporadic forays into Calcutta between 1942 and 1946, the trade volumes never returned to their conventional levels. The occupation of Tibet by the People's Republic of China in 1950 sealed the borders and the Lhasa branch of the family was forced to emigrate from their home of nearly 200 years. They did so in 1957, claiming Indian citizenship by virtue of their status as subjects of the erstwhile Dogra state of Jammu and Kashmir.

But it was not solely in the termination of their trade or even, indeed, their physical exile from the homeland, in which the intimate stories of the effects of the partitions on Ladakhi families, the Khwajas among them, is to be found. We know that migrations and settlements were a widespread phenomenon in Inner Eurasia, as were adaptation to new lands. However, the emergence of hardened boundaries as a result of the creation of modern 20th-century states in China, India and Pakistan, and new questions of identity and belonging began to have social and, perhaps more importantly, psychological effects on the lives of the inhabitants of frontiers turned into borderlands.

With the termination of their traditional vocation, an entire 20-something generation of Ladakhis, including of the Khwaja–Radhu family, was forced to rethink its future. The change they were confronted with was no less than psychological exile into a new world. It was traumatic because of its suddenness and its qualitatively different character from the changes they had experienced so far in the memory that had been handed down to them. To begin with, there was the historically idiosyncratic and legally ambiguous dispute over J&K. Then there was the question of having to contend with choosing a new identity for themselves. Were they 'subjects' of the state? Where they 'citizens' of India by virtue of the status of the state until 26 October 1947? What were they to make of their cultural connections with Tibet in the future? Or were they potentially putative 'citizens' of Pakistan by virtue of their territorial claims according to the two-nation theory?

These questions were being answered by events taking place far away in Delhi, Karachi (the capital of Pakistan at that time) and London. Other questions were closer at hand. One was the now-persistent communal divide, to which Ladakhis were introduced immediately after partition. Until now, the two communities had lived in relative peace, but separately. Although interreligious marriages were not uncommon, one of couple would adopt the religion of the other. Nor was there a pretence at a vague ecumenism between Buddhists and Muslims in Ladakh.

As war broke out between the newly formed states of India and Pakistan over the already 100-year-old state of J&K, small contingents of paramilitary companies flew into Ladakh to secure it from attack by the Pakistan army. Towards this a local home guard, representing all communities, was hurriedly formed and its members deployed in what must have been a somewhat caricatured local 'cabinet' of Buddhist, Muslim and Christian members consisting of ministers of health, revenue, defence, armaments and labour, amongst others (interview with Major [retd] Khwaja A. Rahim, 3 May 2008).

At this same time, some Muslims from Leh and Kargil were victimised and killed in a display of communal suspicion (ibid.), albeit considerably muted in comparison to the orgy of violence witnessed in the central lands of India and Pakistan. Ladakhi Buddhists, however, refused to succumb to such instigation; indeed, in one case, a patriarch of a prominent Buddhism family—the Kalons—fiercely protested the anti-Muslim sentiment, threatening that any harm to Ladakhi Muslims would come over his dead body (ibid.). But if there was any idyllic atmosphere of coexistence, it was shattered between 1947 and 1950, never to return to the earlier levels. One manifestation of this was a representation to the central government of India by Ladakhis that should the demands of Sheikh Mohammad Abdullah for a radically autonomous J&K be met, Ladakh would demand that they be allowed to accede to Central Tibet.[26]

Part of the reason for this representation by the Ladakhis had less to do with communal bigotry and was sparked by the radical land reform then being advocated by the National Conference in J&K. In Ladakh, such a measure directly affected the centuries-old ecclesiastic landholdings, which was resented by the monks, prompting an adversarial approach against 'Kashmiri dominance'.[27] But the larger picture was at the same time simple and more complex, as Ladakhis were thrown into a cauldron of uncertainty.

The uncertainty was real, and although the contours of its meaning for the immediate future only became decipherable after almost a decade, its intensity and effect in an immediate sense is difficult for us to gauge more than half a century later. The 1947–50 period effected Ladakh in other ways. It had relied on Lhasa for its stimulus in culture and, for the Buddhist community, religion for a millennium; but now, novice monks could no longer travel to study at the great monastic colleges of Tashilungpo, Sera, Drepung and Ganden in Central Tibet. Traders found a new world that they did not recognise any more. Even the connections between the nomadic and sedentary populations, which was largely a barter economy—pashmina wool and dairy products for commodities for Kashmir and beyond—began to change into a cash economy, changing relationships. Much that had been recognised became uncertain and strained.

In the ultimate analysis, the political, social, economic and psychological uncertainty meant that the youthful generation of a large segment of Ladakhis—Buddhist, Muslim and Christian—had to contemplate doing something that was, for them, unusual, that is, get a job.[28] It was no different, for example, for the Khwaja–Radhu family. This meant that they had to leave their familiar surroundings and what were relatively secure future vocations that were handed down by their forebears into lands and activities that were unfamiliar and alien. And it happened within a span of two decades after partition as members of this family left Xinjiang, Tibet and, eventually, even Ladakh as they spread themselves throughout the world, settling in what were to them far off lands, including newly independent India and Pakistan, England, Hong Kong, the United States, Canada and the Middle East. It was a series of partitions—exiles, both physical and mental.

UNDERSTANDING CHANGE AND COPING WITH EXILE

It is a well-established fact that partitions, and exiles that result from them, have played a large part in the political landscape of new states and, therefore communities, since the end of World War II, or the postcolonial world. South Asia, in a sense, led the charge in this trend and the psychological effects of it were deep and lasting. In the last quarter-century, its effects on the 'central'—which is to say the parts that were close to the power centres—lands of the colonised have been considerable. However, its consequences of the borderland peripheries has been little studied. Indeed, we would not be wrong in suggesting that a neocolonial attitude towards these lands has retarded a serious look at them. But as we have just seen, the frontier lands were also directly effected, albeit the latter not been fully analysed in that context.

The main thrust of my hypothesis is that the borderlands were not only effected, but that this has happened more radically and over a longer period of time. It began with economic changes as early as the early 19th century, when borders started to assume an overstated importance whereby they were tightened, policed and controlled to the detriment of the populations that lived along them. The process of decolonisation intensified this trend because as a whirl of new states were created and unnatural lines ran through ethnically, linguistically, culturally and economically interactive societies, they became even more isolated and 'left behind', so that their alienation from the so-called mainstream and even from each other became nothing less than traumatic. The shocks experienced in the peripheral populations of South Asia were different and more intensified than those experienced by the central populations of postcolonial South Asia in, for example, Punjab or Bengal. There were uprooting and separations in the latter populations too, of course. But these were different in that they were visible and grossly violent; but being power centres, they were also studies and addressed, albeit not necessarily adequately. In the peripheral populations, the changes were insidious, unaddressed and with hidden, long-term social consequences.

Political change, however, was not a stranger in the frontier lands. Ladakh, for example, began to experience political change through a thousand years of its history, as briefly recounted earlier. But beginning in the middle of the 19th century, the changes were conceptually different in that it impinged on the lives of the people more directly, isolating them as frontiers became borders and the pace picked up as changes in state consolidation, transport, communications and, most recently, information started to accelerate. In this last section of this essay, I want to hint at how these changes result into a growing desperation that can translate as trauma in Ladakh and, if fact, the entire periphery of Himalayan society.[29] How does a society, like Ladakh's, cope with this problem. Let me try to answer this question by narrating two incidents of a personal nature.

My maternal great-grandmother, Molay, was 13 years old when she left Leh after her marriage. She was almost 100 years old when she was forced into exile from Lhasa in 1957 in the wake of the occupation of Tibet by the People's Republic of China. It was not the first time that Tibet had been invaded by external forces, and Molay herself had experienced two previous invasions in the first decade of the 20th century. As an adult during these invasions, she was old enough to have vivid memories. She told us how they fled into the hills and other parts of Central Tibet for a few weeks and then returned. But this occupation was different. It was the first time as, once she crossed the border into Kalimpong in India, she was exposed to the full force of modernist development when she encountered a myriad of cars, trucks, trains and heard about aeroplanes. As a young boy in the 1960s, I spent a good part of my holidays attempting to answer her questions about the workings of the radio ('I sometimes think they must have found little people to put inside this box'), the aeroplane and the idea of communicating via the telephone. My answers would never satisfy her.

The penultimate challenge came in 1969. Molay was well over 100 by then. Neil Armstrong and his crew had landed on the moon and it fell to me to tell her about this historic event. And when I did, there was a long silence. It was as if she was trying to collapse, in those few seconds, the events between the Copernican revolution, the invention of the steam engine and the landing on the moon. After listening to her objections to such an outlandish thought, I showed her the photograph of the event in the newspaper. It was a picture of Neil Armstrong as he stood at gravity-less attention in front of the flag of the United States, saluting. She peered at the picture for a long moment, chuckled and retorted: 'How do you know this is a picture taken on the moon? It could be anywhere in Tibet!'

The second incident occurred in the first years of 21st century. I was in Leh at the invitation of the Indian chapter of Pugwash, the international activist organisation against nuclear proliferation and for conflict resolution. The agenda for the meeting was a conversation on relations between India and China. After the formal discussions, the organising committee invited local opinion makers for an informal dialogue. Ladakhis, in the context of the dispute regarding J & K, are considered a Delhi-friendly audience. But at that time there was some speculation in the media about a possible exchange of territory between Delhi and Beijing. India would concede, ran the speculation, the Aksai Chin region in the west, which China has occupied since the 1962 war, for Tamang in the east, which China claimed as its territory. The Pugwash group found, in the Ladakhis present, a hostile crowd when the discussion veered towards this topic. How could Delhi even *consider* giving away Aksai Chin, which is Ladakhi territory, without consulting them? The group, mostly from Delhi, was taken aback at the resentment and it was a topic of continued discussion over dinner that evening. The incident was instructive in that it illustrated how the loss of control over your immediate surroundings was a logical outcome of the idea of the nation-state. In other words, given the theory of the modern notion of statecraft, Delhi was not obliged to discuss with Ladakhis the decision or the consequences of this putative deal with China.

My reason for taking the time to narrate these incidents is to illustrate two things. First, that an individual can absorb far-reaching changes that impinge on their life by either ignoring them or having a sense of resignation. Molay chose to ignore it as an absurdity and resign herself to what she considered a crime against natural law—she characterised the moon landing as a sin. Ignorance, in this case, was bliss. It took her a few seconds to grapple with such rapid and drastic change. How long does it take an entire society? This question brings me to the second incident. Namely, that societies do not have the luxury of ignoring developments that change them as a collective, but through a process that is considerably more complicated; it takes a collective a lot longer. The Ladakhis at the Pugwash meeting were, in effect, rejecting the late 17th-century Westphalian concept of the nation-state.

To conclude, what does the story of the effects of the last century and a half of regional history, colonial withdrawal and partition say about the dilemmas of the modern age, using Ladakh and the societies it represents, as a case study? These quandaries show themselves as paradoxes: in history, they need to be seen as a process in which diversities converge at a certain point; in economic terms, they manifest themselves as the strain between global inclusion and local specificities; sociologically, they are represented in the pull between homogeneity and divergent interests; and in politics, the dilemma is an escalating tension between the demands of hegemony and those of self-governance at the smallest units of society.[30]

What,, then is the dilemma of our age? In a word, it is change, which by any reckoning is not a new phenomenon, with a difference.[31] A change that is unprecedented in its qualitative depth and its temporal pace. All the major religious traditions, including the Indic and Semitic, address this question. As do the philosophical traditions of the West. Indeed, Buddhism, the dominant confessional tradition of the Himalaya, speaks of the contemplation of change as one of its central philosophies. However, the change that the Tibeto-Himalayan world has experienced in the last 70 or so years has been different; one that has been at a pace that can only be described as brutal, and on a scope that has no precedence.

As described in the story of the Khwaja–Radhu clan, between 1940 and 1950, they experienced a series of radical breaks, partitions and exiles in their ways of life that might be described as 'discontinuist' in the Giddensian sense.[32] It represented a break with everything they possessed in the accumulated knowledge of their immediate world and effected every aspect of their lives: personal relationships, vocation, business interests and notions of education. The pace of this change is hard to imagine. Today, my generation tends to tease our parents about the 'shock' of their having to look for jobs. But for the young adult generation of the Khwaja–Radhu family of the mid-20th century, it was nothing less than traumatic to see their traditional world come apart. In this sense, it was not the trauma of emerging from an isolation, Ladakh having been at the crossroads of trade in the western Himalaya, but that of being hurtled into the new century, from a mentally melancholic existence into one having to grapple with everything ranging from the sheer quantity of conserved and received wisdom to radical social theory, from a barter to a cash economy and from the automobile to the landing on the moon within a space of a few decades.

The difficulty was in understanding what was happening, *as it happened*, without the respite of a period of transition and which required them to alter, suddenly, their sense of belonging and identity. Overnight, from being a frontier land, Ladakh became a borderland. The difference between the two might be described as that between, in relation to their environment and livelihoods, being interdependent, interactive, dialogic and being competitive, confrontational and suspicious. In the preceding few pages, I have described the experience of change in Ladakh as being radical, sudden, alienating, insidious, imperceptible and traumatic. It is impossible for all this to happen and not influence, detrimentally, the self-image of a people. It has affected our interpretation of history, our political outlook, our interpretation of religions and our understanding of who we are. We feel threatened about our identities, have become increasingly isolated in our relationships and progressively ignorant as to our place in the world. It has made us uncertain.

To end with this thought would hazard being accused of pessimism, even cynicism. That is not the intent of this essay. So let me end on a note that is realistic in the possibilities for the future of Ladakh, the Tibeto-Himalaya and South Asia as a whole.

What is done is done. We cannot roll back history or turn back the clock on notions of 'progress' and 'development'. But for any solution to the problems that the processes have generated, an understanding of the complexity of perspectives in interpretation is critical. My aim has been to highlight three perspectives with regard to partition and its aftermath, primarily for Ladakh, but also for the rest of the Himalayan societies.

First, the partition of the subcontinent has been part of a larger, worldwide phenomenon that took place in the wake of decolonisation and the march to 'modernity'. It is a phenomenon that has distanced us from our traditions and confronted us with a situation—historically, socially and politically—that is far more complex than we often realise. It is a battle that we will have to engage in individually, communally, nationally and internationally.

Second, we tend to believe that 'remote' regions like Ladakh, or even the entire Tibeto-Himalayan complex, are not as effected as the 'central' regions by historical events such as the partition of countries. Nothing could be further from the truth. In fact, a case can be made for an even greater acuity in the negative consequences of political adjustments such as partitions because of their location in border areas and their lack of participation in the discourse surrounding their future. This essay discusses Ladakh, but a similar argument can be made for all the cultural enclaves we find along the length of the Himalaya inclusive of the sovereign states sandwiched between the more powerful power centres in New Delhi, Beijing and Islamabad.

The third point I wish to make is that while we cannot deny the sobering reality of change—rapid, radical and unforeseen—that confronts us today, we will be better able to cope with it if we could accept the growing homogeneity in our world, while realising at the same time that it does not need to translate into hegemony. It requires a sensibility that will allow us to enjoy diversity, both immediate and global, while accepting that the journeys of the individual enclaves of uniqueness do not have to be divergent ones.

As part of the phenomenon of modernity and decolonisation, political partitions have played a significant role in solutions towards the transfers of power from the colonising to the decolonised, even as territorial acquisitiveness became a part of the repertoire of the newly formed independent states. As a result, they have brought about immense uncertainties for the peoples who are directly affected by them. It is a foundational injustice. It is the lessening of the experience of uncertainty—persistent, hidden and invidious—that will go a long way towards healing the wounds of partitions.

NOTES

1. I am grateful to *Zubaan* for the invitation to its 2008 speakers' series entitled 'Partition: The Long Shadow', which has resulted in this essay and provided me with an opportunity to think about a subject that has led to a better understanding of my state of Jammu and Kashmir, of which Ladakh is a part, in the context of Inner Eurasian history and civilisations. A good portion of the material for the hypotheses presented here was consolidated during my three-year tenure—even if I was unable to complete it—as the Maharaja Gulab Singh Chair Professor at the University of Jammu in 2004. I am grateful to the Gulab Singh Foundation for its generosity in awarding me the grant.
2. The total population of Ladakh is less than 250,000.
3. It is important to point out here that the term 'Ladakh' applies to both Leh and Kargil. Tourist accounts of it and even non-specialist papers tend to refer to Leh as Ladakh and Kargil as somehow separate from it, a tendency that the peoples of Kargil, rightly, often object to. Also, for reasons of context, I have confined myself to the portion of Ladakh that is on the Indian side of the Line of Control in the now-divided J&K. However, the arguments presented here would hold equally true for Baltistan, which was part of the old Ladakh *wazarat* of the Dogra Kingdom in its entirety between March 1846 and October 1947.
4. This is a term that describes the milieu of the Himalaya that has seen, over a millennium, a gradual penetration of Tibetan language, civilisation and religion from the north and Indic languages, civilisation and religions from the south, influencing many cultures along the length of the Himalaya. In this context, it is over looked that Tibetan civilisation is to be found in five sovereign countries today: large parts of western China, Tibet proper, Bhutan, India, Nepal and Pakistan. It is this complex that is referred to as the 'Tibeto-Himalaya'. Another dimension of this mountainous complex of cultures that is often ignored is the plurality of the terrain, ethnicities, languages, dialects and religions that define it.
5. The term 'globalisation' has increasingly been used to describe the emerging new world order. However, given the nascence of that development, I find it helpful to use other terms that allow us to grasp its full impact. 'Convergence' is one such term, which was being employed in the early 1970s. Some other terms are 'connectedness' and 'conjuncture'. For the latter terms, which convey other nuances, see Darwin (2007:18).

6. For some classic and sweeping histories of Inner Eurasia see Lattimore (1967) and Grousset (1970). A more recent history of the Eurasian landmass is to be found in Soucek (2000).
7. It was this argument that drove Csoma de Koros (1784–1842) of Hungary to make an encyclopaedic study of the language, religion and culture of Tibetan. See Mukerjee (1981) and Duka (1890).
8. A comprehensive cultural history of Tibet, the wellspring for the Tibeto-Himalaya, is Stein (1972). See also Shakabpa (1967). There have been several general histories of various periods of Tibetan history and civilisation since then, a list of which would be overly specialised. Kapstein (2006), however, might be mentioned as an excellent summary of the past work.
9. The authoritative work on this and the earlier periods of Tibetan history and its expansion is Christopher I. Beckwith (1987).
10. The title 'Dalai Lama' is a compound of the Mongol word, *taale*, which means 'ocean', and the Tibetan word *lama*, which means 'the high one'. Hence, 'The high one, ocean [of wisdom]'.
11. A good popular history of Chinggiz Khan is Man (2004). The best scholarly account is the translation of his biography from the Mongolian original. See Cleaves (1982).
12. It bears mention here that there was an earlier model for this relationship when, in the 13th century, the Mongol ruler of China, Khubilai Khan, established a monk–patron relationship with the abbot of the Shakya order of Tibetan Buddhism. It is not discussed here for reasons of space.
13. For a history of Ladakh see Francke (1907). Though somewhat dated, it is the first in a European language. Another popular account is Rizvi (1996). For a specialised history, although less readable, see Petech (1977). It covers the history of Ladakh up to 1842, when it lost its sovereignty to the Dogras.
14. For a good cultural history of Ladakh, see Snellgrove and Skorupski (1977). Later studies have added to this study, including specialised ones such as Linrothe (1999).
15. For a biographical and historical account of Gulab Singh, see Pannikar (1930) and Singh (1974). Both accounts also give a fair summary of the historical conditions of the time. A definitive history allowing us to determine whether Gulab Singh was lucky military adventurer or deliberate strategic statesman is, however, still wanting. Hashmatulah Khan's *Tarikh e Jammu o Kashmir* (1936), is a comprehensive summary of the Dogra kingdom that, albeit elliptically, provides us with an

appreciable insight into Gulab Singh's extraordinary abilities. However, the book is inaccessible to the non-Urdu reader.

16. The name of the new state that Gulab Singh created in 1846, and its subsequently famous nomenclature as 'Jammu and Kashmir', has often resulted in a disregard of the fact that Baltistan–Ladakh became a part of the Jammu raja's (later maharaja's) kingdom by conquest well *before* the more well-known region of Kashmir.
17. The idiosyncrasies of Tibetan orthography leave open the question of whether the word for this mission is *chag* or *phyag*. Both are pronounced the same, with minor dialectal variations. (The word *lo* means 'year' and its meaning is not disputed.) The former spelling means 'break' and may be a reference to the break between missions, which were often subject to several variables. The latter spelling would make it a compound of the word *phyag tshal*, which translates into 'to pay obeisance or tribute'. I have adopted the spelling *phyag* after Beckwith (1987: 199).
18. For a personal and intimate account of the last tribute mission of 1942, see Abdul W. Radhu's *Tibetan Caravan* (1981). It has since been republished under the more marketable title of *Islam in Tibet*, although the author rejected the title. The book serves to highlight the fact that it was a Muslim family that carried the tribute for a century. It is also a valuable work that gleans from oral accounts of other participants in the Central Asian economy of Ladakh.
19. We often assume that the age of European colonisation was the first. As recent studies have argued, this is a partial understanding of history and that 'colonisation' cuts across the east-west divide. See Darwin (2007: 1–6).
20. The city-states were the so-called 'khanates' of Khiva, Bukhara, Khoqand and others (Soucek 2000). The khanates were of a much earlier provenance, of course. But in the middle of the 19th century they began to be established in a modern context, in reaction to Russian expansion of the time.

    Much of the already cited Great Game was brought about by the territorial covetousness with which the contemporary imperial powers, including France and Russia, eyed the prize of British India. The gamesmanship is said to have been sparked by a letter, which fell into the hands of the British intelligence, from Napoleon Bonaparte to the tsar just before the French invasion of Russia, in which the tsar was asked to prepare to go on a joint campaign to wrest India. For a discussion of the Anglo-French rivalry in Europe that spilled onto their colonial possessions, see Jasanoff (2005).

21. A contrary view is presented in Rai (2004), who argues, with considerable justification, that the Dogra rulers were anything but plural in their governance. However, two points need to be emphasised. First is the importance of context in time: namely, the relativity of the politics of the age; second, her study is limited to the relationship between the Dogra Jammu and Kashmir, not the state in its entirety during the century of Dogra rule, which also included Gilgit, Baltistan and Ladakh.
22. For a sensitive and masterly treatment of this perspective of history, see Zeldin (1999).
23. For an anecdotal sketch of the Radhu clan, see Radhu (1981). The family also finds mention of its activities in many travellers' accounts of the 19th and early 20th centuries. Among the more well-known of these are Hedin (1909–13) and Pallis (1939). The family also finds mention in several works of scholarly research, such as Gaborieu (1973) and Rizvi (1996).
24. Hedin also mentions the family being entrusted with the *lo phyag* mission some 50 years before his encounter with its patriarchs.
25. In this context, the reports of the *aksakal*s would go to the resident in Kashmir in the case of Ladakh and to the consul general in Kashgar or Urumqi in the case of Yarkand.
26. A copy of the manuscript in my possession. Interestingly, this document was signed by a Muslim representative as well.
27. A modern history of Ladakh from 1947 onwards will have to address this radical break in the uniquely harmonious coexistence between Buddhism, Islam and Christianity in the high Himalaya. There is an attempt to address this in Kaul and Kaul (2000), but it is a partisan account. However, it does provide an unintended window into the genesis of the divide in Ladakh.
28. The Christian community of Ladakh has been ignored by the scholarship on the land until recently. However, though very small, its contribution to Ladakhi society has been disproportionately large especially in the fields of education, research and even as professionals. A listing of these accomplishments would be long both in deed and in personalities. There exists now some good work on Ladakhi Christians, but a full fledged study of the Christians of Ladakh is still needed in order to fully understand the late modern history of the western Himalaya.
29. It is relevant to mention here that given the tensions between political equity and politicking—of economic realities and material greed and

of administrative practicality and callous opportunity—almost all the borderlands of the Indian Himalaya experienced intra-country partitions that further fragmented them psychologically, socially and economically. See, for example, the carving out of artificial entities out of the north-eastern states of India, of the Indian Punjab and of Uttar Pradesh. In the case of J&K, its disputed nature has resulted in even more radical partitions (the plural is important here). These internal partitions, without prejudice to the legitimacy of the motivations for them, which involve partisan politicking, in their ultimate effect prolong the trauma of separations, fragmentations and alienations, all of which have become an instrument of state policies.

30. This argument is exemplified by the debate between what is being called the 'clash theory' and by the generic term 'globalisation', which has been much theorised. See Huntington (1996) and Stiglitz (2002).
31. The discussion on this, for reasons of space, is necessarily limited. Jurgen Habermas, Anthony Giddens and others have led a vigorous discussion on it over the last quarter of a century, although largely in relation to Europe and North America pertaining to the last 300 years or so. The effect of change in time and space on this part of the world, and particularly 'nested' subcultures and societies, offers an opportunity to test their theses clinically, in a collapsed time frame of 100 years or less. It is this that is suggested in this essay, although such an undertaking would be a much expanded work.
32. Anthony Giddens (1990: 5) used the term to describe the qualitative nature of the changes taking place in the world as a whole. Also see Giddens (1985). It would appear that the Himalaya might provide a living 'laboratory' to test this theoretical frame.

REFERENCES

Beckwith, Christopher I. 1987. *The Tibetan Empire in Central Asia*. Princeton, NJ: Princeton University Press.

Cleaves, Francis Woodman. 1982. *The Secret History of the Mongols*. Cambridge, MA: Harvard-Yenching Institute.

Darwin, John. 2007. *After Tamerlane*. New York: Penguin.

Duka, Theodore. 1890. *The Life and Works of Alexander Csoma de Koros*. London.

Francke, A.H. 1907. *History of Western Tibet*. London: W.W. Partridge.

Gaborieu, Marc. 1973. *Recit d'un voyageur Musalman au Tibet* (Tale of a Muslim Traveller in Tibet). Paris: Shadow.

Giddens, Anthony. 1985. *The Nation-State and Violence.* Cambridge: Polity Press.

Giddens, Anthony. 1990. *The Consequences of Modernity.* Stanford, CA: Stanford University Press.

Grousset, Rene. 1970. *The Empire of the Steppes: A History of Central Asia* (Naomi Walford, trans.). New Brunswick, NJ: Rutgers University Press.

Hedin, Sven. 1909–13. *Transhimalaya* (3 Vols). London: Macmillan.

Huntington, Samuel. 1996. *The Clash of Civilizations and the Remaking of the World Order.* New Delhi: Penguin.

Jasanoff, Maya. 2005. *The Edge of Empire.* New York: Alfred Knopf.

Kapstein, Matthew T. 2006. *The Tibetans.* London: Blackwell.

Kaul, Shridhar and H.N. Kaul. 2000. *Ladakh through the Ages: Towards a New Identity.* New Delhi: Indus.

Khan, Hashmatulah. 1991 (1936). *Tarikh e Jammu o Kashmir* (The History of Jammu and Kashmir). Mirpur: Sharada Book Centre.

Lattimore, Owen. 1967. *Inner Asian Frontiers of China.* Boston, MA: Beacon Press.

Linrothe, Robert. 1999. *Ruthless Compassion.* London: Serindia.

Man, John. 2004. *Genghis Khan: Life, Death and Resurrection.* London: Bantam.

Mukerjee, Hirendra N. 1981. *The Great Tibetologist Alexander Csoma de Koros.* New Delhi: Sterling.

Pallis, Marco. 1939. *Peaks and Lamas.* London: Cassell.

Pannikar, K.M. 1930. *Gulab Singh.* London: Martin Hopkinson.

Petech, Luciano. 1977. *The Kingdom of Ladakh.* Rome: Istituto Italiano per il Media ed Estremo Oriente, Rome.

Radhu, Abdul W. 1981. *Tibetan Caravan.* Paris: Fayard.

Rai, Mridu. 2004. *Hindu Rulers, Muslim Subjects.* New Delhi: Permanent Black.

Rizvi, Janet. 1996. *Ladakh: Crossroads of High Asia.* New Delhi: Oxford University Press.

Shakabpa, T.W.D. 1967. *Tibet: A Political History.* New Haven, CT: Yale University Press.

Singh, B. Satinder. 1974. *The Jammu Fox.* Carbondale, IL: Southern Illinois University Press.

Snellgrove, David and Tadeusz Skorupski. 1977. *The Cultural Heritage of Ladakh.* Warminster: Aris & Phillips.

Soucek, Svat. 2000. *A History of Inner Asia.* Cambridge: Cambridge

University Press.

Stein, R.A. 1972. *Tibetan Civilization* (J.E. Stapleton Driver, trans.). Stanford, CA: Stanford University Press.

Stiglitz, Joseph. 2002. *Making Globalization Work*. New York: W.W. Norton.

Weber, Max. 1965. *The Sociology of Religion* (Ephraim Fischoff, trans.). London: Methuen.

Zeldin, Theodore. 1999. *An Intimate History of Humanity*. New Delhi: Penguin.

CHAPTER 2

From Conclusions to Beginnings

My Journey with 'Partition'

RITA KOTHARI

As I begin to write this paper, there is a postcard on my desk (dated 5 February, 2013) from someone who, upon reading a newspaper discussion of my recent work, says my claim about the continuing role of Partition in shaping identities is "unscientific." Science, avers the writer of the postcard, "does not believe in such biases." The discourse on Partition in India today is characterized by an increasing realization (largely among scholars) of its constitutive and shaping role in the postcolonial realities of Indian citizenship. However silence and denial about Partition continue in the public sphere, despite overt and implied reminders of Partition's 'unfinished business'.

As recently as last year an article titled "No Country for Pakistani Hindus" (Vij-Aurora, 2012) laid bare the persecution of 3.5 million Hindus in Pakistan. Their move to India for safety is fraught with betrayal and rejection. Instances of refugees seeking citizenship as they arrive at the borders of Bengal, Rajasthan and Kutch remind us how inconclusive the Partition event has been, and how its ramifications persist even seven decades after. In the process of studying the 'effects' of the Partition 'event' scholars find themselves grappling as much with the present as the past. Hence contemporary writing on Partition focuses on border-crossing, anomalous citizenship and fragmented politico-social collectives. At another level, Partition scholarship also took what I consider as a testimonies' turn in the 1980s by moving from the high-politics and blame-game of 'who was responsible for Partition' to archives of memory. My engagement with Partition reflects the turn, and it is in that spirit of 'the personal intertwined with historical' that I trace my journey below.

PARTITION: A CONCLUDED EVENT

I remember watching in the eighties the first few episodes of the television serial *Tamas* before they were abruptly taken off the air. The episodes had been so absorbing, and the adrenalin rush so high that I had felt let down by its abrupt end. This and Khushwant Singh's *Train to Pakistan* had formed for me the 'core' of my Partition experience. It wasn't common to read or share books in my house, but I clearly remember watching *Tamas* with the entire family. The historical event of Partition we were watching on the screen was also the very event that had wrenched my parents out of their homeland. My mother was only seven, hence too young to understand, but my father was a teenage boy and had within him vivid memories. When I look back on those days now, I wonder why nobody mentioned (or thought) of *Tamas* as a familiar story. Why did my siblings and I watch without thinking of this as also our parents' story? I would learn many years later that although Sindh and Punjab had been geographically and culturally close, their experiences of Partition were vastly different. I would also understand many years later, that of all Partition migrants the Sindhis have willed themselves to forget Partition most successfully. When you meet Sindhis this forgetting does not come across as repressed memory, but as a pragmatic and mercantile decision to move ahead with life. Some of them even told me, 'Arre, it was a good thing, we left a well and came to an ocean.' Falzon relates the Sindhi experience of Tangiers when it was a duty-free haven until it was integrated with the independent kingdom of Morocco. Until then, it had served as a locus for imports and exports for the Sindhis who bought consumables from Hong Kong and exported them to Europe. When Tangiers ceased to be a duty free haven, the local commercial landscape changed, and the Sindhis adjusted themselves to different markets in Asia. (Falzon, 2005) Thus, entrepreneurial studies on Sindhis show how they have traditionally turned historical circumstances around to suit themselves, and this inventiveness that they brought to bear upon the Partition experience obfuscated for them and others the untold price they were paying.

There were also those who went through the experience but hadn't named it as Partition. I remember taking my aunt, a mother of ten children, (counting only the ones who survived) to a homeopath. When she was asked questions about her life, and where she grew up, she replied 'Sindh.' 'Sorry?' said the homeopath. He had not heard of a region called Sindh. My aunt clarified, 'Hum Sindh mein, woh jab Hindustan-Pakistan hua, tab yahaanaaye.' Understanding dawned upon the doctor and he immediately said, 'To aap 1947 mein aaye.' Now it was my aunt's turn to feel sheepish, 'Saal to nahin pata.' My aunt, Pushpa, passed away some months ago; before she died she wanted me to tell her about my trip to Karachi because that was where she had grown up. While I was interviewing her husband Udhavdas Makhija, she was very keen to tell me how she had travelled ticketless in a ship from Karachi to Bombay, and how when the ticket collector was on the lower deck, she would escape to the upper deck. My uncle didn't let her finish the story, because he insisted he had more important things to tell. Such conversations took place in my family only once I had decided to interview people. In the years of my growing up it would seem Partition was not only incidental but irrelevant. It was over and done with; a conclusion both for me and those who remembered it as 'Hindustan-Pakistan.'

THE BURDEN OF REFUGE: SINDH, GUJARAT, PARTITION

My academic engagement with Partition began around the year 2000. Partition was not a question I asked but an answer I had received when I was following two strands of thought I observed among Sindhis in Gujarat – shame and anti-Muslim sentiment. The shame or disavowal of Sindhi identity, I discovered, was a response to the hegemonic view among Hindu Gujaratis that Sindhis were dirty, immoral, uncouth and 'Muslim-like'. The anti-Muslim sentiment was the Sindhis's anger directed against an ethnicity they were being collapsed with and the 'reason' why they had to come to India as penniless and stateless refugees. The two tied in with each other, almost inextricably, in an interview I did with Maya Kodnani. Kodnani was a former Member of the Legislative Assembly, now serving time in prison for her 'alleged' role in the massacre of Muslims during 2002.

The process of tracing the 'roots' of Sindhi identity in India took me to an imagination of Sindh, pieced together through people's memories (including those of my family) and interviews carried out with migrants. These were juxtaposed with archives of other kinds – letters, refugee records, histories, pamphlets, literature, newspaper articles, resisting in the process an act of smooth and seamless translation of a region I had not lived in. It is beyond the scope of this paper to summarize the socio-political context of Sindh formed in no small measure by its being a frontier region that shaped the 'Hindus' and 'Muslims' more through linguistic commonality than religious difference. Continuous with shared cultures of the song and story, was a complex economic dimension by which the Hindus had cornered in Sindh lands and professions, mirroring the RSS, Muslim League and Arya Samaj in the twentieth century.

Unlike Bengal and Punjab, Sindh was not 'partitioned,' rather its Hindu minority (or most of it, barring the ones in rural Sindh such as in the Thar Parker district) fled to India. The modalities of travel from Sindh ensured relative safety, avoiding the dangers of angry mobs crossing borders in both directions, that is, Muslims from India to Sindh and Hindus from Sindh to India. A large number of Sindhi Hindus travelled by sea and came directly to the ports of Bombay, Porbandar, Veraval and Okha in Gujarat. The ones who travelled from Sindh came directly into Pali in Rajasthan thus avoiding the violent cesspool in north India. In the process of discussing modalities of travel, I have also drawn attention in the book *The Burden of Refuge* to the fortification class provided to the very rich Sindhi Hindus during Partition. The money-lending Sindhis of Shikarpur, for instance, had a well established network in places like Bombay and Bangalore, a definite advantage in their resettlement in India. The professional class among the Sindhis, the Amils, who traditionally worked as administrators in the courts of the Talpur

Mirs and eventually in the British bureaucracy during colonial times also found corresponding jobs in a divided India. And yet, these are exceptions. A majority of Sindhis lived in refugee camps fighting even to this day their ownership of the land they occupied. The well-to-do Sindhis moved out of camps, and also shed in the process practices that identified them as Sindhis. I have discussed this in the context of Gujarat, a society that has earned immense admiration for its economic and developmental opportunities as well as intense censure for its intolerance of non-Hindus. Meanwhile, both the hatred and shame seemed more common to the generation that had 'interpreted' Partition through their parents' experience. The migrants who had to leave Sindh and come to India recounted harrowing tales of 'arrival,' and the indignity of life as refugees, but seldom blamed Sindhi Muslims for their misery. The following interaction between government officials (carried out in 1948) points to the perception of Sindhi Hindus refugees in India:

S.L.Karandikar:
It is found in many instances that the refugees behave as if their miserable lot is the creation of people in this province. They must be told, sometimes with brutal frankness, that we have very little responsibility for what has happened to them. Of course in their misfortune we are one with them, we sympathise with them…but they must be told that they cannot turn themselves into a nuisance and if the Govt. has bowed down to their sentiments it is not because they have proved themselves to be a nuisance. That must be made clear to them. If I understood the Hon. Member Babubhai Patel, he said that many of the refugees want to live in cities because they have come from cities. Well, they cannot be sticklers; they cannot be choosers.

…if all the refugees who have come to this province by some misfortune of their own or misfortune of ours…they can at the earliest, be assimilated, not by putting all of them together, 5 lakhs of them, but by spreading them all over the province.

B.G. Kher:
…unfortunately the class of people who has come here is not accustomed to any manual labour. They belong either to the class of petty traders, shopkeepers or workers in offices and other

white-coated occupations. We first offered to settle them in the Kalwahtaluka on farms, and we are quite prepared to settle a colony. We found that although about a hundred went there, within a very short time they left the place, because they were not accustomed to the poverty, to the food, and to the climate and other things. The Punjabi farmers, however, who had come immediately took to it; and many of them are settling there. But our Sindhi friends are not accustomed to the kind of life that you find in Kanara and other districts.

(Correspondence between B.G.Kher and S.L.Karandikar, File No. 64/102/49. New Delhi: Government of India, Ministry of Human Affairs, National Archives.)

UNBORDERED MEMORIES

A Sindhi writer, G.L. Dodeja has a fascinating account of Sindh in an essay titled, 'Sindh jee Saar' (The meaning of Sindh, 1984) The river Indus, referred to 'Sindhu Nadi' by the Sindhis, provides a first person narrative of the history of the region. The river and language are both feminized as a woman's body, and construct upon that site the ebbs and flows of different periods in Sindh's history. In a complex and discursive formulation, the account begins with an invocation to the well-known Hindu cultural nationalist, Veer Savarkar and goes on to describe the glory that was Sindh, where the Vedas were composed. A rich civilization that she was, the female narrator tells the reader, her importance was recognized by the British, not the Mirs who ruled Sindh before them. However, the British ran ships across the river, measured it, built canals, bringing trade and prosperity. On the banks of this river lived both Hindus and Muslims in harmony, and the latter continue to miss their Hindu brethren. The glory of this mother can be restored by bringing Hindus back to the river/language/region.

Inhabiting the narrative is nostalgia for Sindhi Muslims as well as a myth-like narrative of the origins of Sindhis as the 'first and real' Hindus. Clearly such historical constructions form one of the myriad responses of a community that became a linguistic minority from being a rich, well-heeled, socially and politically powerful section of Sindh. What is particularly fascinating about this (written) story as also others is how the Sindhi refusal to deal with its past and move on as pragmatic mercantile people contrasts with the luxuriant nostalgia in the literary-imaginary space. From the historical and sociological concerns of *The Burden of Refuge* (2007) I moved to the contours of sentiment in *Unbordered Memories* (2009). The encounter with fictional narratives added a layer of complexity in that, it showed how the Sindhi Hindus felt comfortable being sentimental about Sindhi Muslims with whom they shared intimate histories. Perhaps in an environment of suspicion, anger and disapproval of their being intruders who arrived from Pakistan, everyday life did not give them the opportunity to do so. Partition writings in *Unbordered Memories* elude the template of 'utopias-becoming cesspools of violence' that we have come to associate with Partition. For instance, Mohan Kalplana's pre-partition account (below) is imbued by his commitment to the RSS, intimacy with Sindhi Muslims and a general flamboyance. I am told by Sindhi Muslims that Mohan Kalpana is remembered 'there' like a film icon of his times.

> The bomb exploded in Shikarpur colony and Prabhudas Bittani died. At four o'clock one morning, the guards surrounded our place. Few of them came upstairs and they had torches and pistols.
>
> Thrusting a torch upon my face, one of them demanded to know,
>
> 'Is this an RSS office?'
>
> 'This is a home.'
>
> 'Are there women?'
>
> 'They have gone to India. We will also leave in a few days.'
>
> 'We need to carry out a search.'
>
> 'Why?'
>
> 'For arms.'
>
> 'Arms? In here? I am a student. I wish to go to India and become an actor one day.'
>
> 'Open the door. All of it.'
>
> They entered. A petrified Chiranjeev informed me, 'The building is under military surveillance.'
>
> I instructed him, 'Tell them you are my servant if they ask you. You look untidy enough to be convincing.'
>
> I had hidden the cartridges among the tulsi plants in the balcony. Had they found those, we would have surely been arrested and

hanged. They looked at our faces, conducted a perfunctory search and left. Bhabhi said it was not a good idea to continue to live in this place. She rented a place at Ratan Talao. Meanwhile, almost all branches of the RSS had closed down. My maama's friend was a Muslim who, in order to marry a Hindu girl gave himself a Hindu name, Bhagwaan. He got me job as a tracer in the PWD at the Karachi Sadar Bazaar. I was to earn 70 rupees per month. It made me really happy. Those were very different times. On 6 January, 1948, mohajjirs from Bihar filtered into Sindh and instigated riots. They killed thousands. Some of them came to Ratan Talao to loot. A mob came to attack our house.

A young man entered with a knife.

Bhabhi said to him, "Does Islam teach you to attack women and children? What will you gain by doing this? Don't touch my children, you can kill me if you like."

There would have been bloodshed if I was present, but I was in my office. I had been told that bhabhi spoke with such conviction that they just left. A mischievous fellow from amongst the crowd took away my pair of white trousers that was hanging on a peg. I could not get over the loss of those white trousers for a long time. Each time I wore them they reminded me of Nyazi. Even now when I wear white clothes, I miss her.

I went to and from work by tram. Occasionally I would visit the mohalla where we used to live. Its charm had paled, it now wears a deserted look. No movement of any kind. Jammu Dada, who on the days of Moharram whipped himself till he bled, would soulfully say, 'So yaar, you will also go away from Sindh.' He was a boxer, and he could beat people to a pulp, but he avoided knives. These men were the magistrates of our mohalla. A ruffian entered this mohalla only at his peril. He was sure to get blows from Jammu dada.

But one day someone named Jaffrey Dada who had come from Bihar, entered the mohalla and beat Jamu dada up. Sindhis always get roughed up. Jamnu hotel used to be right below my house and sent forth to my ears all day long the songs of Pankaj Mullick and a duet from the film Jugnu sung by Mohammed Rafi and Noorjahan:

Yahhan badle wafa kabewefai ke siva kya hai/hui
Mohabbat bhi dekha, mohabbat mein bhi dokha hai/hui

What exists here but betrayal
I tested love, which is equally unfaithful

I continue to have this record. I used to think that I would go to India and marry Noorjahan, never mind if she is older. I have loved her dearly. But when I came to India, she came into Pakistan. I had made Shaikh Ayaz and Rashid Bhatti listen to this in the bungalow at Juhu Beach….

Mujse pehlisi mohabbat mere mehboob na maang.
Don't ask me my love, for that old passion

When the non-Sindhis wreaked terror upon Hindus of Sindh, they trembled in fear and lost all hope. The day dawned when we also packed our things and hired a camel cart to go to the port of Karachi. I noticed many books belonging to Sindhis being sold at 2 annas each near the Karachi Idgah ground. I bought quite a few books that day. It was perhaps 16thJanuary, 1948 and I was completing the thirteenth year of my life. With every moment, the camel-cart was taking me further and further away from my Sindh, my nation, my mother Sindhu. I passed along Burnes road, D.J. Sindh college, Kacheri road, gaadikhaato, light house, Bunder road municipality, Bolton market….Jamai Dada spotted me…he was on his bicycle and he moved along with one hand resting on the cart. "Bhau are you going away for good?"

"No," I replied, "I will come back." His eyes misted over and he quietly went away.

Back? Me? To Sindh, of all places? In the wispy smoke of my cigarette I still see my Karachi, that camel cart, and the journey of the uprooted. The cat tried very hard to jump out of the tub, but its walls were larger than mountains. What can one do?

Sighs have lost warmth, silences wilted….

(Kalpana, 2009: 63-66)

The account, suffused with sadness, nostalgia and of course sentiment, contrasts significantly with post-partition accounts by the same writer. Partition narratives by Sindhis, whether in the form of oral testimonies or narrative fiction tend to communicate much more bitterness about resettlement than any interaction with Sindhi Muslims. This is as true of ordinary people as RSS ideologues. I have discussed elsewhere the impact of the RSS on Sindh, and how the religious and political lineages of someone like Advani go back to the roots of the RSS in Sindh. If, despite deep affiliation with the RSS, Kalpana's account is imbued with warm and romantic memories, I wish to take you to another account of an individual from a Muslim League family. If Kalpana was a Sindhi Hindu reminiscing on a pre-partition moment after coming to India, what I am about to share with you now is a post-Pakistan moment, when the Hindus have gone leaving behind their homes and memories for the Sindhi Muslims. While the memories, wistful ones, stayed with the Sindhi Muslims, the homes very often went to the Mohajjirs, the penitence of which is to be found in the excerpt from Sheikh Ayaz below:

> Most of my relatives were associated with the Muslim League, and they had a pejorative name "Muhatma" for Gandhi. In fact my closest friend Wajid Ali Shaikh was the president of the Muslim League in Shikarpur and played a leading role in the incident of the Masjid Manzilgah. Had the movement of Masjid Manzilgah not taken place, Allah Bux Soomro would not have lost his life. Had Allah Baksh Soomro not been assassinated, the Sindh Assembly would not have supported the Pakistan resolution. Once Pakistan came into existence, the Muslim Leaguers of Shikarpur who had played a formative role, began to rule Shikarpur as if it was their own fiefdom.
>
> The Hindu migration from Shikarpur began much before March 1947. Hindus were going away leaving behind home and hearth, with mere locks on their properties.
>
> In those days I was a law student, and meant to appear for my final examinations. I was in Shikarpur to quietly prepare for my examination.
>
> Meanwhile, I had learnt to wrestle very well from my days in Karachi, especially at the akhada near Metharam Hostel. Every single day, I would do my exercises there, and go to the ghats of the Neti-Cheti temple for a swim. (I remember reading Savarkar's autobiography especially the part where he mentions how, when the English held him captive and were transporting him by ship, he had jumped into the Suez canal and swum his way to Cairo. From Cairo, he had gone to Paris where he wrote his revolutionary book about the revolt of 1857.) I had exercised so intensively and regularly that my body was as malleable as dough and I could slip through window grills.
>
> In the 1947 migration, thousands of Shikapuri Hindus had

abandoned their homes and belongings by simply locking them, in the hope that the riots would eventually be over, and peace would prevail and they would return home then. Colonies upon colonies in Shikarpur suddenly vanished in the exodus.

Subsequent to migration, a couple of my relatives began to steal at midnight. They would break open the locks on the houses of the Hindus and walk away with everything they could. Once, while they were discussing their various exploits in my presence, I told them, "You people are educated. What will you do if you get caught someday?"

One of them answered, "Out of the question! We can't get caught. You see, we go in the dead of night when it is completely dark and deserted. We take a damp towel and cover the locks with them, and then we start hammering away at the lock and manage to break open the lock noiselessly. We quietly pick up things, and bring them home." I thought for a bit and then said, "I will also come with you tonight."

In the eerie quiet of the night, the four of us headed out of our homes. We went to the neighbourhood behind us and stood facing a mansion owned by a renowned Hindu seth. There was an iron lock on the main entrance. One of my relatives covered it with a dripping rag and hammered at it hard, five or six times. Soundlessly the lock came unfastened. We walked into a house. There was a sitting-room, a divan, and three bedrooms. Of these, two were locked from the outside, while one was closed from inside but one of its windows was open. My relative wanted to break the locks first but I restrained him, "I will go inside and undo the latch." I put both hands through the iron grill and pulled myself up. I slithered through the barred window like a snake and jumped into the room. I lit a matchstick and flicked on a switch. It seemed as if the occupants had closed the room some days ago, and gone out. Clothes and towels lay neatly folded in the almirah. Next to it were some iron trunks that had locks on them. Beside them on the floor lay a cotton doll that had a plait and two little breasts made of cloth. The doll was naked. I couldn't tell whether the doll was Hindu or Muslim. I held the doll in my hands, and stood gazing at it. I tried to imagine its little owner who must have crossed Khokhrapar and gone over to Bombay or Banaras or Calcutta, empty-handed. I continued to gaze at it for a long time, and in the meantime my relatives got tired of waiting for me. They called out my name several times, but when I didn't respond, they finally began to strike at the lock. They continued to strike...to strike...to strike....

(Ayaz, 2009: 53–55)

Ayaz's haunting words, 'to strike... to strike' testify to the ruptures Sindhi Muslims underwent when the Hindus left Sindh. The search for what Partition did to the sociology and memory of Sindhi Muslims unearthed many such poignant accounts as both testimonies and fictionalized narratives. From the preoccupation of Sindhi Hindus in the earlier work, I moved towards memories on both sides, evident somewhat in the book *Unbordered Memories.*

The Muslims in Sindh witnessed the emptying of shops, homes, and businesses. Partition for those in Sindh was also the making of Pakistan, about contestable claims of 'owning' and 'belonging' in the new nation, of competing forms of Islam and forceful classifications of being either Muslim (as defined by the new forces that came to 'represent' Pakistan) or a 'minority'. The stories expanded the zone of experience and nation, including now questions of whether Partition needed to be separated from the formation of territorial borders. It marked a beginning of seeing Partition beyond synonymies of religion and nations, and spatialities as 'here' and 'there.' In the literary-linguistic reasons, these also got diffused because Sindhi speaking Hindus and Muslims across India and Pakistan constitute for each other an important (and only) audience. The following summary of a story based on a 'real' conversation bears my point out:

Jethanand, the protagonist of Gobind Khushalani's short story 'Kahani Kismet Jee' escapes from Sindh under life-threatening circumstances, and arrives in India as a penniless stranger, only to rise to riches in some years. In his old age, he feels the need to turn his attention to his community and roots, only to realize that the Sindhi language that forms the basis of both has begun to disappear from the lives of the Sindhis. The narrative so far is constructed of the stuff of post-Partition Sindhi success as well as failure in India. However, the narrative irony of this particular story lies in the fact that Jethanand requests his old friend Qasim in Pakistan to send him a Sindhi primer, which he and Qasim had jointly published for their firm. The primer was meant to teach the language to the new immigrants – the Mohajjirs in Pakistan – but now Jethanand needs it for his own community in India. The two friends share nostalgic moments and also the agony of Sindhi language on both sides of the border. They bond over the marginalization of Sindhi (despite the benign nation-state in India, and because of draconian measures of Pakistan) in the subcontinent.

MEMORIES AND MOVEMENTS

Given the dearth of Sindhi writers, and more so the audience, the emergence of a new writer named Kaladhar Mutwa, created waves in the Sindhi literary community in India. Mutwa is a pastoralist by occupation, Muslim by religion and rural in terms of demography. He writes in Sindhi and captures the world of Banni Grasslands, a region adjacent to the western boundary that divides India from Pakistan on the Rann of Kutch. To a predominantly urban Sindhi literary world in India, Mutwa brings a new dimension, rerminiscent of the Sindhi rural life left behind by the Hindus in Pakistan. Invested with nostalgia, authenticity and validation of the Sindhi literary genius, the Hindu Sindhi literary community celebrated Mutwa's welcome.[1]Mutwa became the reason why I visited Banni, a region that stretched my understanding of Partition from a temporal event that generated movements in 1947 creating discrete spaces, to one where ongoing processes of border-making and transcending take place and movements are made suspect.

Although in the writing of the *Burden of Refuge*, I do mention perfunctorily 'Sindhi Muslims' in India, it is a fact that until I visited Banni, Sindh had seemed to be 'out there' where Sindhi Muslims lived. Both certitudes had to be questioned along the way. Banni is Sindh, at least in people's memory and imagination. Prior to the 1965 legalisation of the border between India and Pakistan, the pastoralists would move between Sindh and Kutch, taking their cattle wherever they could find fodder. Their houses up until the 1970s were mostly temporary, re-thatched each time they returned from places like Badhin and Mirpur in Sindh to Banni. Subsequent to the Indo-Pak conflict on the Kutch border in 1965, what is called the Kutch award – a legalised border – separated Kutch from Sindh, demarcating what was different, and dividing what was similar. People and cattle had to restrict their movements: they had both become Indian citizens without realizing it. And yet the cultural imaginary of Sindh is intense and hectic in the region, generated and sustained through memory, songs, stories, embroidery, media, phone-calls, and forms of physical (now through visas and passports) as well non-physical movements to Sindh. After the pioneering contribution by Farhana Ibrahim who discusses the subliminal presence of Sindh in Kutch and Kutch's relationship with Gujarat, I followed up with Banni in Kutch, a 'region' that sees itself as 'Sindhi' rather than Kutchi or Gujarati.

> Hashim Halepota is in his seventies. A tall and impressive looking man, Hashim Dada truly looks like an Afghan. Dressed in a printed lungi and kameez, with a patko thrown on his shoulder, he walked up to me at Hotel Sham-e-Sarhad one day. We talked about this, that and the other – Sindhi folk songs, qaafis, embroidery and so on. He suggested strongly that I meet Dr. Rajaram Lakhani in Khavda. Dr. Lakhani had moved from Sindh to Kutch, and had established a successful medical practice. "He is an educated person, you will get to know a lot from him," he said. Although I have developed some wariness of 'educated' people who come with recommendations, I went along with Hashim Dada because I liked him too much to refuse. The journey was also a ruse to be able to talk to him in a casual manner. On our way to Khavda, Dada Hashim showed me to the left a patch of the Rann, and pointing, he said, "We used to go from here on camels. We bought our groceries from Sindh. This was much closer to us than Bhuj is today."
>
> "But, Dada, in the years that you were unable to go to Sindh, and your relatives could not come here, how did you and your future generations sustain this relationship?" I asked him.
>
> "What would you do if you had to live in America for some years? Would you forget your family? Would you not talk to your daughter about them, so that when she grows up she may want to see them? And this is not even the distance of India and America. It is more like Ahmedabad and Surat. In reply he said, "what has also helped is that the Sindhi language survived, largely because of the Koran. When the border happened, it did not sink in properly. We kept thinking it was all 'out there'. In a matter of time, we would be able to go to Sindh again. Two or three decades went by, and we could

> not manage to head there. Some people tried to go, not believing that something had drastically changed. They got into trouble. So we sat quietly, keeping Sindh in our consciousness. Now the routes have opened up again, and I have been there twice in the past three years." (Interview, 28 February, 2009)

Unlike the Bengal borderlands, the demarcation of Banni as a border region did not coincide with Partition in 1947. It came about quietly as a consequence of much contested lines along the western boundary through the Rann of Kutch. However, the 'performance' through which the boundaries near the last village in Dhordo are controlled reminds people of a watchful state, which stopped their access to pastures as well as people in Sindh. But borderlanders also develop counter-narratives in which the 'historical significance' of the border that separates them is minimized, and a 'selective remembering and forgetting' re-conceptualises the space that the state intervenes in. When situated in the context of Partition and its preoccupations, readjustment of spatial maps and their alignment with mental geographies opens up a relatively under-researched aspect. The tragic effect that Partition had upon the people of Banni was not manifest in movement, but the fact that *movements had to be arrested.* This also makes me question the temporal marker of 1947 as the nucleus around which Partition is understood and theorised; rather, I suggest a shift of focus to state fragmentation and borderland traumas after the official Partition was over. Of interest to me are the also the assumptions underlying the international border, making the inhabitants of Banni 'subjects' of Partition without being officially so.

The people of Banni make legal (but not necessarily licit) movements to Sindh, I have elaborated both on the emotional charge as well as silences built around their visits. Schendel makes a persuasive argument and says that 'the state's pursuit of territory – its strategy to exert complete authority over social life in its territory *produces* borders and makes them into crucial markers of the success and limitations of that strategy' (2005: 3). He defines 'borderland' as a zone or region within which lies an international border, and a borderland society as a social and cultural system straddling that border. Banni's evolution as a 'border region' where the Border Security Force monitors every movement in the region is the price its mobile populations paid for the making of the nation-state. Their movements are arrested, and in all policies they are assumed to be sedentary. Thus Banni has been required to cope with multiple shifts in its ecology, and the constant presence of the Border Security Force that watches movements in and out of Banni. The cultural ecology of Sindh that Banni strives to nurture and maintain has no place in the meta-narrative of the Indian nation-state because its origin and sustenance come from what is perceived as the "enemy" country, Pakistan. Urging us to recognize the structural forms of violence that state arrangements and nation-making projects engage in, Banni also draws attention to questions of citizenships which are divided, anomalous, and in every case, far from fully realized.

Gujarat, where Banni is situated, does not see itself as a region having much to do with Partition. As such, even the people of Banni associate Partition with the influx of Hindu Sodhas who arrived in Kutch after the Indo-Pak war of 1971. In the Sindhi spoken by people in Banni, there are no references to 1947 by phrases such as 'Hindustani-Pakistan' or 'Virhango' (separation) or 'ladpalayan' (exodus) used by the Hindu Sindhis to refer to Partition. However, people in Banni do have the boundary as a reference of both space and time; and the rupture is evident when they talk of times before (jadain Sindh chhuthuyi, literally meaning, when Sindh was free). Sindh ceased to be free, or rather Banni ceased to be free in claiming its relation with Sindh not in 1947, but at least twenty years after.

Tewari and Ben-Ari rightly urge us to see partition in lower case, not only as an essentialised event in 1947, but one that forms the 'basis for long practices such as identity, work, memory and inspiration, and the very bases on which different societies are organised' (2007: 21). Through Banni, I draw attention to partition as an organizing principle for nations and communities, and also critique the specific understanding of migration and violence in Partition studies. As Zamindar notes, it is to 'stretch our understanding of 'Partition violence' to include this long, and in some sense ongoing, bureaucratic violence of postcolonial nationhood, and to 'place partition at the heart of a twentieth century of border-making and nation-state formation' (Zamindar, 2008). The structural violence that the people of Banni went through the by being denied the right to visit their ancestral families in Sindh, the routes to fodder and livelihood in Sindh that were forever denied to them and the governmentality by which their natural movements became illegitimate seek revision in our understanding of violence and migration as two attendant consequences of Partition. Violence here is not physical, but one perpetrated upon identity, and the impact through number of people who migrated needs to be revisited to understand people whose movements were arrested. The nostalgia about a lost homeland so central to Partition literature is manifest here in nostalgia for a land that informs identity and is tantalizingly close, but out of bounds. On the other hand, identity, considered to be naturally ensconced within the bounded state of Gujarat, remains uneasy and disconnected. The story of Banni invites a re-appraisal of Partition categories and brings Gujarat yet again into focus as a Partition zone, not by the coming of Sindhi Hindus (who live in Kutch among other places) but Sindhi Muslims who found themselves on 'this' side of the border without having to or wanting to choose.

From thinking of Partition as an event that had concluded before I was born, to recognizing its shaping presence in my own life and around, from not hearing of Sindh in my community to unearthing its subterranean occupation in memory; from seeing Gujarat and Sindh as two mutually exclusive spaces to discovering their diffused and intertwined histories on the border of Kutch, my journey with Partition graduated from a conclusion to a beginning.

NOTES

1. The fact that he was a Muslim, and a large majority of the post-partition Sindhi community in India follows the Hindu right-wing Bharatiya Janata Party did not seem to matter to this equation. The ambivalence does lie, and sometimes surfaces, however, this is not the place to discuss it.

REFERENCES

Ayaz, Sheikh (2009) 'Life, a mere dream,' in Rita Kothari (ed and trans.) *Unbordered Memories*, New Delhi: Penguin.

Dodeja, G.L. (1984) *Sindh jee Saar* (The meaning of Sindh) Ulhasnagar: Harish Dodeja.

Falzon, Mark-Anthony (2005) *Cosmopolitan Connections: The Sindhi Diaspora 1860–2000*. New Delhi: Oxford University Press.

Ibrahim, Farhana. (2008). *Settlers, Saints and Sovereigns: An ethnography of state formation in Western India*. Routledge.

Tewari Jassal, Smita, and Eyal Ben-Ari (2007) "The partition motif: Concepts, Comparisons, Considerations" in *The Partition Motif in contemporary conflicts* ed. Smita Tewari Jassal and Ben-Ari Ayal. New Delhi: Sage.

Kalpana, Mohan (2009) 'Hunger, love and literature' in Rita Kothari (ed and trans.) *Unbordered Memories*, New Delhi: Penguin.

Kothari, Rita (2007) *The Burden of Refuge: The Sindhi Hindus of Gujarat*. New Delhi: Orient Blackswan.

——— (2009) *Unbordered Memories*. New Delhi: Penguin.

——— (2013) *Memories and Movements: Borders and Communities in Banni, Kutch* (Gujarat). New Delhi: Orient Blackswan.

Schendel, Willem van. (2005) *The Bengal borderland: beyond state and nation in South Asia*. London: Anthem.

Vij-Aurora, Bhavna (2012) "No Country for Pakistani Hindus" May 7, 2012, *India Today*, pp. 18–23.

Zamindar, Vazira Fazila-Yacoobali (2008) *The long partition and the making of modern South Asia: refugees, boundaries, histories*. New Delhi: Penguin–Viking.

CHAPTER 3

A Unique Grace

KAVITA PANJABI

All displaced people carry with them a profound nostalgia for the lost homeland. Yet, not everyone has the courage to actually go back there, even for a visit, even when it becomes possible to do so. My dad, chacha, and mamas, all retired men, now in their eighties, had not set eyes on their hometown, Shikarpur, since 1947. We had grown up hearing of the sacks of golden grain at home; the *sheeras* made everyday; the kababs at Haathidwar; the classrooms in which they learnt their *aliph, be, pe*; the picnics by the Sindhwah (a canal of the Indus), and learning to swim in it. All their lives they had wondered what had become of these places, what they may have begun to look like in the decades that followed; just once more they yearned to go back to the Sindh of their childhood, to see Shikarpur. Yet, ten years ago, just as we were on the verge of actually getting their visas for Pakistan, they all let the plan drop abruptly. The reason given was that they (who regularly went on holidays together even twice a year), could not fix on a time convenient to all of them. Why, after half a lifetime of longing for their childhood home, I wondered, had they suddenly decided against it, just when it was becoming possible to do so? The precise reason still remains a mystery to me, none of them will talk about it. The only thread that takes me towards a reason is the fear Dad had voiced, when I was preparing to visit Shikarpur on the way back from a peace conference in Karachi the year before that. He had said, on a halting, broken note: 'You will find nothing there…they will have razed all our homes to the ground…nothing will be the same…' Maybe they had all stepped back at the last moment because of the fear that the lost homeland carries no more the sense of home, that it can remain intact only in memory?

What, then, in the now, can the sense of a homeland be that is no more a home? Had they dared to step out from memory land into the reality of Sindh, how would they have related to it? Even if their houses still existed (as dad's did, I saw[1]), they did not have the same concrete, intimate referents of home, of their families, their possessions, their land. What, I wondered, could a homeland mean without a sense of actual territorial possession?

—

After the Partition the sense of homeland attached to Sindh in each one's intimate being had to be replaced by the sense of 'the enemy' attached to it by one's new nation state. Few of us today may understand what it meant to be torn between the love of a homeland, and fierce loyalty to an emergent nation and its leaders; and to be forced to choose between the two. The pressure to prove oneself a loyal Indian, especially if one had come from what became Pakistan was immense. Evidence of similar pressures in Pakistan too are still resonant in the very naming of the Mohajir Quaumi Party, with the term *mohajir* or refugee indicating a continuing split in the populace into insider and outsider.

My father was one of those who had fled from Pakistan to India. When we teased him, in the seventies, referring to him as a Pakistani, for his homeland was in Pakistan, he would respond vehemently, exclaiming, 'Don't ever call me a Pakistani! When I lived in Sindh it was India; the moment it became Pakistan, I left it to come to India; I have always been an Indian.' Even as he has always been an Indian, so too his home had always been in India, moving with him when he moved; but the homeland, Sindh, had to be left behind. Tragically emptied of the intimate sense of home, it had to be determinedly refilled with the political sense of the 'enemy land'. Or so I thought.

His personal sense of homeland, still based in his childhood in Shikarpur, Pakistan, seemed to be at complete odds with his passionate political loyalty to the Indian nation, with the former rarely being articulated in the early years; yet both, I now realize, were simultaneously integral to his identity. An entire childhood, spent hiding behind sacks of dry fruit that my grandfather exported to Iran, hanging out at Chandruhalwai's at Hathidwar, playing truant in school, cooking mutton in sealed clay pots at picnics by the canal, rushing to Maddua Ma's rescue when the bone of the famed Pallo[2] got stuck in her throat, and she purportedly brought the town down with her screams – these were all located in Shikarpur. Yet all of these still lived on in him, as did his love of India, his deep admiration of Gandhi and Nehru, and his own investment in the future of India. As we grew older, and as the trauma of the Partition gradually subsided, he began to share his memories of his childhood and youth. What is now Pakistan was as intrinsic to his identity as India was, irrespective of the political borders that divided one from the other. The Sindhi identity of his childhood and the Indian identity of his adulthood, rather than being disjointed and conflicting dimensions of his being, had found continuity in it; together, they comprised an identity that was actually, to use Mufti's evocative phrase, "at odds with the geometry of selves put into place by partition." (274) Within him, his lived realities of Shikarpur and Bombay dovetailed into each other; outside, they were positioned on opposing sides of this geometry of borders.

Did the 14 million dislocated people of the Partition all lead schizophrenic lives, and submit mutely to the will of politicians, to the regimes of their nation states? We did resist. We resisted this imposition of borders, and the institutionalization of enmity, across the forcibly divided realms of our shared culture. Thousands of ordinary families continued to meet across these frontiers, hundreds of marriages are still being forged across them. Scores of extraordinary writers and poets that this traumatic history threw up, protested against the forced divide, the inhumanity of the times. The haunting words Faiz Ahmed Faiz penned in the midst of the violence of independence still pierce through this history into the present: *'Yeh subah woh toh nahin/ ki jiska intezaar thhaaha mein…'* ('This dawn is not the one/that was the much awaited one';) Saadat Hasan Manto represented the blurring of all lines of Hindu and Muslim, self and other, *desh* and *dushman* in his depictions of the bestiality to which all had succumbed – his *Siyah Hashiye* or *Black Borders* is powerful testimony to this savage blurring. Even in that culture of grotesque violence, we were one; it was our shared culture.

Qurratul-ain-Hyder later dwelt upon the threads of love and belonging that continued to hold people in webs of relationships across the divide so strongly that even decades after the partition the warp and woof of these threads continued to put to test the jingoism of the borders. Akhtar-uz-zaman-Elias, author of *Khwabnamah*, the Bangladeshi magnum opus of the partition in the East, said, even as late as the nineties, when one of his legs had to be amputated in a Kolkata hospital, 'I've always claimed I've lived with one foot on either side of the border. Now I'm leaving one foot behind on your side for ever – and of course I've made sure it's the bad foot!' Transformation of painful reality into poignant irony was his hallmark, and the parodying of enmity in confident chuckles of intimate friendship his signature. Such tropes have become as much a part of our shared culture across the borders as has the chauvinism which they keep challenging.

—

Some say the sense of a homeland left behind forever remains as a powerful memory of loss, handed down from generation to generation. Yet, indefatigable creatures that we human beings are, we do carry our sense of home with us and remake it as we traverse geographies and histories; so this shadow of loss does gently fade into the past as the endeavour to live in the present takes over. This remaking of homes could have been a testament of our resilience, and also our creativity, across all the barbed wire borders erected on the face of this subcontinent. Then why have many of us so carefully nurtured the sense of loss across generations, to a point in the present when it is this loss, rather than the resilience, that structures our identities? It is ironic, because now this loss, far from being our own experience, is but a memory borrowed from our parents and grandparents.

Why do we hold on to this sense of loss even when it is not directly ours? Maybe because it was nurtured as a badge of our people by our loved ones, our parents or grandparents, who were uprooted and displaced forever? Maybe. But it's also time to ask some hard questions. The suffering was very real, very painful; and deeply admirable the resilience with which people dealt with it. Yet, how can such suffering become the badge of a tribe that has wronged as much as it was wronged? The partition was no holocaust experienced by one community at the hands of another, more powerful one – it was an event of reciprocal violence, of a deeply ironic 'equality' in which the violated was also the violator, the oppressor also the victim.

Yet we do hold on to the sense of historical loss. And loss seeks redemption. When such loss becomes the badge of an entire dislocated population, then it implicitly targets those responsible for it, it demands compensation, reparation, justice. But, in this case, from whom do we seek redressal, who is to redeem our losses? The very people whom we violated? Who hold us responsible? Could we ever make amends for the losses they incurred due to us? Sometimes loss is irredeemable.

—

Yet what happens when this need for historical reparation is as compelling as the loss is irredeemable? The millions who lost their homes and lands on both sides, who lost loved ones in barbaric ways, certainly understood this as massive historical violence; and violence too seeks reparation. Is this a civilizational dead end, in the face of which we can only continue to wage wars and tear each other apart?

A reconciliatory force may of course be forged anew, but can it be forged from a blank slate? Or be built upon a forcibly suppressed history of mutual violence? Wherein lies the possibility of reconciliation that is capable of restoring the broken continuity of a history divided?

If, at times like this, when loss is irredeemable, can reparation be forged *elsewhere* than in the compensation of past losses? Let us not forget that partition was an experience not only of loss but also of betrayal, of violence, of indignity, of humiliation. It is this history of betrayal, indignity and humiliation that continues to haunt us even in situations where refugee populations have actually rebuilt their homes, regained their lost security, and forgotten the loss of loved ones whom they may never even have known. Yet, there is also a mutually shared sense of violation, shared across the very divide that became so painful. It is deeply ironic, that the devastating sense of being profoundly violated be shared with none less than the very violator; but it is also, maybe, a leveller, also, albeit paradoxically, a sharing that actually grounds some hope.

Can reparation be forged then in the acceptance of mutual loss, but also in a realization of a shared history of trauma and dispossession, such that none can understand each better than the other? Can it grow thus from the cultivation of a sense of mutual belonging to each other in the troubled post-Lapsarian present too, not just in an idyllic pre-Partition past? Is there, somewhere, a powerful force of such a shared history, waiting to be acknowledged, still capable of bringing us together?

Maybe it is time to acknowledge that in this shared experience of violation we belong with each other. We are inextricably, ontologically, bound to each other in having violated each other simultaneously, in having suffered simultaneously, and in equally abysmal ways. It is a sense of belonging with each other that 14 million people and their 42 million descendants and millions of other countrymen and women all know – but this knowing seems to have been swept away under the carpet of history. For, to acknowledge such mutual identification in suffering is also to acknowledge such mutual culpability in the exercise of evil.

It is time to acknowledge this mutual culpability, for the stakes are high, very high indeed. Our defense budgets, inflated by our mutual enmity, take away substantially from our food, health and education budgets; the grand performance of hostility at the Wagah border everyday keeps thousands of children hungry, sick and illiterate in both our countries. Acknowledgement of mutual culpability may not immediately pave the way for forgiveness, but at least it does for mutual acceptance. Hannah Arendt evocatively expressed the radical evil of the holocaust as a 'structural element in the realm of human affairs' in which human beings 'are unable to forgive what they cannot punish…and unable to punish what has turned out to be unforgivable.' (241) Because the ravages of the holocaust could be neither punished nor forgiven, they transcended the potentialities of human power. Yet, the Partition was not the holocaust. It was not a unilateral drive by one race to annihilate the other; it was the same people, divided into two religious communities, reducing each other to sub-human levels in a terrifying mutual reciprocity. It comprised a grotesque mirroring of culpability, a twinning of this structural element of radical evil. The evil of the holocaust transcends the potentialities of human power because one community of people subject another to unthinkable abjection, abjection that could neither be punished nor forgiven; but the mutuality of the evil of the partition demands, ethically, a mutual reparation within the realm of human affairs, however difficult it may be. Mutual culpability could call for mutual punishment, but that could only perpetuate a chain of further violence; what is more rational is the move towards mutual acceptance, mutual forgiveness. A mutual acknowledgement of culpability, a joint mourning for the lives we took, a shared atonement for the sorrows we wreaked upon each other, all have the potential to propel both sides towards reconciliation, to end the cyclical recurrence of violence. Violence between nations may be forcibly stopped or pre-empted by international forces or economic considerations, but the impetus to violence in human beings can only be stemmed by coming to terms with pain – the pain of being violated as well as of having violated. The question then is, do we have the courage to acknowledge our own culpability each to the other, have the will to build on it anew, with the inspiration to forge constructive civilizational bonds across this impasse? The mutual evil may have transcended human realms, but the power of mutual forgiveness resides in human realms.

—

Actually, it seems that a poignant and painful sense of belonging with each other – poignant in the sense of loss of shared living, painful in the acknowledgement of the mutual violation - has always characterized popular wisdom since 1947. Such wisdom is carried in the oral narratives of the undocumented interactions of daily life, and in the unheeded insights of literature. The tragedy is that such wisdom of everyday life, and the creative relationships it engenders, is efficiently swept away beneath the camouflages of political expediency – it does not make it to the pages of history, far less policy.

There seems to be an unspoken tension, in fact an inverse relationship, between political mappings of identity, and personal or literary mappings of affect across the borders of India and Pakistan. Political and institutional cultures are marked by a shrinking, jingoistic partitioning of languages, religions and culture across these borders; simultaneously, personal narratives and literary writings transcend these very borders in nuanced, complex, and ever expanding trajectories of remembrance and re-connection. [1]

What does it mean to continue to belong affectively to the lived culture of a 'lost' land across the border? On the other hand, what are the costs of claiming exclusive ownership of the texts and sites of a once shared culture? A contradiction persists between affective cultural belonging across political borders and the chauvinistic erasure of cross border elements in culture. The latter facilitates claims of exclusive proprietorship of literary canons by institutions on each side of the border. In this internally contradictory cartography of cultural relations between the peoples of India and Pakistan, the workings of the literary and personal domains offer substantial challenges to the workings of institutional culture, creating a significant subterranean field of tension that calls for attention – and offers some hope for the future.

In India, Urdu has been distanced into the realms of Muslim (read Pakistani) culture, even as our Hindustani, that resonated so richly with the echoes of Perso-Arabic heritages, has been confined into the straitjacket of an obtuse sanskritized Doordarshan Hindi, such that none of the Hindustani populations of this country would recognize their lived realities in it. Pakistani television, on the other hand, has systematically divested its Urdu of the indigenous Khadiboli, and invested it instead with a baggage of Arabic that makes is as alien to the lived culture of this subcontinent today as it would have been in the time of its founder Amir Khusrau. Pakistani text books begin with the Sultanate and the Mughal rule, as if history did not exist before the arrival of the Muslim rulers, even as India struggles to compensate the 'loss' of Mohanjodaro and Harappa to Pakistan, and digs away furiously in Lothal and Dholavira to establish its own claim to the antiquity of the Indus Valley civilization. In mainstream literary scholarship Radha and Krishna are now mere 'Indian' elements, irrespective of the fact that Pakistani qawwals such as Bahauddin and Razauddin continue to sing poignantly about their *viraha*; and while Jhule Lal and Mast Qalandar have become dear to us again, through the popularity of festivals of sufi music, they are nevertheless perceived as Pakistani elements adopted by a progressive Indian population. Literary and cultural institutions of India claim Faiz, Manto and Noor Jehan as their own, despite the fact that these legends lived their last in Pakistan, and the nature of their politics and creativity put all political borders to shame; on the other hand Rabindranath is claimed as an exclusively Indian poet – catch any Indian institution acknowledging him as a Bangladeshi too – irrespective of the facts that he happened to be the creator of Bangaldesh's national anthem, was born there, wrote most of his important early works there, and had also resisted the partitioning of Bengal by launching a massive festival of *rakshabandhan* across the political divide.

The ways in which we construct our personal, literary and cultural maps across the borders call for some reflection. In fact, 'the modes and forms in which memories of the pre-partition past are popularly kept alive' (Mufti: 262) pose questions of immense importance for cross-border scholarship, and cross border relations too - and they have only just begun to be explored.

Aamir Mufti's work is one such instance that analyses both, the everyday means by which ordinary people in Pakistan unsettle the finality of the partition, [3] as well as the cultural resources of Sufism that a poet like Faiz drew upon to represent an experience of self that spans across the communal and nation-state divides.[4]Referring to the forms in which people keep memories alive at the everyday level, Mufti observes that

> In Pakistani cities, such as Lahore, Karachi, Hyderabad, and Rawalpindi, which were cleared of their large Hindu and Sikh populations within months of August 1947, the signs of these erstwhile residents are ubiquitously present-in the sight of sealed-off temples, in street and neighborhood names that continue to be used despite municipal attempts to erase them, in the signs of the

> "other's" tongue above doorways in the old quarter of any city. The memories and stories of older eyewitnesses, the tales travelers tell of revisiting long-abandoned homes, the enormous font of verbal genres—folk songs, nursery rhymes, proverbs, and popular tales about characters such as Birbal and Mullah Dopiaza – are among the many everyday means of unsettling the finality of partition, of disconcerting the self with its own uncertainty. (262)

Unsettling the finality of the partition. One 'story' that does this with the gentlest, yet most enduring impact, is that of my friend's Suman's[3] mother Seema's return to her childhood home in Gujranwala in the early eighties. Suman's father, a senior government officer, had been invited to a bilateral meeting in Lahore, and her mother was permitted to accompany him on that trip. Seema's family had fled their Gujranwala home when she had been but a toddler of three. All she remembered of that house were the lovely green blue tiles across which she used to crawl, fascinated by their colour and design. Suman's grandfather was still alive at the time of this trip, so Seema went to her father and got the address of their family home in Gujranwala from him. After the meeting, Suman's parents made their way to Gujranwala. As they disembarked from the car, and began to walk through the loaded fruit orchards towards the house, flashes of recognition began to hit Seema. When they reached the doorway of the house they looked up at the name above the arch, and did a double take – the nameplate still said 'Kapoor Haveli.' An elderly woman answered the door and found the two strangers standing there. After what seemed like an aeon, Seema finally found her voice: 'Ye Kapoor Haveli hai?' she asked quietly. The woman took one long hard look at them, then whipped around and ran back into the house calling out excitedly, '*Aaoaao, dekho, kaun aaye hain! Ghar ke maalik aaye hain!*' Come, come, see who is here! The owners of the house are here!

The entire household, sons, daughters-in-law, grandchildren, came streaming out of their rooms at this unbelievable call as Suman's parents continued to stand at the doorway, still uncertain of what their reception would be like. The woman of the house came back and ushered them into the sitting area in the hall with an uncanny sense of familiarity. What ensued was a series of narratives about how that family had fled India in 1947, how they had been given this house to live in upon presenting their papers of property left behind, the family members they had lost to Hindu marauders on the journey here, and how Seema's family must have encountered a similar fate at the hands of Muslim attackers too. Across the hours the uncanny sense of familiarity solidified into inexplicable bonds as the conversations surged forth over all possibilities of accusations or forgiveness – both sides found in the other a deep, nuanced understanding, a gentleness that comes with reflection, a sense of mutual belonging that only wounded communities can experience with each other.

As the stars flooded into the dark grey twilight, Seema and her husband got up to take their leave. The woman of the house stopped them, '*Nahin nahin, aap yahan se khaali haath kaise jaayenge, ek tohfa toh leke hi jaana parega.*' No, how can you go away empty handed from here, you will have to take at least a gift. Seema protested, saying they were there on an official trip, they could not possibly receive any gifts. '*Nahin, kam se kam ek chadar toh le hi jaani paregi.*' No, you will have to take one chadar at least, was the firm response. Looking around in desperation Seema suddenly glimpsed something from a remote past – a few pieces of half- broken tiles lying in the corner of the room. Blue green in color, they still carried the familiar designs imprinted on the toddler's mind as she had crawled across them forty odd years ago. She raised her hand hesitantly, pointing with a shaking finger, then suddenly found her hand steadying itself. She pointed firmly at the broken tiles of her memory and laid claim to them, as firmly as the woman had insisted on giving her a chadar, and said: 'I want those.' Unsettling the finality of partition can sometimes lead to an unshakeable certainty too, as many families such as these would have experienced, but maybe never articulated.

Mufti attributes the immense popularity of Faiz on both sides of the border to the fact that his poetry is 'a site for the elaboration of a selfhood at odds with the geometry of selves put into place by partition.' Extremely valuable about this staging of selfhood in Faiz's poetry is that it takes division seriously, 'refusing to treat it as merely epiphenomenal, as in the unity-in-diversity formula of Indian nationalism.... In fact, it suggests that division, the indefinitely extended separation from the beloved, constitutes the very ground from which union can be contemplated.' (Mufti 248)

As Seema had reclaimed her past with the gift of those tiles in Gujranwala, someone else in Sindh had reclaimed my family as his own, with his gift of Sindhi sufi songs. This is how I had written about this when it had happened ten years ago:

> In Karachi, Nandita [my friend from Bombay] introduced me to Junejo, the chairperson of Jiye Sindh Mahaz, a Sindhi nationalist organization. Junejo had given up his job in the Karachi Development Authority as an engineer and registered as an independent advocate in order to work for the Mahaz. An extremely attentive, gentle person, he welcomed me like a long lost friend, and soon had me narrating my family history to him, in Sindhi. He then responded saying that he was going to move a resolution demanding that all the Sindhis who had been forced to flee Sindh should be allowed to come back and resettle here if they wanted to. The thought of my father who had spent a lifetime distancing himself from Sindh because it was now in Pakistan, who when teased about being a Pakistani would reply angrily, saying: 'Pakistan did not exist when I lived in Sindh; I have always been an Indian' flitted through my head. Nandita and I burst out, almost in unison, 'Let them just be able to visit Sindh first.'
>
> At the end of this conversation, he asked me what he could do for me in Karachi. When I told him I was looking for music I already knew was not easy to come by – songs of the faqirs, the poetry of Abdul Latif, Sachal Sarmast, Shaikh Ayyaz, and the folk songs of Mai Bhagi, Sindh's legendary singer - his eyes lit up. I'll get them for you, he promised. When I pleaded for addresses of shops instead he just looked at me firmly and said, 'What will take you eight hours to locate, I will find in two hours. You have very little time here.'
>
> Our paths did not cross the next day. On the third day, Nandita said he had been looking for me. We found Junejo talking to a group of people, but upon seeing us he disengaged himself from them, and came up to us, his right hand buried in his *jhola*. 'I was looking for you yesterday. Here's what you wanted.' Saying this he dug into his bag and took out five cassettes, obviously well used. I immediately realized that it was not easy, even for local Sindhis, to locate the music I'd wanted – these were his own cassettes.

> I looked at this person, a stranger until two days ago, in complete wonderment, and exclaimed, 'But these are yours, how can you give these away to me? And they are not even available easily, I know.' 'Take them, they're for you,' he said. I stood there, perplexed, 'I don't know what to say, *aap apni cheezein mujhe sab kaise de de rahein hain?*' Why are you giving away your own things to me? He looked at me sadly and said, '*Aap kya hamaare apne nahin hain? Aur vaise bhi, hum aapke kitne karzdaar hain…aap logon ko hamne yahan se nikaal jo diya tha.*' Aren't you one of us as well? Besides, we owe you so much… after all we drove you out of here.

Unable to deal with the intensity of this history of pain and guilt I just looked at him mutely, then walked away.

Now Junejo is for me, he is as for for my friend Nandita Bhavnani, Dada Junejo. He calls every time he comes to Bombay, leaves gifts for me with her, as an elder brother would. The pain and guilt have mellowed, a sense of belonging remains.

Today, even as I write this, I suddenly realize how I had not been ready to understand my pious grandmother Bhabi's sense of belonging with mullahs in the act of prayer. Bhabi's narratives of being persecuted by sword and torch-bearing marauders as she fled down the lanes of Quetta clutching on to her two sons, desperately seeking safety, had traumatized me as a child, which is maybe why I had not been ready to understand, even ten years ago, what I had written then:

> Bhabi would always chide my brother and me for not praying to god. '*Tanwwan tab kadi bhagwana jo naalo bhi na vatthanda aayo*', she would remonstrate – 'You never bother to even utter god's name'; and pointing in the direction of the mosque outside our window she'd say, 'Tanwankhon tah ho mullah suttho ahey, deenyan mein panjhha dafaa pehinje khudakhe tab yaad kando ahey. Even that mullah is better than you, he calls out to his god five times a day.' I of course had been taken aback at such a show of magnanimity in her appreciation of the mullah, even as she continued to refuse to touch any food prepared by Muslims.

I remember with a start today that what she had not said *pehinje khudakhe,* his khuda, she had actually said *bhagwanakhe*, using the same word for his god that she did for her own. In my complete immaturity

I had been unable to understand, I still remember struggling with this memory when I was writing, thinking I must have heard wrong, she must have said khuda, not bhagwan. Somewhere, maybe in the solace she found in her prayer, she must have come to accept that her bhagwan was also the mullah's god. In prayer she had settled her scores. In her religiosity she related more to the devout mullah of a religious community that had hounded her than she did to her own godless grandchildren.

The language of faith, that had become a vehicle of such enmity in 1947, can also become a language of the most profound offerings of the human soul, as I was to learn in Lahore in 2001 and then again in Karachi in 2003. I had written:

> On one of the first cab rides the last time, in 2001, my curious cabbie had launched into an animated conversation about borders and separations, about families divided, and then ventured onto the 'tough' discussion that many an Indian and Pakistani choose not to get locked into – about Kashmir. This time it had been surprisingly easy. When I said the peoples of Kashmir should have the freedom to decide their future for themselves, that India and Pakistan had already wasted millions of rupees and thousands of lives in mindless violence and wars across half a century, and that these resources and lives could have well enriched homes and schools in both our nations, he responded in enthusiastic agreement, albeit in some surprise that we found ourselves nodding in such agreement. After a moment of reflection, he asked, *'Aap ka mazhab kya hai?'* What faith do you belong to? He showed complete disbelief when I said I had no mazhab, no religion. *'Yeh kaise ho sakta hai?'* How can that be? *'Koi to mazhab hoga, aap Hindu hain, Mussalman hain? Kisi ishwar, ya phir Allah peh to aapka bharosa hoga?'* You must belong to some faith, must be a Hindu, or a Muslim? You must believe in some god? Ishwar or Allah? *'Haan hai,'* I responded quietly. *'Insaan mein hai. Sirf insaan mein.'* Yes, I have faith in human beings. Only in human beings. The man looked at me as if thrown into bewilderment – but I was wrong. It was the astonished joy of recognition, of having heard the echoes of a long lost friend in me – a friend who many years ago had won him over to the terse beauty of this belief in human beings. This time he won me over, as he smiled, *'Aapne to ha maare dil ki baat keh di.'* You've spoken the words of my heart. Yet the language of

> the spirit clearly occupied a much higher place in his being than the language of the heart. For, after a few more lanes of companionable silence in this new found bonding, he turned to me and made me an offering. An offering of the highest order that a believer can make: '*Aap hamaara mazhab kyon nahin apna leteen hain?*' Why don't you make my religion your own?

He was not drawing me into the fold of his religion – he was offering it to me, to make my own.

And then in Karachi two years later:

> The closest I was to come to that sense of a sacred transaction was to be on this, my third trip to Pakistan, when we visited the *mazaar* of Abdullah Shah Gazi the most revered *pir* of Karachi. This was famed to be the oldest Muslim shrine in the sub-continent. Feica and Uttam [friends from Karachi and Kolkata] had already descended the stairs back onto the city road. Krishnadi [my friend from Kolkata] and I were lingering at the windows watching the waves in the sea behind, and also witnessing the desperate hope in the wailing of the woman who had brought her sick child to the mazaar. The vivid red, green and gold of the *chadars* offered to the *pir* flooded our senses in the morning sunlight. As we turned a corner to move towards the door, a man who had been sitting at a low table in a corner got up slowly, went to the altar in the centre of the room, and beckoned to us. We walked up to him, a bit uncertainly. Before we knew it, he had swung the red, green and gold of a *chadar* around each of us and pulled the ends to the front, draping us in the finest he had to offer. We stood rooted to the ground, speechless. All we could do was look at him, and each other, with feelings as yet inexpressible. Two atheists stunned by the blessedness of grace – and that too in an 'enemy' nation.

As we made our way down the stairs in a stupor, Faiz's dua rang out in my ears, loud and clear:

Aaiye haath uthaayen hum bhi
Come, let us raise our hands in supplication

Hum jinhe rasmedua yaad nahin
We, who do not remember the ritual of prayer

Hum jinhe soze mohabbat kesiwah
Who, except the passion of love,

Koi but, koi khuda yaad nahin
Do not remember any idol, any god.

I do not know how my father would have related to his homeland if he had ever revisited it. I only know that I belong to it now in inalienable ways. The question of any territorial ownership does not arise for me, I have never, ever, thought of any part of the terrain of Sindh as my land. The question of political ownership – India's ownership of Pakistan, or even of just Sindh – would now be a violation of grace. Of the grace with which the cabbie in Lahore opened the doors of his profoundest beliefs to me, of the grace with which the man at the mazaar of Abdullah Shah Gazi enveloped us in the protective *chadar* of the revered *pir*. It is a grace of spirit that the people of India and Pakistan and Bangladesh have cultivated, instinctively, caringly, resolutely, across the territorial and material divides of politics and nation. It is a grace that is nurtured by the very divides it keeps demolishing, a grace that draws us into belonging, with each other, across the treacherous barbed wire of the borders. It is a unique grace, of claiming belonging without possessing.

NOTES

1. See my *Old Maps and New: Legacies of the Partition* (Seagull Books, 2004) for an account of my trip to Shikarpur, and the narratives of other journeys to Pakistan.
2. The river Indus used to be rich in Pallo, the same as the famous Ilish fish of Bengal.
3. Names changed.

REFERENCES

Arendt, Hannah, 1958,1998. *The Human Condition*. Chicago and London: Chicago University Press.

Mufti, Aamir. 2004. "Towards a Lyric History of India". boundary 231:2, pp. 245–274.

A GOOD EDUCATION

{Acknowledgement: SARAI-CSDS Independent Fellowship}

Texts by Amiya Sen are from *Aranyalipi* (The Forest Chronicles), based on her interactions and experiences in the refugee camps of Dandakaranya. Translated from Bengali by Bhaswati Ghosh

Bye Babu. Be good and don't be naughty. See you in the evening.
1975, it must have been.
The moment my mother left for work, I was the Prince of 7, Kasturba Niketan, a rehabilitation home for partition refugees, tucked in a corner of Lajpat Nagar, New Delhi. My government servant-grandmother, blessed with staff quarters here, took care of the roof above. For me, the day was blissful in the company of Dadu, my retired grandfather and Didu—my in-and-out grandmother—who would return in time to feed her grandson.
Where from?
Reba Mandal from Khulna
Now hurry up will you?
AMIYA SEN
Assistant Superintendent cum Matron, Kasturba Niketan

Much of Didu's day would be spent in taking stock of the sarkari kindness, scheduling lives of the widow inmates and their children. But evenings were private, strictly for her grandson and endless storytelling.
Once upon a time in our house in Barisal, now in Bangladesh...
It's quite late. Go to sleep now...
Go to sleep child. Tonight's story is not for you...
And once I slept, would begin Didu's second life, her writing. Late into the night, when the world slept, her stories based on her daily encounters would awake to light and freedom. Passionate and possessed, writing was her only refuge from a clerical, ruthless world of files and forms.
The Statesman

DANDAKARANYA
MADHYA PRADESH
Dear One,
Welcome to the Dandakaranya Project.
The Raipur station isn't far from these
desolate plains. This place feels peaceful
but on its edge. I am told right now 35,000 are
living here in Mana Camp. Farmers, sweet-makers,
blacksmiths, potters and cobblers from East Bengal.
Unlike us, the privileged who moved at the very outset,
these are the real lambs of partition. Pushed by the
unanticipated attack of death, they reached the Indian border.
The very sight of them made the West Bengal government
scream, 'There's no space here—we can't accommodate them.'
Despite being unlettered and helpless, they show such dignity!
But who will understand! We are such a self-oblivious race.
152

I WANT YOU TO HAVE US MILK
This is a result of America's magnanimity. While others got Patton tanks, we got unlimited milk powder. We should remain grateful to America. Please bring your cup and stand in a queue!
USAID
I am here on work. Simply put, here my job is to counsel and convince mothers to send their kids to Delhi. The government promises these children a good education in Kasturba Niketan. I never felt the scheme was bad yet my fear was, would they agree? They would have to let go of their children for years! That's exactly how it was meant to work. These boys and girls wouldn't be returning before they could be on their own. We are talking of 15–20 years. Here, their world changes within minutes; who knows if Mana Camp will exist when they return? Even if it does, these destitute women might get lost in the deep crannies of the forest.
153

In *Apple Cart*, Bernard Shaw described the working of a democratic government: as fire engulfed a house, the fire brigade was called. Before the firefighters arrived, not only did the house turn into ashes, but a new building had replaced the old one. But how could the firemen leave without fulfilling their obligations? Before leaving, they ensured the new building was drenched. Brick by brick.

Dear one, couldn't something better have been planned for them? Couldn't there be a home similar to the one in Delhi somewhere in West Bengal—a familiar land?

Anyway, the project's focus was education. For this reason, it wasn't feasible to take the entire family to Delhi. I hadn't revealed to them that along with their children, they were going to lose their dole money too. Still, I fought on with my dilemmas—remember I was here on work.

'Please don't break up families.
If they get separated now,
they might never be reunited.
Please try to take entire families.'

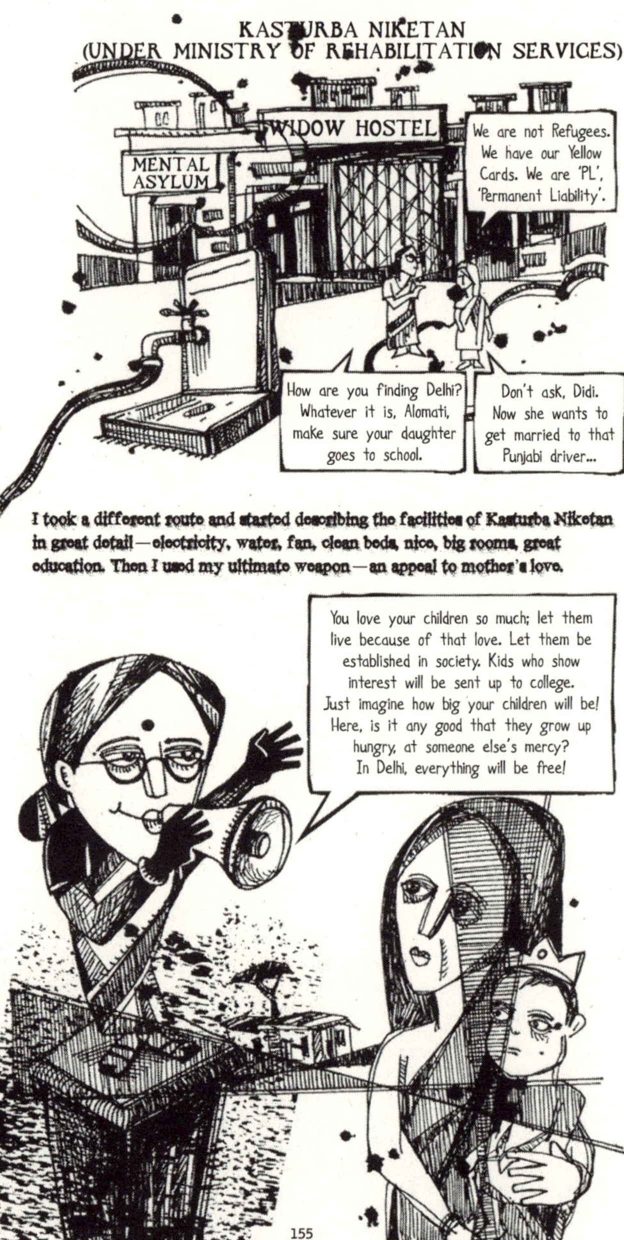
KASTURBA NIKETAN
(UNDER MINISTRY OF REHABILITATION SERVICES)
WIDOW HOSTEL
MENTAL ASYLUM
We are not Refugees. We have our Yellow Cards. We are 'PL', 'Permanent Liability'.
How are you finding Delhi? Whatever it is, Alomati, make sure your daughter goes to school.
Don't ask, Didi. Now she wants to get married to that Punjabi driver...
I took a different route and started describing the facilities of Kasturba Niketan in great detail—electricity, water, fan, clean beds, nice, big rooms, great education. Then I used my ultimate weapon—an appeal to mother's love.
You love your children so much; let them live because of that love. Let them be established in society. Kids who show interest will be sent up to college. Just imagine how big your children will be! Here, is it any good that they grow up hungry, at someone else's mercy? In Delhi, everything will be free!
155

With 165 Punjabi and 125 Bengali families, most of the Bengali lot at Mana Camp were transferred to Kasturba Niketan in 1967. Kasturba Niketan had three adjacent buildings—an administrative building, a hostel for Bengali widows and their children, and a mental asylum. Often the asylum inmates would sneak into the widows' hostel creating havoc for the caretakers.

For Didu, being a Bengali did not make life any bit easier. For the widows she was 'adminstration', hence responsible for the life they lived. And since they both spoke the same language, she would often receive a generous dose of their curses. On a good day, she was just one of them.

As for me—the grandson of 'adminstration', I enjoyed getting pampered from all sides.

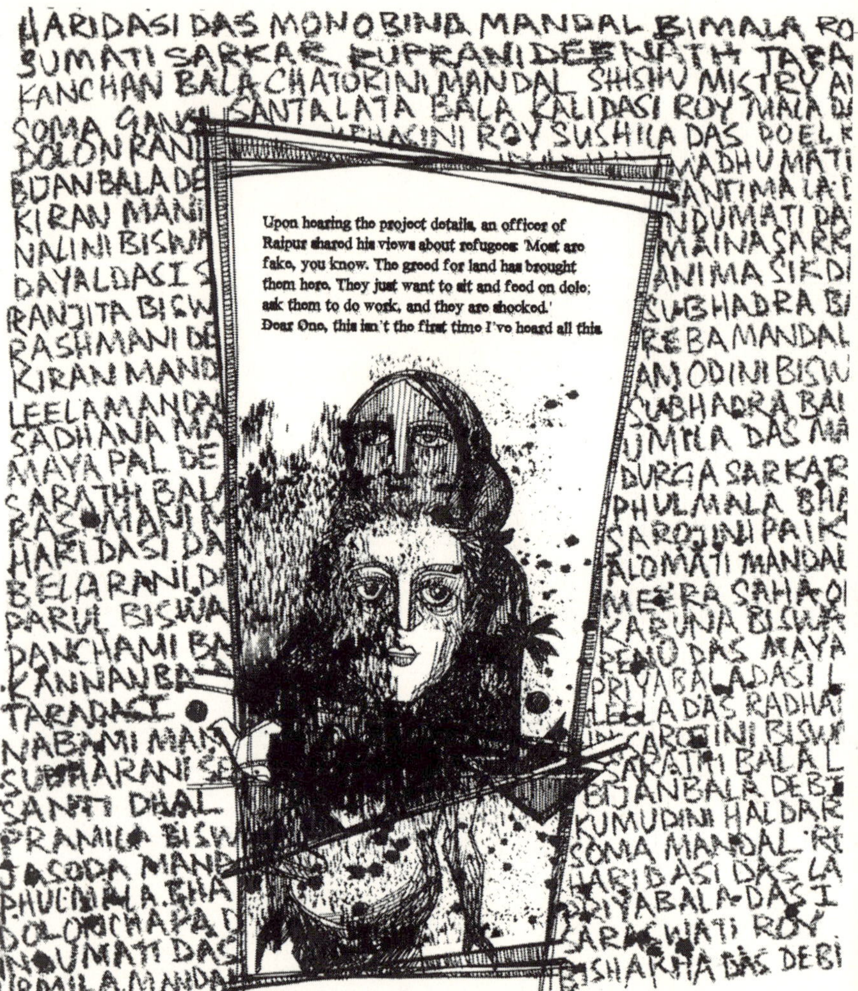

No one came forward to heal the physical or mental wounds of this helpless lot that not only suffered violence, lost their loved ones, but were also rendered homeless and insecure. Instead, they were packed like sardines inside train coaches. Before they could gather their bearings they found themselves in unfamiliar territory. The riverine lot were now landlocked burdens on the state. But, Dear One, who made it so difficult? On the other side, Pakistan's policy shows no confusion. Its policies with regard to minorities in East Bengal are no different from its attitude towards Pakhtuns and the other minorities of NWFP. Therefore, heaping blame on Pakistan is futile.

In the end, most of the mothers relented. When they agreed, my heart ached with a void. Where will these children return after 15 years? Will they have even a faint memory of Mana Camp then? Even if they do, will they find their mothers eagerly waiting for them?

Dear One, you are a man and might laugh at this. But I am a mother and all those thoughts crossed my mind. Seeing some of them agree, I shivered. I had played the devil's advocate.

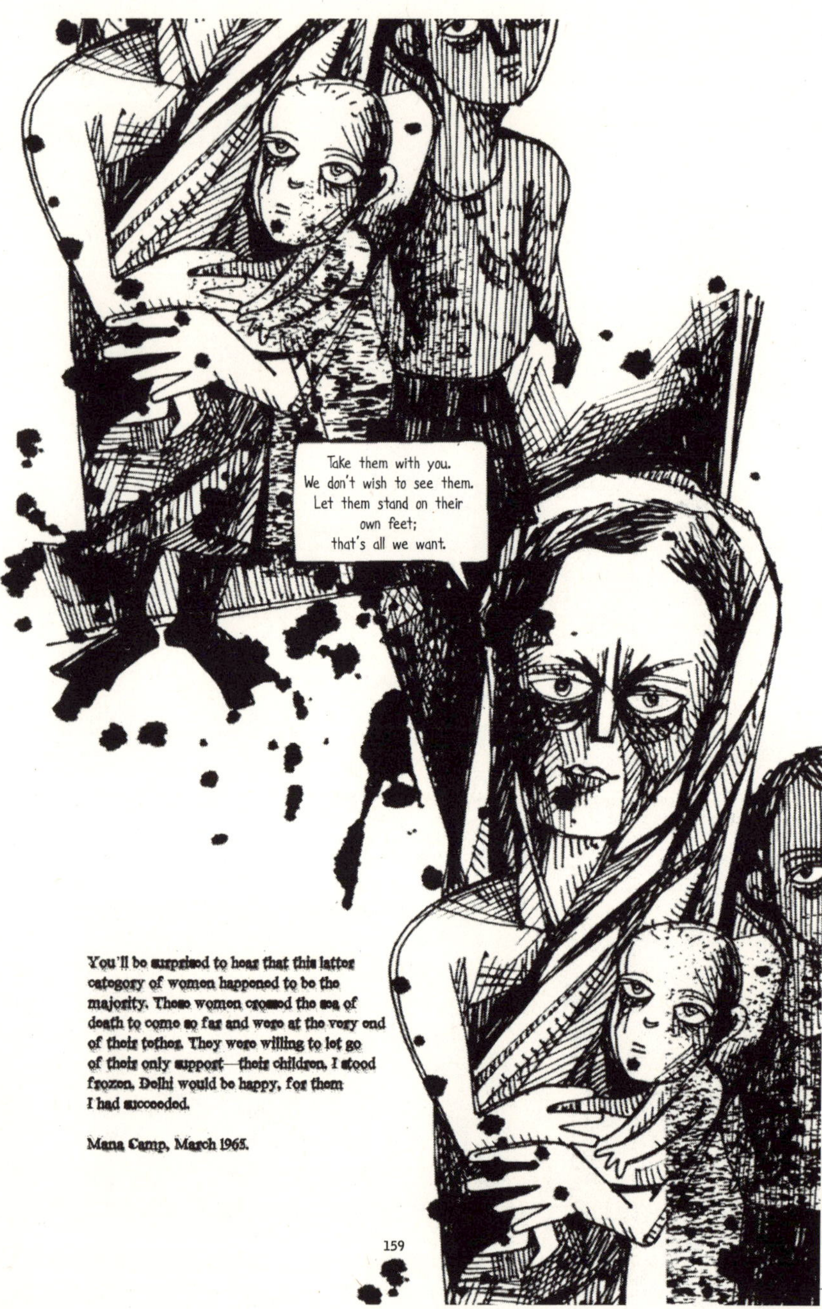
Take them with you.
We don't wish to see them.
Let them stand on their own feet;
that's all we want.
You'll be surprised to hear that this latter category of women happened to be the majority. These women crossed the sea of death to come so far and were at the very end of their tethers. They were willing to let go of their only support—their children. I stood frozen. Delhi would be happy, for them I had succeeded.
Mana Camp, March 1965.
159

It's time we sent Babu to a school. I've made some enquiries. There's a new one...
That Blue something? But... that's English medium...
Yes...on Feroze Gandhi Marg. In a big house...
But...that's English medium! How will he learn Bangla then?
Forget Bangla. Let him go to school, get some education...
We need to do this urgently. That's the only way we can keep him away from these refugee kids
Aaah! Refugee Kids huh? If they are refugees...
The Statesman

Suited-booted, enjoying the privilege of being held by the refugee kids. Kasturba Niketan, Lajpat Nagar, New Delhi.

VISHWAJYOTI GHOSH

is the author of the graphic novel *Delhi Calm* (HarperCollins India, 2010). His comics are regularly published in various journals and anthologies, including *When Kulbhushan Met Stockli, Ctrl.Alt.Shift Unmasks Corruption* and *Pao Anthology of Comics.* He is also a member of the Pao Comics Collective.

In 2009 he published a collection of postcards based on classified ads titled *Times New Roman & Countrymen.* Vishwajyoti Ghosh is also the author of the cartoon column *FULL TOSS.* Associated with Inverted Commas, a communication collective, he is currently wrapping up a mapping project in the working clusters of Gurgaon.

He lives and works in New Delhi.

AMIYA SEN (1916–90)

is a Bengali novelist and short story writer whose writings have been published in various Bengali journals, including *Desh, Jugantar,* and *Basumati.* She engaged with the world of migrants and refugees through most of her writings.

Apart from her non-fiction books, *Aranyalipi* and *New Delhi-r Nepathye,* she also wrote *Shonai Shono Rupkatha,* a children's book and a memoir of her childhood engagement with the Indian freedom movement.

CHAPTER 5

Partition and the Politics of Citizenship in Assam

SANJIB BARUAH

In the past few years Chief Minister Tarun Gogoi of Assam has been speaking in favour of extending refugee status to a section of the unauthorised Bangladeshi migrants living in his state. The Assam government, he says, will make a proposal to the Centre to that effect ('Assam CM Bats for Asylum to Migrants' 2013). But the idea is not exactly new. Ever since the partition of 1947, many in India have been saying that India has responsibilities towards those who had found themselves on the 'wrong' side of the border, and that accommodating partition refugees is a historic obligation of the Indian state. In making his case, however, Gogoi cites international norms. 'Seeking political asylum in a different country by the people of another country,' he said, 'is not a new thing. This has happened elsewhere in the world as well. So, granting refugee status to those who had left their country of origin under certain compulsions is not wrong' ('Gogoi on Refugee Status for Bangladeshi Migrants' 2013).

Yet the citizenship status of cross-border migrants from Bangladesh – and before 1971 from East Pakistan – has long been an emotionally charged and polarising issue in Assam, sparking street protests, civil disorder and violence, even though the chief minister has tried to present his proposal as if it is unrelated to any of that. Thus, referring to the much-discussed Assam Accord of 1985, according to which migrants crossing into India after 25 March 1971 are non-citizens – which is the current Indian law – Gogoi said his proposal for refugee status would not violate its stipulation because his proposal is about those who are forced to migrate and not those who migrate voluntarily ('Gogoi Pitches for Refugee Status' 2013).

A certain amount of ambiguity is probably unavoidable in any talk of asylum and refugees. 'Despite the use of the term "refugee" in popular everyday speech,' says a study of refugees and the international states system, 'the actual meaning behind the concept remains unclear' (Haddad 2008: 23). The term is both normative and descriptive, and there is ample room for manipulating its meaning. Faced with growing numbers of asylum seekers, politicians in Western countries generally prefer a narrower definition, and apart from trying to physically stop potential claimants from entering their countries, they try to 'limit the scope of any definition by tightening the procedural and substantive requirements necessary for the individual to satisfy criteria for refugee status' (Haddad 2008: 25). Gogoi, however, does not try to define the term 'refugee' narrowly. If anything, he gives it an unusually expansive meaning.

Refugee status, he says, 'should be given to all, irrespective of the person being a Hindu or a Muslim' ('Gogoi on Refugee Status for Bangladeshi Migrants' 2013). This allows him to say that his position, or rather the Congress party's position, is not the same as that of Hindu nationalists.[1] At a press conference in April 2012, he said, that while the Bharatiya Janata Party (BJP) talks only about refugee status for Hindus, he is interested in extending the same to 'Buddhists, Christians and Muslims along with Hindus' ('Gogoi Wants Refugee Status for Bangladeshis' 2012). But what it means in concrete terms, especially vis-à-vis Muslim migrants from Bangladesh, is unclear. It would be hard to make the case that they face religious persecution in Bangladesh. Gogoi's message, however, was less expansive in the speeches he made in 2011 at election rallies in the Barak Valley. He then specifically spoke of 'the Bengali Hindus of Assam' as deserving refugee status since 'persecution forced them to migrate from Bangladesh' ('Pollvault 2011' 2011).

No one disputes that unauthorised cross-border migration from Bangladesh to Assam does occur, though the estimates vary enormously. This essay does not enter the debate on numbers, but proceeds on the assumption that the number is significant. As Kamal Sadiq (2009: 37) puts it, 'illegal immigration' in places like Assam is 'invisible' only in the sense that 'publically, no one has systematic data, but if one digs deeper, the state has confidential estimates based on reports and surveys by intelligence or police agencies'. Sadiq's book *Paper Citizens* is a study of a few world regions where 'illegals' are welcomed 'both as economic workers and as political actors' (ibid.: 168). Apart from Assam, he finds evidence of 'illegal immigrants' voting in significant numbers in parts of Malaysia and Pakistan as well. The widespread use of illegally acquired identity documents to circumvent state regulations or to access public benefits makes this possible. He describes the process as follows:

> As soon as an illegal immigrant enters... [the] country, he/she starts seeking some form of citizenship documents to legitimize his/her entry and stay. This is a cumulative process. Illegal immigrants accumulate a variety of documentation over time, as they ease their way into citizenship. Each piece of documentation – plastic or paper – brings an additional layer of legitimacy until, finally, the illegal immigrant becomes 'visible' as a citizen (ibid.: 113).

In the case of Assam, the phenomena can only be understood when put in the context of the partition of the subcontinent, and the civil war between East and West Pakistan that led to the emergence of Bangladesh in 1971. The latter too produced a major refugee crisis that deeply affected Assam. India had militarily supported the Bangladesh liberation war and any pretence of border control was abandoned during that period.

Gogoi's promised proposal for refugee status follows earlier moves in Assam's post-partition history that sought to deal with the reality of unauthorised large-scale migration from across the border. The ambiguity of the citizenship status of a significant number of people living in Assam has been an explicit issue, or a subtext, in a number of major political battles in the post-partition history of Assam.

MANY PARTITIONS

> The decision about the creation of Pakistan had just been announced and people were indulging in all kinds of surmises about

> the pattern of life that would emerge. But no one's imagination could go very far.

This is how 'We Have Arrived in Amritsar', Bhisham Sahni's (1989: 180–81) classic short story on partition begins. It evokes the uncertainties created by the decision to divide India. The characters speculate on whether Jinnah, the founding father of Pakistan, would relocate there or continue living in Bombay. 'Why should he leave Bombay? I think he'll continue to live in Bombay and continue visiting Pakistan,' says the narrator. The characters try to guess whether the towns of Lahore and Gurdaspur would be part of India or of Pakistan (ibid.).

Historians today reject the notion of partition as a single decisive one-time event. Gyanendra Pandey emphasises the 'extraordinary uncertainty' of the period. He writes:

> A fact that is easily overlooked today, precisely because of the categorical establishment of India and Pakistan as separate, sovereign states on 15 August 1947 is that it was just ten weeks before that date, in early June 1947, that the formal, constitutional partition of British India was finally decided upon (Pandey 2001: 39).

The idea of Pakistan did not begin as a quest for separate sovereign statehood. It was 'perfectly compatible with a federal or confederal state structure covering the whole of India', and as late as the summer of 1946, as Ayesha Jalal (1998: 93) reminds us, 'the demand for a wholly separate and sovereign state of "Pakistan" remained open to negotiation.'

During the years leading up to 1947, there were at least three different conceptions of partition, writes Pandey (2001: 40): 'The meaning of Partition was worked out step by step in 1947–8 and afterwards.' There was no single chronological rhythm to the process. Nor can it be understood by assuming that the process has led inevitably towards the consolidation of two (and later three) bounded national spaces. If 'there are many different stories to be told about 1947, many different perspectives to be recovered' (ibid.: 44), in the case of Assam, the meaning of partition has been unfolding slowly over decades through a torturous process.

THE WEIGHT OF THE PAST

In order to understand postcolonial Assam's persistent difficulties with the question of citizenship of post-partition migrants, one must begin with the fact in the early part of the 20th century, when Assam was under British colonial rule, it was official policy to encourage the settlement of Muslim East Bengali peasants in Assam. The people of deltaic eastern Bengal are known for their remarkable mobility: they move frequently as rivers change course and are adept at starting new settlements. In the 19th and 20th centuries, the region's worsening economic conditions accelerated emigration (van Schendel 2005: 210–11). Assam came within the orbit of East Bengali emigration when British colonial officials began trying to attract settlers to make 'productive' use of Assam's 'wastelands'. Partition did not reverse this logic of a land frontier. The flow of people from one of the subcontinent's most densely populated areas to a relatively sparsely populated one couldn't suddenly be switched off. Indeed, the borders created by partition, as Willem van Schendel puts it, impinged on East Bengal's 'demographic scenario of increasingly desperate "self-rescue migration"' (ibid.: 211). Ironically, the pressure on Assam only intensified after partition. It generated a massive movement of Hindus, while the economically induced migration of poor Muslim peasants continued.

During the last two decades of colonial rule, however, the policy of settling East Bengali Muslim peasants in the 'wastelands' of Assam began facing stiff resistance. As a result, the provincial government was forced to introduce certain restrictions on areas where immigrants could settle. The Muslim League opposed those restrictions. Their position on the issue merged with the call for Pakistan and the demand that Assam be part of it. During the closing years of British colonial rule, it became an emotionally charged and divisive issue, and it gave the partition debate in Assam a particular inflection that is deeply etched in local memory. Unfortunately, the rest of India – and our political classes – have almost no knowledge of this important period of Assam's history.

Another relevant piece of history is that Assam as a British colonial province included the Bengali-speaking and populous district of Sylhet. It became part of East Pakistan/Bangladesh in 1947 as a result of a referendum, which the Mountbatten Plan had stipulated because of Sylhet's peculiar position of being part of 'predominantly non-Muslim' Assam but being contiguous to Bengal, which was 'predominantly Muslim' (quoted in Chakrabarty 2004: 176). Since so many partition accounts are focused on the division of Bengal and Punjab, Sylhet's separation from Assam has been aptly called 'a forgotten story of India's Partition' (Dasgupta 2008:18). Given the district's religious demography, it was not a surprise that a majority of Sylhetis voted to join East Bengal, which became East Pakistan. Except for a part of Karimganj subdivision – the four police station areas of Patharkandi, Ratabari, Badarpur and a portion of Karimganj – the rest of Sylhet district became part of East Pakistan/Bangladesh. Its separation from Assam is sometimes referred to as Sylhet's return to Bengal because of district's historical and cultural affinity with the latter. Prior to 1874, when it became a part of the newly constituted chief commissioner's province of Assam, Sylhet was a part of Bengal.

Tensions between the predominantly Assamese-speaking Brahmaputra Valley and the predominantly Bengali-speaking Surma Valley – which apart from Sylhet, also included the district of Cachar – were a constant in the political history of British colonial Assam. This is the context of historian Amalendu Guha's (1977: 319) characterisation of the Sylhet referendum as 'a life-time's opportunity for the Assamese leadership "to get rid of Sylhet" and carve out a linguistically more homogeneous province'. Indeed, the outcome of the referendum was 'greeted with immense relief and hope by Assam', though obviously Assam, in this context, refers mostly to the Brahmaputra Valley. The relief, however, was 'momentary and short lived', for Assamese leaders did not foresee the massive migration of Hindus from Sylhet and the rest of East Bengal that was about to start once partition became a reality (Bhattacharjee 2012: 218–19). 'Over the next few years,' as Anindita Dasgupta (2008: 19) writes, 'large numbers of Sylheti Hindus from the ceded parts of Sylhet district began to relocate to the Indian North-East, particularly to southern Assam, where they had established considerable economic and social networks in the period 1874–1947.' Southern Assam is what was then the district of Cachar. Those parts of Sylhet's Karimganj subdivision that did not become part of Pakistan were now attached to it. In terms of the contemporary map of Assam, southern Assam refers to the predominantly Bengali-speaking Barak Valley: the districts of Cachar, Karimganj and Hailakandi. A fundamentally different set of memories of partition prevails in this part of Assam compared to those in the Brahmaputra Valley.

An important clue to understanding the difficulties that post-partition Assam has had with the question of citizenship of migrants from East Pakistan/Bangladesh is clearly the history of emigration from the same region to Assam during the British colonial period. A quotation that often appears in writings on immigration to Assam – and cited in support of very different arguments – is from C.S. Mullan, a British colonial official responsible for the census report of 1931. He famously predicted that, 'Immigration is likely to alter permanently the whole future of Assam and to destroy more surely than the Burmese invasion of 1820, the whole structure of Assamese culture and civilization.' In another thirty years, he said, it was not improbable that 'Sibsagar district will be the only part of Assam in which the Assamese will find itself at home' (cited in Das 1989: xi).

The distinguished historian Amalendu Guha (1977: 212) had termed Mullan's formulation 'mischievous and blatantly fallacious', aimed at setting 'the Assamese and the immigrants… against each other'. But viewed from today's vantage point, one has to recognise that the demographic transformation of Assam did indeed take place pretty much along the lines of Mullan's prediction. It has led to significant shifts in the state's demographic balance and it continues to have major consequences for Assamese politics, and for the way the meaning of partition has unfolded in Assam. But contrary to Mullan's prediction, as Monirul Hussain (1993: 207) points out, 'the entire East Bengali Muslim peasant community' adopted Axomiya or Assamese as their mother tongue. This produced a cultural politics very different from what Mullan had in mind. This has led M.S. Prabhakara (1999) to comment that the real fears of the ethnic Assamese in the Brahmaputra Valley are rather different from the 'standard' view. It is not so much that they fear that Bengali speakers would eventually outnumber them or that Assam's demographic transformation presents a danger to the very existence of Assamese language and culture. Their real fear, says Prabhakara, is that the new generation of Assamese speakers – mostly Muslims of East Bengali descent – would claim Assamese as their own language, 'stealing away, as it were, a crucial cultural patrimony which defines the Assamese people' (ibid.).

CITIZENS, REFUGEES OR FOREIGNERS? MULTIPLE FRAMES

Ambiguities of citizenship are not unique to post-partition India. There is probably no place on earth where the legal lenses of the citizen–foreigner binary shapes everyone's perception of who belongs in a country and who does not. There are multiple perspectives in India on the unauthorised migrants crossing the partition border. I will use the term 'frame' to talk about these different ways of seeing and interpreting. In the eyes of some people, unauthorised migrants crossing the partition border violate the territorial sanctity of the post-partition national space. To others, their presence may be illegal, but licit. Whether they are Hindus or Muslims is important to some. To others, the year a person crossed the border is crucial. At least that is how Indian citizenship laws define citizenship in post-partition India. Others see another important set of values, the land rights of indigenous peoples, as trumping the claims of cross-border migrants to citizenship and land rights. Perhaps these competing frames align our mental maps with our inner moral geography.

It is possible to distinguish two dominant frames in the perception of cross-border migrants in post-partition India: the Nehruvian non-discriminatory frame and the soft Hindu nationalist frame, soft because it is not associated only with Hindu nationalist groups and has resonance well beyond this political circle. The laws on Indian citizenship reflect the Nehruvian non-discriminatory frame. They continue to embody the spirit of the Nehru–Liaquat pact of 1950 that the leaders of India and Pakistan signed amidst fears of further outbreak of violence against religious minorities. They tried to draw a line and 'maintain a kind of status quo of populations' (Singh 1984: 1059). As a result, Indian law does not distinguish between Hindu and Muslim arrivals from Pakistan or Bangladesh, except in the context of the immediate post-partition years, and that too only by implication. Both categories of migrants are foreigners. If they wish to become Indian citizens, they can do so, but only through a legal process akin to naturalisation. However, when it comes to Hindus, the frame of India's citizenship laws is not necessarily the most authoritative.

The former Indian foreign minister Jaswant Singh, and one of Hindu nationalism's best-known moderate voices, suggests that the continued migration of Hindus to India is 'the compelling logic of the consequences of partition' (ibid.). It is unlikely that Singh would see Muslim migration as part of the same 'compelling logic'. Radical Hindu nationalists are not as subtle about the distinction. An article in a Hindu right publication speaks of a 'sinister plan' to turn Assam and the rest of North-East India into a Muslim majority region (Mall 2004). The Vishwa Hindu Parishad's Praveen Togadia once called on the Indian government to 'capture one or two districts in Bangladesh, acquire space and send these infiltrators there' (cited in van Schendel 2005: 233). There is little doubt about the implicit definition of a 'Bangladeshi' in Hindu nationalist discourse; it certainly does not include Hindus.

But there are other frames through which the migrant from across the partition border is viewed in India. In the Brahmaputra Valley, there is a distinct regional patriotic frame that is shaped by the particular history that I have outlined earlier.[2] As I have indicated, since British colonial times, Assam has stubbornly resisted being treated by its rulers as a land without people or with very few people. Land frontiers, after all, are not natural; they are made by humans. It is unequal political power, and often conquest, that turns territories inhabited by some people into frontiers for other people. Once the modern politics of numbers was introduced, it was probably inevitable that 'whose land is it?' would emerge as the key question in Assam's politics. Indeed, local resistance had forced changes in its settlement policy well before partition, and it defined the battle-lines vis-à-vis partition. If in pan-Indian circles there is insufficient understanding of this and other such frames, it is partly because India's 'retrospectively constructed' official nationalism seeks to ignore and delegitimise 'the multiple alternative strands of popular nationalism and communitarianism that lost out in the final battle for state power' in 1947 (Jalal 2001: 741).

The citizenship debates in post-partition Assam parallel disputes over the policy of settling 'wastelands' with East Bengali Muslim immigrants in the colonial era. In 1937, Jawaharlal Nehru visited Assam as president of the Indian National Congress amidst a raging controversy over that policy. But he called on the Assamese to give primacy to 'national' problems over 'provincial' ones, and he labelled the Assamese concern with East Bengali immigration 'provincial'. The Assamese public intellectual Jnananath Bora wrote a scathing critique of Nehru for refusing to appreciate Assam's predicament. If so-called provincial issues have a lower priority for the nation, he said, the answer surely lies in making Assam independent: a *deś* (country) rather than a *pradeś* (region). The collision of frames continued to play out in the period after independence. In the 1980s, when the United Liberation Front of Assam (ULFA) appeared on the scene, a new generation explicitly reclaimed Bora's intellectual legacy (Kar 2011: 53–54).

It is hardly surprising that tension between the regional patriotic frame and the pan-Indian frame came to the fore immediately after partition when serious differences arose between the Assam government and New Delhi on the question of settling refugees. The Gopinath Bardoloi-led Congress government tried to restrict the number of refugees being resettled in Assam on the grounds that there was insufficient land available to accommodate them. A state government circular issued in May 1948, said:

> In view of the emergency created by the influx of refugees into the province from East Pakistan territories and in order to preserve peace, tranquility and social equilibrium in towns and villages, the government reiterates its policy that settlement of land should be in no circumstances made with persons who are not indigenous to the province (cited in Chaudhury 2002: 64).

In a letter to the Assam chief minister, Jawaharlal Nehru said that Assam 'was getting a bad name for its narrow-minded policy'. The position that Assam did not have enough land to accommodate refugees, he said, was unacceptable: 'It is patent that if land is not available in Assam, it is still less available in the rest of India.' According to a careful historian of this controversy, Nehru treated the Assam chief minister's judgments 'with little respect' and displayed 'impatience and condescension' (Barooah 1990: 29–30).

These developments are not unlike those that occurred in the Pakistani province of Sindh over settling Muslim refugees migrating to the Pakistani side of the border. The prime minister of Sindh, Muhammad Ayub Khuhro, had expressed reservations about Sindh's ability to accommodate as many refugees as demanded by Pakistani leaders. By December 1947, while over 4 million refugees were resettled in West Punjab, only 244,000 were resettled in Sindh. Pakistan's minister for refugees and rehabilitation, Raja Ghazanfar Ali, chastised Khuhro for his unwillingness to resettle more refugees in Sindh. By complaining about the burden of refugees on his province, Ali said that the Sindh prime minister was raising the 'virus of provincialism'. Indeed, Khuhro was later dismissed from his position partly because of his stance on refugee resettlement. The episode 'not only strengthened Sindhi sentiment against the center, but also encouraged the precedent of executive action against elected representatives, which boded ill for the future' (Talbot 2010: 36). One can say the same about the Indian political establishment's reaction to the Assam politicians' reservations about refugee settlement, and its effects on the future relations between Assam and New Delhi.

On the other hand, as it should be clear by now, the Barak Valley has nurtured very different memories of partition, and its perspective on the question of the citizenship of cross-border migrants – of Hindu migrants to be precise – is fundamentally different from that in the Brahmaputra Valley. The same applies to the neighbouring state of Tripura where, with the settlement of large numbers of partition refugees, Bengali Hindus became the state's numerical majority as well as its dominant face. In this regard, Assam's Barak Valley (and the state of Tripura) is not unlike cities like Delhi, where Hindu refugees provide support for political parties and organisations that are seen as sympathetic to refugees just as in 'the politics of Pakistan Punjab cities like Lahore, Sialkot, Multan, and Gujranwal… cannot be understood without reference to the refugee dimension' (ibid.).

MANAGING THE AMBIGUITIES OF CITIZENSHIP

It was during the six-year Assam Movement in 1979–85 that the rest of India became somewhat familiar with its tangled 'foreigner' question. For the first time in the history of postcolonial India, political developments in Assam received coverage in the national press over an extended period. The leaders of the movement claimed that as many as 4.5 to 5 million people in the state, that is, 31 to 34 per cent of the population in 1971, could be foreigners and that the state's electoral rolls included the names of hundreds and thousands of such foreigners. The infamous massacre in Nellie where about 2,000 people, mostly Muslims of East Bengali descent, were killed, occurred during the 1983 state Assembly elections, which were boycotted by supporters of Assam Movement. Significant changes were made to Indian citizenship laws during and after the movement. The Citizenship Amendment Act of 1986 effectively gave de facto amnesty to all those who had crossed the border into Assam in the quarter-century following partition, irrespective of whether they were Hindu or Muslim. But how did Assam manage to keep a lid on this issue for more than three decades before it blew up?

After the tensions over refugee settlement in the immediate post-partition period subsided, the state's ruling Congress party settled down to a creative way of managing the ambiguities of citizenship status. They took a non-discriminatory and open-to-all approach to the electoral rolls and avoided the troublesome matter of sorting out who was a refugee and who an illegal immigrant. Inclusion in the electoral rolls became a part of the Congress's patronage system controlled by local political brokers. Almost any adult in Assam could get his or her name included in the electoral rolls. This arrangement allowed Assam to postpone indefinitely any effort to seek a resolution of the foreigner question. As I have indicated, this was possible because what is involved in the exercise of franchise in India is not a formal certificate of citizenship, but a rudimentary document like a 'ration card'. The Japanese scholar Hiroshi Sato (2005: 103–4) talks of the 'fault lines' between the normative definition of citizenship in Indian law and the actual exercise of franchise being based on rudimentary documents. In Assam, these fault lines arguably became the epicentre of a veritable political explosion in 1979.

Ironically, what upset this applecart was not any action or statement by a radical local nationalist. In 1978, no less a constitutional authority than India's chief electoral commissioner made an astounding series of statements. S.L. Shakdher spoke publicly of the 'large-scale inclusions of foreign nationals in the electoral rolls'. Seemingly unaware of the political firestorm he was about to set off, he warned that 'a stage would be reached when the state may have to reckon with the foreign nationals who may in all probability constitute a sizeable percentage if not the majority of population' (Asom Jagriti 1980: 12). The words became the lightning rod for the Assam Movement. The campaign mobilised enormous popular support, but there is little doubt that at the same time it made a large segment of Assam's population quite anxious. While the campaign couched its argument in constitutional and legal language, labels such as Bangladeshis, illegal immigrants and foreigners that gained currency, sounded menacing to many.

The holding of elections became highly contested affairs during the Assam Movement. The Parliamentary elections of 1979 could not be held in most parts of the state because of organised opposition – they were held in only a couple of 14 constituencies. The exceptions, predictably, were the two constituencies in the Barak Valley. The Assam Accord, signed in August 1985, which ended the movement agreed on various 'cut-off dates' of entry into India. Immigrants from East Pakistan who entered Assam before 1 January 1966 would be formally made citizens or, more accurately, would be deemed citizens. Those who came between 1 January 1966 and 24 March 1971 would be disenfranchised for 10 years. Those who came after 25 March 1971 and stayed were supposedly going to be detected, their names deleted from the electoral rolls and expelled. However, as we shall see, the law to put this into effect did not quite do that. In 1986, India's citizenship law was amended to take into account the Assam Accord: it clarified that non-citizens who entered Assam between 1966 and 1971 would enjoy all rights of citizens except the right to vote for 10 years. There were fresh elections in Assam after the signing of the accord, and a new political party formed by the leaders of the Assam Movement won a majority of seats and formed the new state government. However, prior to it, the Indian

Parliament, at a time when most of Assam had no representation because of the 1979 election boycott, had passed the Illegal Migrants (Determination by Tribunals) Act (IMDT Act) in 1983, severely limiting what the new state government could do on the question of 'foreigners'.

The IMDT law, the Assam Accord and an amendment to the Indian citizenship laws in 1986 together formalised an Assam exception to India's citizenship laws. Of these three, the IMDT law was the most important. Its expressed purpose was to establish tribunals for making 'the determination in a fair manner, of the question whether a person is an illegal migrant' so that the government is able 'to expel illegal migrants from India'. The preamble of the law refers to a day that, ironically, resonates more in Bangladesh than in India. The rationale for the IMDT Act was as follows:

> A good number of the foreigners who migrated into India across the borders of the eastern and north-eastern regions of the country on and after the 25th day of March, 1971, have, by taking advantage of the circumstances of such migration and their ethnic similarities and other connections with the people of India and without having in their possession any lawful authority to do so, illegally remained in India (Government of India 1983).

The date 25 March 1971 was when the Pakistani military crackdown of the liberation struggle in East Pakistan began, initiating a massive exodus of displaced people to India. The date is important because, according to a bilateral agreement signed with India in 1972, Bangladesh took responsibility for those who moved to India after that date and agreed to take them back. What is left unsaid in this agreement, and explicitly provided for in the 1986 amendment to the citizenship law, is more important. In effect, all migrants from East Pakistan, whether Hindu or Muslim, who came before 1966, are deemed to be Indian citizens by default, since Bangladesh as a successor state to the Pakistani province of East Pakistan explicitly does not take responsibility for them. The same applies to those who came between 1966 and 1971, except that a commitment was made to the leaders of the Assam Movement to delete their names from the electoral rolls for 10 years. Thus, the status of all Hindus and Muslims who migrated to Assam from East Pakistan during the quarter-century following partition was made legal without an explicit declaration of amnesty or conferral of citizenship.

The IMDT Act was designed to insulate more recent immigrants from Bangladesh – those who came after 1971 – from the application of India's ordinary citizenship laws. Indeed, it specifically applies to only those who crossed the Indo-Bangladesh border after 25 March 1971. It is a perhaps a rare example of a law guaranteeing an unauthorised foreigner the protection of something akin to a judicial process making deportation difficult, if not impossible. Under the Foreigners Act of 1946 that applies to cases of disputed citizenship in India as a whole, the burden of proving citizenship status is on the person concerned. The IMDT Act reversed the burden and spelt out an elaborate procedure for a third person registering a complaint about someone being an illegal immigrant. The person making the complaint had to reside within the jurisdiction of the same police station as the person 'in relation to whom the application is made is found or resides'. This was a fairly solid protection since the solidarities based on local residential and ethnic networks were likely to be indifferent to the legal distinction between citizens and foreigners. The law even specifies an application format for making complaints, and provides that a complaint could be rejected if it was deemed 'frivolous' (Government of India 1983).

Abdul Muhib Majumdar, an influential lawyer and politician, played a key role in crafting the law. He pointed out the tension between the Indian reality of very few people possessing a major citizenship document like a passport and the standard procedures for enforcing citizenship laws being premised on documentation. 'The Foreigners Act,' he said, 'is applicable *to foreigners only, like those with passport(s) who have overstayed in the country*.' When 'the suspect claims that he is *not* a foreigner,' said Majumdar, 'there is no provision in the Act to deal with him under such [a] situation'. As a result, he explained, there was a need for a 'judicial trial', which he said the IMDT Act provided (Ahmed 2005, emphasis added).

In political terms, with the IMDT Act the Congress party managed to present itself once again as a dependable provider of security to Muslims of East Bengali descent in Assam and win elections, even though it had to temporarily make room for the Asom Gana Parishad (AGP), the regional party now articulating the aspirations behind the Assam Movement. The Act was extremely successful in terms of what it tried to do. But from the point of view of supporters of the Assam Movement, it was a disaster. As the Indian Supreme Court noted in its 2005 ruling, it created 'insurmountable difficulties' for the government in the identification of unauthorised immigrants living in Assam. Thus, even though enquiries were initiated in Assam in 310,759 cases, only 10,015 persons were declared illegal immigrants and only 1,481 of them were deported till 30 April 2000. This was 'less than 0.5 per cent of the cases initiated' (Supreme Court of India 2005).

BEHIND THE POLITICS OF 'VOTE BANKS'

A widely held view of the IMDT Act was that it

> made the makeover from migrant status to 'legal citizens' of the State relatively uncomplicated. Political leaders have not only prevented the existing machinery from identifying and deporting aliens, but have legalised their presence through instrumentalities like generous distribution of ration cards and even citizenship certificates (Routray 2003).

The term 'vote bank' frequently appears in reports and commentaries on elections in Assam to describe the patronage system that facilitate voting by non-citizens. The term is used pejoratively: it invokes the image of hordes of people voting as a bloc along ethnic lines, at the behest of political fixers doing the bidding of powerful politicians. Voting in this manner is seen as the opposite of the model rational voter of liberal political theory. However, for people whose citizenship status is ambiguous, this mode of voting can also be seen as rational political behaviour – voting in exchange for protection by political patrons.

Indeed, a striking feature of elections in Assam is that thousands of poor Muslims of East Bengali descent go through enormous trouble in order to exercise their franchise. Trains to Assam at the time of elections often carry large numbers of poor people of East

Bengali descent – some living in slums in other parts of the country. They travel to Assam to vote in the villages and towns they are registered as voters. In Guwahati – North-East India's commercial hub – there is noticeable shortage of rickshaws and vegetable peddlers on election days because many people in these occupations leave the city and return to places where they are registered to vote. Voting is clearly more important to them than to many of India's upper- and middle-class citizens. Only a concern for security could explain why some of India's poorest political subjects are such earnest voters. Inclusion in the electoral rolls and the act of voting holds out the promise of not being subjected to police harassment as a 'foreigner'. It is hardly surprising that many of them spend their hard-earned money not only on travel, but also forfeit their meagre earnings of a day or more just to be able to vote.

Upendra Baxi (2001: 925–26) once wrote that modern India's 'developmental politics' have forged national markets for large numbers of unorganised migrant labour criss-crossing the country. In those labour markets, he said, Indian citizens have become 'subjects without rights' all over again. This segment of India's labouring poor probably has a significant cross-border component. There is no way of figuring out who among the multitudes of the working poor in Assam – people working in building and road construction sites, brick kilns, agricultural fields, shops and small business establishments, people pulling rickshaws, vegetable peddlers, and child workers in respectable households and in roadside food stalls or those picking garbage – is a Bangladeshi and who is not. Random conversations with people in these occupations suggest that a significant number of them are seasonal migrants from other parts of India – including some rural-to-urban migrants and people moving from one part of North-East India to another – as well as from Bangladesh. While it is frequently assumed that all cross-border migrants are potential settlers, the reality may be more complex. While some may settle, others may be circular migrants – some seasonal – crossing the partition border as part of the subcontinent's floating population.

AFTER THE IMDT LAW: NEW UNCERTAINTIES

In July 2005, the patronage system that facilitates voting by non-citizens came under threat when the Indian Supreme Court declared the IMDT Act unconstitutional. The ruling went further than what even the IMDT's strongest critics in Assam could have hoped. Indeed, the Court agreed with much of what the leaders of the Assam Movement were saying. The IMDT Act, said the Supreme Court, encouraged massive illegal migration from Bangladesh to Assam and that it is the 'main barrier' to identifying illegal immigrants. There can be 'no manner of doubt' that Assam is facing 'external aggression and internal disturbance' because of large-scale illegal immigration from Bangladesh (Supreme Court of India 2005).

While the phrase 'external aggression' may have been gratuitous, the Court had little choice regarding its basic argument. For the IMDT Act violates a basic jurisprudential principle: that of equality. This quasi-judicial process available to people with disputed citizenship status applied only to Assam, not the rest of the country. The arrangement may have been a clever political adaptation to the reality of large-scale cross-border migration, but its legal basis was precarious. Yet only a naïve legalist would expect a court to magically settle such a profoundly political question that is ultimately about the birth of the republic itself.

Indian courts and Parliament often engage in 'an iterative game of action-response-rejoinder that can be played out any number of times' (Mehta 2007: 74–75). Faced with state Assembly elections in Assam in early 2006, where the Supreme Court's ruling became a serious liability for the party, the Congress-led government in New Delhi issued two notifications that brought back the provisions of the IMDT Act through the back door. Even though, by the end of the year, the Supreme Court nullified those notifications as well, it gave the Congress enough time to squeak by and win the Assembly elections.

Another significant verdict came in July 2008 from the Gauhati High Court in Guwahati. A 'large number of Bangladeshis' in Assam, it said, play 'a major role in electing the representatives both to the Legislative Assembly and Parliament and consequently, in the decision-making process towards building the nation' ('Bangladeshis in Assam Have Become Kingmakers' 2008). Such pronouncements by authoritative institutions can eat away at the legitimacy of elected governments. By now, high constitutional bodies such the Election Commission, the Supreme Court and the Gauhati High Court have all spoken in favour of drawing a firm line between citizens and foreigners, and have taken the position that non-citizens exercise significant political influence in Assam. The ambiguities of citizenship have once again become a potent source of civil strife in Assam. Thus, in the summer of 2012, when violence between the Bodos and the Bengali-speaking Muslims broke out, a number of media reports and commentaries blamed it on the influx of 'illegal Bangladeshi migrants' into the area. In effect, these accounts portrayed the 'undifferentiated Muslim masses inhabiting western Assam' – many of them descendants of the early-20th-century settlers from East Bengal – as 'Bangladeshis' (Hussain 2012: 37–38).'

Let me now return to the episode with which I began this essay: Chief Minister Gogoi's statements on refugee status for Bengali Hindus in election rallies in the Barak Valley in 2011 and the expansive definition of the term 'refugee' that he proposed. By 2011, the Badruddin Ajmal-led All India United Democratic Front (AIUDF) was emerging as a serious new political force in Assam, cutting into the traditional Congress's support base among Muslims of East Bengali descent. In those elections, the 15 Barak Valley constituencies became critically important to the Congress. In 2009, a BJP candidate had won a spectacular victory in one of the two Barak Valley constituencies, defeating a Congress stalwart. The erosion of support for the Congress among Muslims of East Bengali descent and the Bengali Hindu support for the BJP candidate produced that outcome. The BJP's long-standing position of supporting refugee status for Hindu migrants was widely credited with the Bengali Hindu vote in its favour. Gogoi tried to take the issue out of the hands of the BJP—an issue on which a governing party might be more able to deliver than a party in the opposition. The tactic paid off handsomely. The Congress won 13 of the 15 Barak Valley seats, the Bengali Hindu vote contributing significantly to its success. There was little doubt that Gogoi's advocacy of refugee status played a major role (Deka 2011). At the same time, in view of the growing challenge that the Congress has been facing from the rise of the influence of the AIDUF among Bengali Muslims, Gogoi can hardly afford to be seen as toeing the Hindu nationalist line. His attempt at an expansive definition of the term refugee was designed to appeal to that constituency.

It is doubtful that a seasoned politician like Gogoi expects a dramatic Indian policy shift regarding the citizenship status of unauthorised Bangladeshi migrants in Assam. At least in the foreseeable future, it is unlikely that a publicly announced amnesty to all unauthorised cross-border migrants would become politically acceptable. The notion of refugee status for Muslim cross-border migrants on grounds of religious persecution in Bangladesh will be hard to sustain. At the same time, the political difficulties that the Congress would face in drawing a line between Hindu 'refugees' and Muslim 'illegal immigrants', as Hindu nationalists have proposed, are formidable. It would not only go against the foundational ideology of the post-partition India state that rejects the theory that there are separate Hindu and Muslim nations, it would severely damage the Congress brand—the party's traditional reputation as a secular party—as well. Nevertheless, it seems inevitable that, like the pre-1971 cross-border migrants who were made Indian citizens by the 1986 amendment to India's citizenship laws, citizenship in some form will be conferred on all post-1971 immigrants as well. Gogoi's proposal for refugee status for Bangladeshi nationals and his efforts to give an expansive meaning to the term refugee were perhaps a prelude or a trial balloon.

CONCLUSION

The world since the national order of things (Malkki 1995) became normalised has been famously compared by Ernest Gellner with Amedeo Modigliani's paintings where 'neat flat surfaces are clearly separated from each other... there is little if any ambiguity or overlap'. He contrasted it with the 'riot of diverse points of colour' in the impressionist canvases of Oskar Kokoschka: his metaphor for the world before nations (Gellner 1983: 139–40). One should not expect a Kokoshka-to-Modigliani transformation to descend on the partition's eastern border any time soon. Dealing with the question of migration across this border in more than an ad-hoc and stop-gap manner would require acceptance of the fact that the idea of partition as the creation of two, and subsequently three, bounded nation-states – each functioning on a 'container model of national sovereignty' (Ong 2004: 71) – has never quite matched up with ground realities.

Policies responsive to this reality cannot be made unilaterally in one country. It requires not only cooperation between Bangladesh and India, but also a deeper partnership that, instead of trying to harden the border with stricter policing, accepts the realities of a soft border. Managing a soft border could mean working towards agreements like an Indo-Bangladesh protocol on labour movement to facilitate and document the cross-border movement of people, and the decoupling of citizenship rights from rights of personhood. A labour protocol could take some of the pressure away from the circular migrant who under current conditions has no other option but to look for security by procuring proxy citizenship papers and finding a political patron. A labour protocol and other bilateral arrangements that try to manage the movement of people across this soft border could significantly reduce the strains on Assam's legal and political institutions. That may be a surer road to a stable and legitimate political order in Assam, rather than the ad-hoc and unilateral measures of the past or Tarun Gogoi's ingenious but implausible proposal of refugee status for 'Buddhists, Christians and Muslims along with Hindus'.

NOTES

1. See, for instance, Gupta (2012), who argues: 'India was created as a homeland for all Hindus of undivided India so Hindus from neighbouring countries have moral, social and political claim for right of residence in present day India, and in any case better claim over Bharat than any other refugee.'
2. I use the term regional patriotism following what Ayesha Jalal (2001: 739) refers to as 'regionally specific patriotisms' that predate undivided India's encounter with colonial rule.

REFERENCES

'Assam CM Bats for Asylum to Migrants', *Telegraph* (Guwahati), 11 September 2013.

'Bangladeshis in Assam Have Become Kingmakers: Court', *Hindu* (Chennai), 29 July 2008.

'Gogoi on Refugee Status for Bangladeshi Migrants', *Sentinel* (Guwahati), 11 September 2013.

'Gogoi Pitches for Refugee Status', *Assam Tribune* (Guwahati), 11 September 2013.

'Gogoi Wants Refugee Status for Bangladeshis', *Times of India*, 24 April 2012.

'Pollvault 2011: The Congress Is Doing a BJP Here', *Tehelka*, 2 April 2011.

Ahmed, Shakil. 2005. 'Muslims Forced to Live in the Shadow of Partition Policy', *Milli Gazette*, 5 August. http://www.milligazette.com/dailyupdate/2005/20050805a.htm (accessed 13 September 13, 2013)

Asom Jagriti. 1980. 'Indian Citizens Versus Foreign Nationals', memorandum submitted to Prime Minister Indira Gandhi by Ajit Kumar Sharma and Others.

Barooah, Nirode K. 1990. *Gopinath Bardoloi, Indian Constitution, and Centre–Assam Relations, 1940–1950*. Guwahati: Publication Board Assam.

Baxi, Upendra. 2001. 'Saint Granville's Gospel', *Economic and Political Weekly*, 36(11): 921–30.

Bhattacharjee, Nabanipa. 2012. '"We are with Culture but Without Geography": Locating Sylheti identity in Contemporary India', *South Asian History and Culture*, 3(2): 215–35.

Chakrabarty, Bidyut. 2004. *The Partition of Bengal and Assam, 1932–1947*. London: RoutledgeCurzon.

Chaudhury, Sujit. 2002. 'A God-Sent' Opportunity?' *Seminar*, 510: 61–67.

Das, Susanta K. 1989. *Spotlight on Assam*. Chanderpur, Maharastra: Premier Book Service.

Dasgupta, Anindita. 2008. 'Remembering Sylhet: A Forgotten Story of India's 1947 Partition', *Economic and Political Weekly*, 43(21): 18–22.

Deka, Kaushik. 2011. 'Gogoi's Minority Report: Assam CM Beats Vote Bank Stress', *India Today*, 20 May. http://indiatoday.intoday.in/story/assam-tarun-gogoi-strategy-to-win-assamese-vote/1/138758.html (accessed 26 September 2013).

Gellner, Ernest. 1983. *Nations and Nationalism*. Ithaca, NY: Cornell University Press.

Government of India. 1983. *The Illegal Migrants (Determination by Tribunals) Act, 1983* (enacted 25 December 1983). http://www.satp.org/satporgtp/countries/india/states/assam/documents/Actsandordinences/the_illegal_migrants_Act.htm (accessed 13 September 2013).

Guha, Amalendu. 1977. *Planter Raj to Swaraj: Freedom Struggle and Electoral Politics in Assam, 1826–1947*. New Delhi: People's Publishing House.

Gupta, O.P. 2012. 'Rights of Hindu Refugees in India', *Organiser*, 27 October. http://organiser.org/Encyc/2012/10/27/Rights-of-Hindu-refugees-in-India.aspx?NB=&lang=4&m1=&m2=&p1=&p2=&p3=&p4=&PageType=N (accessed 23 September 2013).

Haddad, Emma. 2008. *The Refugee in International Society: Between Sovereigns*, Cambridge: Cambridge University Press.

Hussain, Banajit. 2012. 'The Bodoland Violence and the Politics of Explanation,' *Seminar*, 640: 37-40.

Hussain, Monirul. 1993. *The Assam Movement: Class, Ideology and Identity*. Delhi: Manak Publications.

Jalal, Ayesha. 1997. 'Exploding Communalism: The Politics of Muslim Identity in South Asia', in Sugata Bose and Ayesha Jalal (eds), *Nationalism, Development, and Democracy: State and Politics in India*, pp. 76–103. New Delhi: Oxford University Press.

———. 2001. 'South Asia', in *Encyclopedia of Nationalism: Fundamental Themes*, Vol. 1, pp.737-56. San Diego, CA: Academic Press.

Kar, Bodhisattva. 2011. 'Can the Postcolonial Begin? Deprovincializing Assam', in Saurabh Dube (ed.), *Handbook of Modernity in South Asia: Modern Makeovers*, pp.43–58. New Delhi: Oxford University Press.

Malkki, Liisa. 1995. 'Refugees and Exile: From "Refugee Studies" to the National Order of Things', *Annual Review of Anthropology*, 24(1): 495–523.

Mall, Jagdamba. . 2004. 'Demographic Invasion of North-East', *Organiser*, 19 September. http://organiser.org/archives/historic/dynamic/modulesedae.html?name=Content&pa=showpage&pid=41&page=29 (accessed 1 May 2014)

Mehta, Pratap Bhanu. 2007. 'The Rise of Judicial Sovereignty', *Journal of Democracy*, 18(2): 70–83.

Ong, Aihwa. 2004. 'The Chinese Axis: Zoning Technologies and Variegated Sovereignty', *Journal of East Asian Studies*, 4(1): 69–96.

Pandey, Gyanendra. 2001. *Remembering Partition: Violence, Nationalism, and History in India*. Cambridge: Cambridge University Press.

Prabhakara, M.S. 1999. 'Of State and Nationalism', *Frontline* (Chennai), 9–22

October. http://www.frontline.in/static/html/fl1621/16210680.htm (accessed 1 May 2014)

Routray, Bibhu Prasad. 2003. 'Assam: The IM(DT) Act—Of Aliens, Natives and Politics', *South Asia Intelligence Review* (Weekly Assessments & Briefings), 1(44): ??–??. http://www.satp.org/satporgtp/sair/Archives/1_44.htm (accessed 26 September 2013).

Sadiq, Kamal. 2009. *Paper Citizens: How Illegal Immigrants Acquire Citizenship in Developing Countries*. New York: Oxford University Press.

Sahni, Bhisham. 1989. 'We Have Arrived in Amritsar', in Stephen Alter and Wimal Dissanayake (eds), *The Penguin Book of Modern Indian Short Stories*, pp. 180–87. Delhi: Penguin Books.

Sato, Hiroshi. 2005. 'Normative Space of the "Politics of Citizenship" in Eastern India', in Kyoko Inoue, Etsuyo Arai and Mayumi Murayama (eds), *Elusive Borders: Changing Sub-Regional Relations in Eastern India*, pp. 83–109. Tokyo: Institute of Development Economics.

Singh, Jaswant. 1984. 'Assam's Crisis of Citizenship: An Examination of Political Errors', *Asian Survey*, 24(10): 1056–68.

Supreme Court of India, Judgment on Writ Petition (Civil) 131 of 2000, 12 July 2005, Bench R.C. Lahoti, G.P. Mathur & P.K. Balasubramanyan. http://esamskriti.com/html/inside.asp?cat=732&subcat=731&cname=imdt_suprem_court_jud_05 (accessed 28 March 2006).

Talbot, Ian. 2010. 'India and Pakistan', in Paul R. Brass (ed.), *Routledge Handbook of South Asian Politics*, pp. 27–40. New York: Routledge.

van Schendel, Willem. 2005. *The Bengal Borderland: Beyond State and Nation in South Asia*. London: Anthem Press.

CHAPTER 6

Reconstructing Marichjhapi

From Margins and Memories of Migrant Lives

JHUMA SEN

Herman Melville wrote: 'In landlessness alone resides the highest truth.' One such truth is that remembering and forgetting sometimes work together in the memory project in myriad ways. While the subject on the margins at the receiving end of history insists on preserving the memory of trauma and tribulation till closure arrives in the form of justice, their more privileged counterparts actively persist in the erasure of the memory of the fringes while remembering to articulate their own as the only memory worth preserving. Bengal's romance with the upper-caste *bhadralok*'s 'traumatic and nostalgic memories of a lost homeland in East Bengal' (Rahman and van Schendel 2003) has dominated the imagination of partition historiography so much that very little or no attention has ever been paid to the bulk of refugees who settled outside Bengal and who had to directly face a lopsided discriminatory rehabilitation policy practised by the government. Needless to assert, they were the *nimnoborgo* (lower caste) and *chhotolok* as opposed to *bhadralok*. Partition's 'missing' link in the form of the felt history of these people needs to be articulated and the silence that shrouds Marichjhapi needs to be uncovered to fill the gap in the migrant's story.

Marichjhapi, or the Marichjhapi Massacre as it is known by those who have chosen to remember it, was the product of a number of factors, including partition, migration, questions of caste, ecology and discriminatory refugee policy, and finally of a reversal in policy adopted by the Left Front government in West Bengal. On a shorter note, Marichjhapi culminates in the forceful eviction of East Pakistani refugees by the West Bengal government run by the Left Front in 1979 from the island of Marichjhapi in the Sundarban region, which resulted in a human calamity. Curiously, such an incident was lost in oblivion till more recently similar state-backed atrocities in the nature of Nandigram and Singur jolted the Bengali imagination to accommodate the history of the untouchable refugees of Marichjhapi.

PARTITION AND THE UNTOUCHABLE REFUGEES

It is a well settled notion that the formation of new states is a refugee-generating process. The formation of a Hindu-majority India and a Muslim-majority Pakistan arguably caused the largest mass migration in human history, with around 15 million people crossing the newly formed border. Several million Hindus migrated from the eastern borders of Pakistan into the states of West Bengal, Assam and Tripura. Migration from East Pakistan happened in successive waves—the first in 1947 after the partition of Bengal, the second after the 1954 riots and a third wave after the 1971 war. Even this demarcation of periods of migration is not an exhaustive one: in 1949–50, migration was caused largely due to communal riots in Khulna and Barisal; in 1956 the adoption of an Islamic constitution by Pakistan spurred more migration; and a million left East Bengal when communal violence erupted in 1964 after the Hazratbal incident.[1] While post-partition 'unrest' can normally be attributed as the reason for the waves of migration, it is also remarkable to observe in this context the composition of the migrant diaspora. Of the 1.1 million Hindus who had migrated from the east by 1 June 1948, about 350,000 were urban *bhadralok*, 550,000 were the rural Hindu gentry and many of the rest were businessmen (Chakrabarti 1990). Similarly, somewhat lower down in the ladder, Hindu artisans also migrated to the west, where their patrons were now settled, calculating that their prospects of resettlement there would be better than living in a turbulent east. The first wave of refugees, the caste elite with education, assets, and kith and kin in the west, found it relatively easy to integrate and assimilate in India.

In sharp contrast, for the majority of the Hindus in East Bengal comprising peasants, sharecroppers and agricultural labourers, migration to the west was identified as a last resort. East Bengal's peasants were 'above all a domestic, stay at home people' (Government of India 1964; also see Chatterji 2010). The majority of them were lower-caste untouchables—the depressed classes. In the east, their only possession was their tiny landholding. They did not have the resource, education, skill or family connections in the west to emigrate and resettle. So, with the migration of the upper-caste and elite Hindus, when suddenly they became the target of arbitrary communal violence, they were faced with the unkind prospect of leaving their modest lifestyle behind and emigrating to the west. Therefore, while the more entitled upper-caste refugees migrated in large numbers in the first wave (between 1947 to 1949), very few lower-caste ones packed up and left. In contrast, the figure rose sharply in late 1949 and early 1950, when they were the targets of terrible communal violence that ripped apart parts of East Pakistan.

Rehabilitation measures adopted for the two classes also remained disparate owing to this reason—while the former, with resources at their disposal, could easily integrate into the mainland of West Bengal, the latter were forced to live on the fringes or, as the new resettlement policies demanded, scattered in different parts of their new nation, most notably in Dandakaranya. It must also be mentioned here that in Calcutta and its vicinity, 149 unauthorised colonies, colloquially termed *jabor dakhal* (forcefully occupied), sprang up to house the *bhadralok* refugees and the encroachment had a smooth sail to legalisation subsequently. Conversely, the *chhotolok* (or lower-caste) refugees were placed in transit camps and forced out of the state. Calcutta, and largely West Bengal, continued to be sanitised of lower-caste presence by a carefully pursued state policy of discrimination in rehabilitation (Byapari 2012).

Before entering into a discussion on the manner in which the resettlement of the untouchable refugee population shaped up, it is important to know who these refugees were. For the most part, they were the Namasudras, earlier known as the Chandals of Bengal, who lived in Dacca, Bakarganj, Faridpur, Mymensingh, Jessore and Khulna in East Bengal. The Namasudra movement had been one of the most powerful political mobilizations of the untouchables in India during the colonial period and had kept the Congress party in Bengal in opposition since the 1920s (Mallick 1999). When the upper-caste Hindu nationalists of the Congress party were evoking the glorious Hindu past in an attempt at nation building, the Namasudras began to look at the present regime under the British, where they had the same legal rights as an upper-caste Hindu, as a far better alternative than the darker past where they were socially, legally and politically at the lowest rung of the ladder devised by caste Hindus. This was evident sometimes through assertions in the form of resolutions declaring that the Namasudra 'community has, therefore, not the least sympathy' with the upper-caste elite Hindus and their agitations, and sometimes by refraining from participating in Congress-led mass political agitations like the Non-Cooperation, Civil Disobedience and Quit India movements (Bandyopadhyaya 1997).

Partition dealt a blow to the Namasudra movement. They lost their bargaining power and became a political minority in both countries. But this was only part of the problem. While the upper-caste Hindu refugees were settled in and around Calcutta, the Namasudras were shunned to the uninhabitable camps in districts of 24 Parganas, Nadia, Burdwan, Midnapore or Cooch Bihar, or forced to settle in inhospitable tracts of Dandakaranya and the Andaman islands (Chatterji 2010.). The once organized and powerful Dalit movement was thus effectively broken.

A word about the state government's refugee 'resettlement' policy must also be mentioned here. This had always been one of careful 'calculation, discrimination and discretion' aimed at dispersion (Bandyopadhyaya 1997).[2] The Namasudras had been at the receiving end of calculated state-practised discrimination bordering on caste preferences and bargaining power. In 1948, when Dr B.C. Roy took over charge of the government, his policy was guided by two main considerations—first, that refugees were to be strongly discouraged from coming to West Bengal and, second, even if, after the best measures taken to keep them out, they ended up in the state, they were to do exactly as they were told (ibid.). The latter meant the refugees had to go wherever the government directed them, which in most cases was outside West Bengal and most certainly out of Calcutta. Admittedly, of the 389 refugee colonies that the government had set up, not a single one was in Calcutta. To complicate matters, these colonies were in places that were deserted by the local population owing to an uninhabitable environment, and hardly any of these colonies were where the refugees would have chosen to live. Not without surprise, therefore, many such 'resettled' families moved out and gravitated back to Calcutta or more habitable localities. The state government took the view that there was simply no land in West Bengal to resettle the population that had migrated, so they had to be forced out and settled in various parts of the Indian Union. The first of such schemes was to relocate them to the Andaman islands, which failed miserably. The second was to relocate them to Dandakaranya.

CHALO SUNDARBAN

The Dandakaranya Project Area (DPA) covered about 77,700 km^2 in the districts of Koraput and Kalahandi of Orissa, and in the district of Bastar in Madhya Pradesh. The process of shifting refugee camps from West Bengal started almost as soon as the DPA was established in 1958. However, from the first day itself, refugees started to leave Dandakaranya as soon as they had settled. In 1978, 10,000 families deserted the place. The reason was not difficult to gauge. The hilly terrain was unsuitable for agriculture, there was no sustainable industry that would allow the settlers to be employed and earn a living, and there was no provision for education or health care. Initially, the refugee exodus from Dandakaranya was blamed on the refugees—that they were 'lazy' and they treated the project area as a 'guest house' for which all arrangements needed to be made. However, in 1964, Saibal Gupta, chairperson of the Dandakaranya Development Authority (DDA) blew the whistle, pointing out that less than 10 per cent of the land was arable and the rest uncultivable:

> Most of the plots did not produce enough food to keep the families who farmed them alive. In this bleak and barren terrain, there was

> no other work by which the refugees could earn a few rupees. Such industries as the authority tried to run, in a hopelessly amateur fashion, were disorganized, unprofitable, mismanaged and usually closed down soon after they were set up. For the brief periods that they were open, they paid their workers scandalously low wages. (Bandyopadhyaya 1997: also see Kudaisya 1997)

Dandakaranya was an area culturally, physically and emotionally entirely removed from the migrants' known world (Jalais 2005; '"Massacre" in Marichjhapi' 2005). This resulted in extensive protest by the refugees in almost all camps in West Bengal as a mark of dissent against the measures of the government to send them to Dandakaranya against their will; in fact, they were served notice of either going to Dandakaranya or quitting the camp within 30 days. Hunger strikes were started by two batches of refugees of Kalabani and Sarasanka camps in the district of Midnapore on 6 June 1961, which spread like wildfire.

Enter the Left Front. They denounced the attempts of the Congress to evict refugees from West Bengal and promised that when they came to power they would ensure their settlement in West Bengal and this would be, in all probability, on one of the islands of the Sundarbans. During the B.C. Roy government in the 1950s and early 1960s, Jyoti Basu, then the leader of the opposition, had presented their case in the Legislative Assembly (see box 1).

BOX 1 Letter from Jyoti Basu to the State Rehabilitation Minister on the Rehabilitation of Camp Refugees

July 13, 1961

Sri P.C. Sen
Minister, Refugee, Relief & Rehabilitation
Government of West Bengal

Dear Sri Sen,
Prolonged hunger-strike by the refugees lasting for more than a month in almost all camps in West Bengal has proved beyond doubt strong reluctance on the part of the refugees to accept the proposal of the Government regarding their rehabilitation in Dandakaranya. As a matter of fact there has been no movement of refugees to Dandakaranya though they have been put to

serious hardships and untold sufferings due to stoppage of doles. For more than a month refugees in almost all the camps have been on hunger-strike to voice their protest. It is unlikely that there will be a change in attitude of camp refugees if they are subjected to further hardships and sufferings. Such experiment is also fraught with serious consequences. Left to their own fate these camps families will hardly be able to rehabilitate themselves properly and will be a burden on the State, I, therefore, urge upon you to reconsider the policy of the Government in respect of rehabilitation of camp refugees to prevent further deterioration in the situation.

The primary issues involved now is not continuation of doles to camp refugees for an unlimited period but their early rehabilitation and restoration of doles till that is achieved. We do not think that the rehabilitation of camp refugees in a manner acceptable to them is so very difficult as is often being suggested by the Government. For example, the families now in Sonarpur group of camps may be easily fitted in Herobhanga Second Scheme. Families now in Asrafabad group of camps may also be absorbed in the camp site which is an abandoned rehabilitation colony, the land of which is already in possession of the Government and in Ashoknagar colony if the families are given facility of changing their category. Coopers Camp can be liquidated in its present site if the government implements the present scheme of converting that into a township with some modification. Families now in Gopalpur and Kaksa camps in the District of Burdwan may also be partially absorbed in Durgapur Industrial area and partially in land elsewhere. Families now in the camps in the district of Midnapur may be rehabilitated in Garbeta Scheme. Such illustration may be multiplied. If the refugees are given due facility for rehabilitation through bainanama scheme as well as change of occupational category in addition to the measures suggested above the rehabilitation of all families is now in camps may be completed within a very reasonable period and with much less cost than in places outside West Bengal. The number of such families is now almost half of what it was earlier and many have found rehabilitation in West Bengal although it was stated by the Government that West Bengal has reached a saturation point. I feel, therefore, that the rest may be found rehabilitation here provided there is willingness on the part of the Govt. The enthusiasm that will be generated among the refugees if such a policy is accepted will be no mean an asset for their proper rehabilitation. It is needless to dwell upon the necessity of restoration and continuation of doles during the period prior to their rehabilitation.

It has been made clear from our side times without number that despite the policy set out above for rehabilitation in West Bengal, there may be families who may be willing to go to Dandakaranya and we do not object to their going.

My views on the problem have been briefly outlined in the previous paragraphs. I believe that there is a scope for discussion on the matter for finding a proper solution to it. I am, however, going abroad for a short period, I shall try to meet you later when I come back. But in the meantime I request you to have discussion with the representatives of U.C.R.C., who will seek interview with you.

Yours sincerely,

Sd.
Jyoti Basu

The same Left Front had also insisted in a letter to Dr B.C. Roy that no refugees would be forced out of West Bengal against their wishes. In the meanwhile, the Communist Party of India—Marxist (CPM) leader and erstwhile All India Council of East Pakistan Displaced Persons' general secretary, Samar Mukherjee, also sent a letter to Pandit Nehru on 27 July 1961 on the rehabilitation of camp refugees (see Box 2).

As late as 25 January 1975, Jyoti Basu, while visiting Bhilai to address an industrial workers' meeting, demanded publicly that the Dandakaranya refugees be allowed to settle in the Sundarbans. He assured that if and when the Leftists were voted to power, their government would bring the refugees from Dandakaranya to West Bengal and take every step to rehabilitate them there. This was reported in Raipur's two dailies, *Naya Duniya* and *Navbharat Times*. Within two years, the Left Front came to power by winning the Assembly elections and forming their government. It was time for the Dandakaranya refugees to remind them of their promise.

A delegation of refugees from Dandakaranya went to Calcutta to meet Basu. As Sunil Haldar, a member of the group of refugees deliberating resettlement in Marichjhapi with the state government,

BOX 2 Letter from Samar Mukherjee to the Prime Minister on the Rehabilitation of Camp Refugees

Ref No. 24/61 27th July, 1961

From: Shri Samar Mukherji, M.L.A.,
General Secretary,
All India Council of East Pakistan Displaced Persons,
93/1A, Bipin Behari Ganguli Street,
CALCUTTA-12

To: Shri Jawaharlal Nehru,
Prime Minister of India,
NEW DELHI

Sub.: Rehabilitation of East Bengal Refugees Now in Camp

Sir,

1. A grave situation has developed due to continued hunger strike by groups of refugees in almost all the camps in West Bengal. The hunger strike was first started by two batches of refugees of Kalabani and Sarasanka camps in the district of Midnapore on 6th June last. Since then it has spread to almost all the camps and at present there are about 100 refugees on hunger-strike in different camps.
2. We do not propose to deal with the various problems of other sections of refugees which are nonetheless acute. We like to restrict us here only to the problems of camp refugees because their solution brooks no further delay.
3. The hunger strike by the Camp refugees was started as a mark of protest against the measures of the Government to send them to Dandakaranya against their will and under compulsion by service of notice on them with the option of going to Dandakaranya or to quit the camp within a period of 30 days. It is far from truth that the purpose of the present movement is to continue payment of doles eternally and to delay the liquidation of camps. On the contrary, the main aspect of the present movement is for the demand of their quick rehabilitation in different schemes started or proposed in West Bengal by the Government and through bainanama scheme together with the facility of changing their occupational category.
4. Such demands by refugees are not only realistic but also can be implemented within a very reasonable period and at a cost

lower than that for schemes outside West Bengal. This will be borne out by the following illustrations. There are about 1000 families now in Sonarpur group of camps. All these families may be rehabilitated in Herobhanga 2nd scheme which was announced by the Govt. long ago but has not yet been implemented for reasons best know to them. About 600 families of Asrafabad Camp may be rehabilitated at the present site of the Camp which is the site of an unsuccessful rehabilitation Colony as well as in the nearby Ashokenagar Colony where a large number of plots are lying vacant. Coopers Camp may be liquidated in its present site if the Goverment implements the proposed scheme of converting the camp into a township with some modification. Families now in Gopalpur and Kaksa Camps in the district of Burdwan may be absorbed in Durgapore Industrial area. Families now in the camps of Midnapur District may be rehabilitated in Carbeta Scheme where it was proposed to accommodate 1500 familes. But only 350 families have been sent there uptill now. It will not be out of place to mention that in reply to a memorandum submitted in 1958 the West Bengal Government said that about 13,000 families may be settled on fallow lands in Garbata. Such illustrations may be multiplied without any difficulty. We can dare say that if the refugees are given due facility for rehabilitation through bainanama Scheme together with the facility for change of category in addition to the measures stated above their rehabilitation in a manner acceptable to them will not prove so difficult as is often suggested by the Government. It should also be mentioned here that the West Bengal Government stated in 1959 that of the 39,000 bainanamas executed by the camp refugees 21 thousand would be implemented. But not more than 50% of those have been implemented. These along with other measures were suggested to the state Government long ago. If these were adopted in time the camps would have been liquidated long ago and the present undesirable situation would neither have arisen nor the question of rehabilitation of camp refugees in Dandakaranya.

5. It should also be made clear that despite such a policy there might be families who may like to go to Dandakaranya. There can be no objection to that. It will thus be clear that the present movement has nothing to do with opposition to Dandakaranya project as a whole. The movement only opposes sending refugees to Dandakaranya against their will when there

is sufficient scope for their rehabilitation in West Bengal in a manner desired by them. It should also be mentioned here that the Chief Minister of West Bengal as well as the Governor of the State gave assurances in categorical terms that no refugee will be sent outside West Bengal against his will.

6. It will be seen that the coercive methods adopted by the Government for sending refugees to Dandakaranya have failed in as much as only 5% of families served with notices have gone to Dandakaranya. A stalemate has reached in respect of rehabilitation of camp refugees. Any further experiment with such a policy is fraught with serious consequences. Left to their own fate these camp families will be hardly able to rehabilitate themselves properly and will ultimately be a burden on the meager resources of the State. A rethinking of the whole question has, therefore, been necessary both for the proper solution of the problem and on human considerations.
7. It is high time that you should intervene immediately into the matter to prevent further deterioration in the situation which will result in loss of life of a few refugees and untold sufferings to many others as well as for a satisfactory solution of the problem.

Yours faithfully,

Sd.
Samar Mukherjee

including the Left Front government, remembers (Bhattacharjee 2010)· in 1977, after Jyoti Basu came to power, 18 of them went to West Bengal to talk to him. Basu, on being reminded of his promise in Bhilai, conceded that if they (the refugees) could rehabilitate and resettle themselves in Marichjhapi, they were welcome to do so and assured them that his government would not create any obstruction like the previous one. A team of Left Front leaders, including minister Ram Chatterjee, two Members of the Legislative Assembly, Kiranmay Nanda and Rabi Shankar Pandey, also visited Dandakaranya on 28 November 1977 (Byapari 2012). Ram Chatterjee again visited with Ashok Ghosh, the chairperson of the Left Front, and it is widely reported that they encouraged the refugees to settle in the Sundarbans, which had been a demand for long by the Left

Front while it had been in opposition. Ashok Ghosh is said to have declared: *'Apnara Paschimbanglay ele Paschimbanglar 5 koti manusher dosh koti haat apnader samarthane gorje uthbe'* ('When you return to West Bengal, 5 crore [50 million] Bengalis will welcome you with 10 crore [100 million] hands') (ibid.; Bhattacharjee 2010). Predictably, '*chalo* Sundarban' ('to the Sundarbans') was the cry that dominated the imagination of the 40,000 people who were to soon migrate to Bengal's wetlands. This was perhaps, finally the return to the hyper-reality of the 'homeland'.

THE SELF-SETTLED REFUGEES

The journey, from Dandakaranya to Marichjhapi, however, was not smooth. During the early part of 1978, the first wave of refugees from Dandakaranya started travelling from Orissa's Malkangiri to West Bengal. They crossed Habra, Barasat, Bali Bridge and finally reached Hasnabad.

Once the number totalled a few hundred thousand, the CPM leaders sought to send them back to where they came from. The Left Front government declared that although they had earlier stated that Dandakaranya refugees would be resettled in the Sundarbans, under the changed scenario that would not be feasible. It was on 18 April 1978 that more than 10,000 refugees crossed Kumirmari and reached Marichjhapi. They declared that they did not want any aid from the government towards their resettlement. They only demanded that they be allowed to stay at Marichjhapi as citizens of the Union of India.

Ten thousand refugees sold their belongings to make the trip to Marichjhapi. But when they arrived, it was to find that the refugee policy had changed, and many were arrested and returned to the resettlement camps. The remaining managed to slip through police cordons and reach their destination at Marichjhapi island and settlement began.

At Hasnabad, the refugees coming from Dandakaranya camped nearly for two months to find proper ways of earning, living, and to gauge the policy and principles of the state government. After staying in Kumirmari without any obstruction from local authorities for about fifteen to twenty days, they entered the plantation, Bagna, Marichjhapi, in 24 Parganas.

Approximately 30,000 settled in Marichjhapi and carried on their business, trade and occupation unaided by the government and solely relying on their enterpreneurial skills to sustain themselves. They provided for themselves food, clothes, shelter, education, health, and other cultural and recreational pursuits from April 1978 onwards. It was said that they built smithies for the production of agricultural implements, pottery units for household units, handlooms for weaving cloth and making of mats from indigenous fibre, centres for building of country boats, fisheries and kitchen gardens. Other production included *bidi*s, baked products, sweetmeats and condiments, handicrafts such as bamboo baskets and woodcraft (Jalais 2005). They built two local bazaars, schools employing local teachers and a private hospital; four dispensaries were also set up. Manufacturing fishing nets was a regular occupation. Thus, they made an attempte to rehabilitate themselves by setting up a home away from home.

Nirmalendu (né Nirmalkanti) Dhali, who started a school in Marichjhapi, offers an account of how they sought to resettle themselves on the island without any state support (Bhattacharjee 2010). A meeting was called by the members of the committee formed immediately after the refugees arrived in Marichjhapi. They identified the immediate concerns—accommodation, drinking water, health, education, maintaining order and discipline, and creating a suitable embankment to hold back the tidal waves. Shanties were made, roads were constructed. Every family was mandated to send one person to assist in building the embankment. Dhali was tasked with setting up a school. It started out as a small collection of shanties with five teachers. In a month's time, the number of students increased to 2,000 to 3,000, and subsequently to 4,000. The number of teachers went up to 25. The township that came to exist as a product of the labour of the settlers was named Netaji Nagar and the school called Netaji Nagar Uchcha Bidyapeeth (Netaji Nagar High School). Dhali, while reminiscing about their efforts in building Netaji Nagar, notes that the settlers attempted to perform their duties with a degree of competitiveness and camaraderie that was unique.

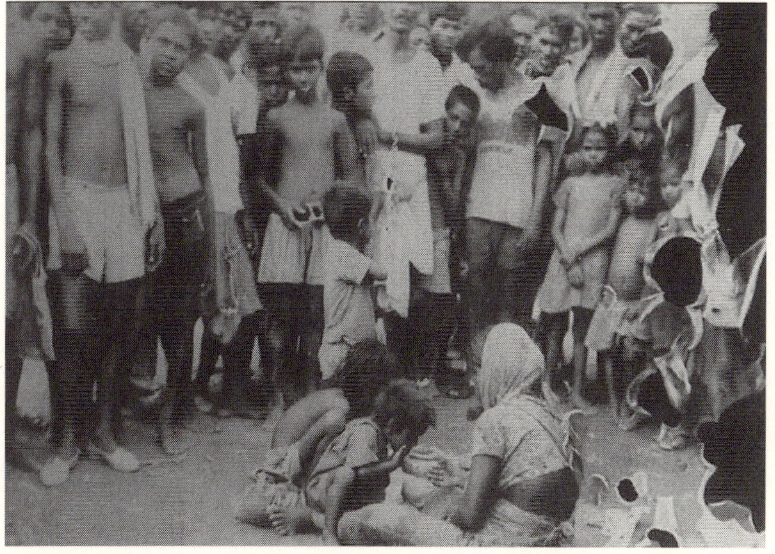

Photos courtesy Tushar Bhattacharya

> We started our new lives with a full arrangement of daily consumption such as living house, school, markets, roads, hospital, tube wells, etc. We managed to find out sources of income, also establishing cottage industry such as *Bidi* factory, Bakery, Carpentry, Weaving factory etc. and also built embankment nearly 150 miles long covering an area of nearly 30 thousand acres of land to be used for fishing, expecting an income of Rs 20 crores per year. That may easily help and enable us to stand on our own feet. Moreover, after one or two years washing by rain water, preventing saline water to flow over those lands will yield a lot of crops such as paddy and other vegetables.
>
> We have distributed lands in Marichjhapi amongst six thousand refugee families in the shape of paras, villages and anchals. Nearly a thousand families built their houses in different plots in group system and have been residing there for about a year. (ibid.)

In short, Marichjhapi could have been an ideal model to be emulated for refugee rehabilitation and resettlement.

THE MASSACRE

The state government, now having flipped on promises made, including by the chief minister, was opposed to the settlement at Marichjhapi and sought to disperse the settlers on absurd charges, including, most notably, the allegation that they were running a parallel government.[3] The settlers were accused of smuggling weapons and assisting in bringing illegal immigrants into West Bengal. The other claim that the government made was that the area that contained Marichjhapi was part of the Sundarban Reserve Forest and hence protected under the Forest Act. There is overwhelming evidence to suggest that both claims are false.

The state government, determined to oust the refugees, launched a veritable war bordering on economic blockade of the settlement. The supply of necessities (including drinking water) were prevented from reaching them, defying all principles of law and justice. This is almost reminiscent of the Spartan blockade of Athens following the Battle of Aegospotami, depriving Athens of the ability to import food grains or communicate. It was said that Athens, on the verge of starvation, was forced to surrender. Marichjhapi, however, still held on, perhaps due to its sheer determination to continue living a restructured life out of the debris of partition.

On 20 August 1978, at about 3 p.m., about 30 steam launches employed by the state government were found to be illegally blockading Marichjhapi to stop any passage of its inhabitants across the river for drinking water and other essential supplies from the village markets of Kumirmari, Mollakhali and Satjelia. It was alleged that the launches carried police officers who attempted to take back the refugees to Dandakaranya. The protesting cries of the settlers brought some local volunteers and social workers to the spot, who appealed to the blockading forces that essential items be allowed to the residents of Marichjhapi. However, this was to no avail and the blockade continued till 8 p.m. But even their persistent presence for 15 days failed to bring back a single family to Dandakaranya. This was followed by an attack by the police on the refugees. The launches ran over 43 boats, breaking them into pieces, and the police also opened fire, resulting in the death of two young boys. The people of Marichjhapi had no recourse but to leave another 157 boats behind to be trampled upon by the agencies of the state that had once welcomed them to set up a home at the very place.

In the course of the attack, a phonogram was sent by S. Chatterjee, secretary, Nikhil Banga Nagarik Sangha to Prime Minister Morarji Desai, with copies to Members of Parliament Subramanian Swami, Sakti Sarkar, Charan Singh and others (Box 3). A second phonogram was sent on 21 August (Box 4).

BOX 3 Phonogram Sent by S. Chatterjee, Secretary, Nikhil Banga Nagarik Sangha, to Prime Minister Morarji Desai and MPs, 20 August 1978

Prime Minister,
Your kind attention drawn to planned massacre of innocent refugees at Marichjhapi, Sundarbans, in your name. Please take realistic stock of situation and kindly allow them to independently establish their stay irrespective of any political compulsion.

About ten thousand built their huts, economic fisheries starting paying dividend regenerating economy locally.

Now seems being brutally uprooted by L.F. Government in connivance with yours who probably is ignorant of exact situation.

REQUEST IMMEDIATELY STOP MARICHJHAPI OPERATION TOMORROW AND RESPECT WHOLE CULTURAL BENGALIS HEART.

Sd.
S Chatterjee.
Secretary,
Nikhil Banga Nagarik Sangha.

BOX 4 Phonogram was sent by S. Chatterjee, secretary, Nikhil Banga Nagarik Sangha to Prime Minister Morarji Desai and MPs, 21 August 1978

Prime Minister,
Humbly appeal—Stop further massacre operation on Marichjhapi Sundarbans refugees. Today all launch services suspended there sine die officially large contingent forces sent not for just return to Dandak. Repeat appeal to P.M. and Morarji must know real situation before making Turkman Gate plus Jallianwalla Bagh blunder.... Must... politics rule or Central Government and civilized India. Kindly Act.

In January 1979, when women from Marichjhapi, in three boats were crossing the river to fetch drinking water from Kumirmari on the opposite bank and were attacked by government forces and capsized, the residents of Kumirmari were infuriated at the sight of this inhuman and barbarous act. Protests erupted and the people's anger was met with four rounds of teargas shells which were hurled at the boats and another five rounds were thrown at the assembled people of Kumirmari. As a result, the three women were left in a precarious condition.

Later, a three-member committee comprising Members of Parliament (MPs) who had visited Marichjhapi submitted a report to the prime minister. The report spoke of the excessive use of force by the state and blamed the state government for the atrocities committed at Marichjhapi. It also slammed the state government's allegation that the residents of Marichjhapi were attempting to run a parallel government.

In the meantime, polarization between factions of political dissenters on the Marichjhapi issue only made matters worse. The refugees also approached the All India Backward and Minority Communities Employees' Federation (BAMCEF) led by Kanshi Ram. However, it was not a powerful organization in those days. Institutions of the central government such as the Scheduled Castes and Tribes Commission that owed an obligation to defend their rights unfortunately did not intervene. The press was alienated.

The refugees refused to give up, although some died of starvation and disease. When police action failed to persuade the refugees to leave, the state government ordered their forcible evacuation. The fateful days were 14 to 16 May 1979:

> Muslim gangs were hired to assist the police as it was thought that Muslims would be less sympathetic to refugees from Muslim-ruled Bangladesh. The men were first separated from the women. Most of the young men were arrested and sent to the jails and the police began to rape the helpless young women at random. At least several hundred men, women and children were said to have been killed in the operation and their bodies dumped in the river. (Mallick 1999)

The refugees themselves had asserted to the visiting MPs that a thousand had died of disease and starvation during the blockade; 10,260 families returned to their previous places of residence; 4,128 families perished in transit, died of starvation or exhaustion; and many were killed in Kashipur, Kumirmari and Marichjhapi by police firings (Atharobaki 1982). Dr Nilanjana Chatterjee states that by the time the eviction was completed on 17 May 1979:

> at least 3,000 refugees had secretly left Marichjhapi and scattered across West Bengal.... At the end of July 1979, a spokesman for the Dandakaranya Development Authority announced that of the nearly 15,000 families who had 'deserted', around 5000 families (approximately 20,000 refugees) had failed to return. The final deadline for them to re-register with the project was extended yet

> again to 31 August 1979 and the matter was considered officially closed. (Chatterjee 1992)

A remarkable incident happened in the meantime. When the government was pursuing its policy of economic blockade, an application was filed under Article 226 of the Constitution of India at Calcutta High Court, demanding a direction to the state and the central governments to refrain from interfering with 'the peaceful existence, life and living, occupation, trade and business of the inhabitants and citizens, residing at Marichjhapi' and *'to lift the illegal and arbitrary blockade and warlike acts of oppression and allow them free egress and ingress from their place of residence and business without hindrance of any kind whatsoever'*. The application underlined that the government was violating inter alia Articles 14, 15(1), 19(d), (e), (f) and (g), and 21 of the Constitution. The Court, through Justice R.N. Pyne, passed an interim injunction against the state specifying that:

> The respondents are restrained from interfering with or creating any obstruction to the supplies of essential commodities such as drinking water, milk, medicine including disinfectants, foodstuff and clothes etc. to the petitioners and other inhabitants of Marichjhapi. The respondents are also restrained from interfering with the petitioners' and other inhabitants' right of ingress and egress from Marichjhapi.
>
> *The supply of drinking water, essential food items and medicines as well as the passage of doctors must be allowed to Marichjhapi. The island cannot be put out of bounds.*

Debabrata Biswas, one of the petitioners representing the settlers in Marichjhapi states how the order brought cheers of joy and jubilation in the otherwise cornered island people. Rice and other provisions came in from different areas after 15 days of blockade. Thousands of inhabitants thundered—*'Amra sorbo na. Amra banchbo'* (We shall not move. We will live.)

However, this jubilation was short-lived. The Left Front government continued to violate the order. In the meantime, two supplementary petitions were filed before the Calcutta High Court, praying that advocates of both sides be allowed to go to

Marichjhapi, inspect the site and submit a report to the court. The government denied that the refugees were being subjected to any blockade and continued in defiance of the court. On 7 May, in spite of the injunction being in operation, 2,500 armed police, including 250 female officers, and hired goons landed on the island. What continued in the successive days has been discussed earlier.

The advocates for the petitioners visited the island, submitted a report about what they had seen, including a ravaged island bulldozed to the ground and facing opposition from state government officers while conducting their inspection. In a tragic twist of fate, when the case was listed next (before another judge, Justice Bimal Chandra Basak), the court dismissed the application on the grounds that it did not want to get into disputed facts on the use of force and that the island was in the reserved forest area. Incidentally, the latter is much a disputed fact. Officers of the government, including the Forest Department and NATMO, deny the assertion made by the ruling government that the area was part of a reserved forest. In a twist befitting the duplicity, the CPM settled its own supporters in Marichjhapi, occupying and utilising the facilities left by the evicted refugees. Ecological concerns were conveniently overlooked. This suitably settles the question whether the dwellers were living in a protected, unauthorised area.

The Marichjhapi massacre never saw an appeal to a higher court. By the time the judgment was delivered, the refugees had been successfully dispersed again and there was no one to fight another battle against the might of the state. The CPM excused itself by making a statement to the effect that 'there was no possibility of giving shelter to these large number of refugees under any circumstances in the State'.

MARICHJHAPI IN *BHADRALOK* MEMORY

Marichjhapi did not live in the *bhadralok* memory in the 1970s, 1980s and 1990s. The complete silence about the incident in the landscapes of upper-caste memory for three decades raises serious questions about the constitution of civil society and the complete collective privileging of the *bhadralok* memory over others. The interrogation of caste in the post-partition memory-building project did not find a place in non-Dalit writing in those three decades—a massacre at the beginning of the Left regime went largely unnoticed, but towards the end of the same government's rule, Marichjhapi came into circulation in public and largely privileged memory. Was it then appropriated by the *bhadralok* to oust a government they didn't want?

The fall of the mighty Left was a combination of several factors, including a mix of both crushing of the rights of the rural poor and the labouring peasantry, as also the discontent of an upwardly mobile middle class whose consumerist dreams of globalized greatness remained unfulfilled during the Left Front's reign. But mostly, it was a peasant rebellion on the familiar beam of land and livelihood that thwarted the CPM and saw its most spectacular electoral defeat. The urban heartland's upwardly mobile middle class was disgruntled at the traditionally 'elitist' issue of corruption among the Marxist *babu*s, which seemed to find a resonance more than the issue of human rights violations in Singur and Nandigram.

In the 2000s, with the resurgence of violent politics against peasants in Nandigram and Singur, Marichjhapi came back in political discussions. Mahasweta Devi (2011), veteran author and social activist says that when Marichjhapi happened, people's experience with the Left Front government was not as bitter as it was during Singur and Nandigram. Marichjhapi, therefore, did not receive the overwhelming attention and support that the other two movements did. This begs the question—what was the politics of the largely urban middle class in lending support to the peasant movement in Singur and Nandigram, and how did it differ from that of Marichjhapi? The middle-class angst against the ruling government consolidated and appropriated the wave of protest on the ground in Singur and Nandigram. The same angst of the Bengali *bhadralok* also went a step ahead and sought to consolidate from the tunnels of history the memories of the untouchables of Marichjhapi in tales of the Left's promises, and the Left's treacheries.

A commendable amount of literature on Marichjhapi, including compilations of reminiscences, interviews, memoirs and opinion pieces – all these have emerged in the period following Nandigram and Singur, in the midst of strong opposition to the ruling government, when it was eminently clear that the sun was likely to set over the Left Front's empire in West Bengal. Images of Marichjhapi have circulated in the form of photographs of its schools, markets, settlements, fisheries, etc. Shailen Chakravorty reminisces how he could only publish a review of a book on Marichjhapi in the 2002 Kolkata Book Fair under a pseudonym and how the same was strongly opposed by the Publishers and Booksellers Guild. This was barely five years before Nandigram. He bitterly adds that in the post-Nandigram phase, the same Marichjhapi became an 'item' to be appropriated by everyone in the new anti-Left wave. With the transfer of power in 2011, from CPI(M) to Trinamul Congress, newly anointed Chief Minister Mamata Banerjee declared ('Sahaj Path in Primary Schools Again' 2011) that her government would investigate the killings in Marichjhapi, which had been a longstanding demand of the survivors.

Marichjhapi, however, changed the course of untouchable politics in West Bengal. Incidents like it were a constant reminder about how the secular politics of the *bhadralok* Marxists had let down the untouchables. Manoranjan Byapari calls Basu, the one who didn't keep the promises he made to the refugees in Dandakaranya, *beiman* (traitor). Others like Sunil Haldar, dub their act as that of *biswasghatokota* (treachery). There hasn't been a single investigation into the massacre or an enquiry into the missing 4,000 people who had settled there in spite of the new government's promise. The 'sensitive' academia has also not paid much attention to the *chhotolok* refugees of the east. What should perhaps be a sordid reminder of this politics of caste and class in refugee 'resettlement' is the name of the village where many of the Marichjhapi settlers live now—Pother Sesh, which means 'end of the road'.

NOTES

1. This refers to the 1964 East Pakistan massacre and ethnic cleansing of Bengali Hindus in the wake of an alleged theft of what was believed to be the Prophet's hair from the Hazratbal shrine in Jammu and Kashmir in India.
2. Pradip Kumar Bose (2010) made a comprehensive study of the literature on refugee studies in his essay, 'Refugee, Memory and the State'.

3. For all data and facts cited, and discussions made in this part, I have relied on the following references: Bhattacharjee (2010), Choudhury (2004), Mandal (2002) and Pal (2009, 2011).

REFERENCES

Atharobaki, Biswas. 1982. 'Why Dandakaranya a Failure, Why Mass Exodus, Where Solution?' *The Oppressed Indian*, 4(4): 18–20.

Bandyopadhyaya, Sekhar. 1997. *Caste, Protest and Identity in Colonial India: the Namasudras of Bengal, 1872–1947*. London: Routledge.

Bhattacharjee, Tushar (ed.). 2010. *Aprakasito Marichjhapi*. Shibnath Choudhury.

Bose, Pradip Kumar. 2010. 'Refugee, Memory and the State: A Review of Research in Refugee Studies', *Refugee Watch*, 36 (December). Byapari, Manoranjan. 2012. *Itibritte Chandal Jiban*. Kolkata: Priyashilpa.

Chakrabarti, Prafulla K. 1990. *The Marginal Men: The Refugees and the Left Political Syndrome in West Bengal*. Lumière Books.

Chatterjee, Nilanjana. 1992. 'Midnight's Unwanted Children: East Bengali Refugees and the Politics of Rehabilitation'. Ph.D. dissertation, Brown University.

Chatterji, Joya. 2010. *The Spoils of Partition*, Vol. 15. Cambridge: Cambridge University Press.

Choudhury, Sibnath. 2004. *Marichjhapir Kanna* (The Lament of Marichjhapi). Kolkata: Srijani Prakasak.

Mahashweta, Devi. 2011. 'Manusher Ghum Bhengechhe' (The People Have Woken Up), Aprakasito Marichjhapi.

Government of India. 1964. *Census of India: 1961*. New Delhi: Ministry of Home Affairs, Office of the Registrar General India.

Jalais, Annu. 2005. 'Dwelling on Morichjhanpi', *Economic & Political Weekly*, 40(17): 1757–62.

Kudaisya, Gyanesh. 1997. 'Divided Landscapes, Fragmented Identities: East Bengal Refugees and their Rehabilitation in India, 1947–79', *Singapore Journal of Tropical Geography*, 17(1): 24–39.

Mallick, Ross. 1999. 'Refugee Resettlement in Forest Reserves: West Bengal Policy Reversal and the Marichjhapi Massacre', *Journal of Asian Studies*, 58(1): 104–25.

Mandal, Jagadish Chandra. 2002. '*Marichjhapi: Noishobder Antorale*' (Marichjhapi: Beyond Silence). Sujan Publication (2002).

'"Massacre" in Morichjhanpi'. 2005. *Economic and Political Weekly* (Letters to the Editor), 40 (25).

Pal, Madhumoy (ed.). 2009. *Marichjhapi Chhinna desh, Chhinna Itihaash* (Marichjhapi: Disintegrated Land, Disintegrated History). Kolkata: Gangchil.

——— (ed.). 2011. *Nijer Kothay Marichjhapi* (Marichjhapi in Its Own Words). Kolkata: Gangchil.

Rahman, Mahbubar and Willem van Schendel. 2003. '"I Am Not a Refugee": Rethinking Partition Migration', *Modern Asian Studies*, 37(3): 551–84.

'Sahaj Path in Primary Schools Again', *Times of India* (Kolkata), 18 June 2011. http://timesofindia.indiatimes.com/city/kolkata/Sahaj-Path-in-primary-schools-again/articleshow/8895606.cms (accessed on 20 May 2014).

CHAPTER 7

The People's Militia

*Communists and Kashmiri Nationalism in the 1940s**

ANDREW WHITEHEAD

'The people's movement of Kashmir', declared the British communist Rajani Palme Dutt in the summer of 1946, 'is the strongest and most militant of any Indian State… Its leader, Sheikh Abdulla [sic], impressed me as one of the most honest, courageous and able political leaders I had the pleasure of seeing in India.'[1] This was warm praise from the austere Palme Dutt. His week-long stay in the Kashmiri capital, Srinagar, in July 1946 came at the end of a five month visit to India which was intended largely to guide and instruct the Communist Party of India (CPI).[2] It arose from a personal invitation from Sheikh Abdullah, the leader of the National Conference, the main nationalist party in princely-ruled Kashmir. By the time Dutt reached the Kashmir Valley, Abdullah had been arrested for leading a mass protest campaign against the maharaja. The same issue of Dutt's *Labour Monthly* that published the account of his trip to Kashmir also carried Sheikh Abdullah's speech in his own defence at a trial in which he was sentenced to three years imprisonment for making seditious speeches.[3]

Dutt, the British-born son of a Bengali doctor, was a doctrinaire exponent of orthodoxy within the leadership of the Communist

* This essay was first published in *Twentieth Century Communism: a Journal of International History* and is reprinted here with permission from the journal's editors and its publisher, Lawrence & Wishart.

Party of Great Britain (CPGB).[4] In the British party, he was more feared than loved; in the Indian party, his stock was much higher. Palme Dutt's *India To-Day*, a huge book first published in 1940 at which time the author had never set foot in India, was enormously influential there. Dutt acted as mentor to the younger party, and the CPI leadership would have taken careful note of his comment that Kashmir was 'the political storm-centre of the Indian fight for freedom'. In his *Labour Monthly* article, Dutt made much of the resemblance of the National Conference[5] emblem, a red flag with plough, to the red flag with hammer and sickle which flew over the bonnet of his car on the arduous road journey from Rawalpindi to Srinagar. In the Kashmiri capital, under the thrall of what he described as a 'reign of terror' established by the maharaja, he attended Sheikh Abdullah's trial:

> the sympathy even among the soldiers and armed guards for Abdulla was visible. When Abdulla entered the court, the entire court with the exception of the judge stood up in his honour – which was more than they had done for the judge. He saw me as he entered and moved away from his guards to shake me by the hand, and we exchanged greetings and I was able publicly to express to him the admiration and support felt for his stand. The proceedings were held up till we had completed these greetings.

A few days later, Dutt button-holed Jawaharlal Nehru, a friend and ally of Abdullah, to advise him against 'letting down the Kashmir fight'. By the end of the following year, Nehru had become the first prime minister of independent India and Sheikh Abdullah was in power in what had become Indian Kashmir.

Rajani Palme Dutt's ringing endorsement of Sheikh Abdullah and the movement against autocracy in Kashmir both reflected and gave impetus to Indian communist activity in this out-of-the-way valley in the Himalayan foothills. Communists helped to shape Sheikh Abdullah's radical campaign against princely rule. In turn, Palme Dutt, it has been suggested, saw in the mass action in Kashmir a potential model for left campaigns, midway between insurrectionism and the restraint advocated by Nehru's Indian National Congress.[6] Yet in the year following Dutt's visit to Srinagar, communists in Kashmir took the lead in organising a popular armed force. Hundreds of young Kashmiris enrolled in the militia, and some saw active service while helping to repulse an invasion by pro-Pakistan irregular forces. The militia bore such leftist imprints as political officers, a women's wing, and a linked cultural front staging popular dramas and organising propaganda.

The establishment of a volunteer force was a remarkable innovation in a part of India where there was no martial tradition. The involvement of women in the militia was even more of a breach with convention in such a conservative region, with little space for women in public life. For Indian communists, too, this was new territory. The party had little history of armed activity, and was sharply critical during the Second World War of Subhas Chandra Bose's Indian National Army, a force raised outside Indian soil which fought alongside Japanese troops. The militia in Kashmir was a revolutionary force – part of a political mobilisation which saw a new political order take shape there. Sheikh Abdullah's advent to power marked the end of more than a century of princely rule, and he became the first Kashmiri Muslim to hold the reins of power for well over three hundred years. The volunteer force, however, was not a challenge to the newly independent Indian state; rather it was established to support Kashmir's accession to India and was equipped and trained by the Indian army. It was a defence force, intended to safeguard the Kashmiri capital from a very real threat of occupation and ransacking by armed Pakistani tribesmen, rather than a propagator of insurgency. When after a few weeks the immediate danger to Srinagar abated, so too did the temper of militia activity. The women's section disbanded, and the men's militia was eventually incorporated into the Indian armed forces.

Kashmir had not been a focus of communist activity prior to the mid-1940s, and it largely disappeared from the party's horizons within months of Sheikh Abdullah's political takeover. When at the close of 1947 the CPI moved towards a policy of promoting a popular uprising in southern India, this amounted to a repudiation of the policy pursued in Kashmir. The communist approach to Kashmiri nationalism in the mid-1940s harked back to the Popular Front period – a practice of working within progressive parties which had mass support. Although communists in Kashmir made no secret of their political allegiances, they did not seek to organise as a separate party. Their influence within the National Conference was considerable, and endured into the early years of Sheikh Abdullah's period in office. As well as their leadership of the militia, communists also shaped an exceptionally radical political programme with the 'New Kashmir' manifesto of 1944. The land reform measures outlined in the manifesto were eventually implemented, and are widely seen as one of the most radical and successful measures of political and social empowerment in South Asia. This article looks at the means by which communists gained influence within the Kashmiri nationalist movement, the nature of the militia which it helped to establish, and the reasons for the failure to develop a mass-based communist movement.

—

The mountain valley of Kashmir was 'great game' territory, part of that inaccessible region of Asia where China, Tibet, Russia and the British Raj all met. The principality of Jammu and Kashmir took shape from the mid-1840s. A century later it was the biggest by area, and second biggest by population, of all India's princely states. The ruling family were Dogri-speaking Hindus from Jammu – in other words, outsiders in the eyes of many Kashmiris – who managed to agglomerate, though never quite bind together, a huge area stretching north from the Punjab plains, through valleys in the Himalayan foothills, to some of the high mountain ranges. The Kashmir Valley was the heartland of their fiefdom, though it accounted for well under half of the princely state's total population and less than a tenth of the land area. It was the centre of the Kashmiri language and culture and of a tolerant Sufi-influenced form of Islam, the religion of more than ninety per cent of the Valley's population. The maharajas were, by and large, wealthy, sporting Anglophiles. They presided over an autocracy where the Muslim majority was disadvantaged, facing heavy taxes and other feudal-style impositions and with little prospect of education or advancement.[7]

The opening of the Jhelum valley road in 1890 for the first time allowed access to Srinagar by wheeled transport and started to chip away at Kashmir's political and intellectual isolation. From the 1920s, increasing numbers of civil servants and army officers descended on Srinagar during the summer to escape the blistering heat of the plains. There was travel in the other direction too. The offspring of Kashmir's tiny Muslim middle class started to secure an education in Punjab or further afield. From the beginning of the 1930s, popular politics began to take root in the Kashmir Valley, and achieved some concessions from autocratic princely rule. Newspapers and public gatherings for political purposes were permitted from 1932. From the start, the example of the Russian Revolution loomed large in the thinking of Kashmir's small group of politically minded youngsters. Sheikh Mohammad Abdullah, the son of a shawl maker, was the most prominent Kashmiri political leader from the early 1930s until his death in 1982.[8]

Sheikh Abdullah was a graduate of Lahore and Aligarh universities and a charismatic leader and orator who rejoiced in the title Sher-e-Kashmir: the lion of Kashmir. The initial political mobilisation, in the face of often severe repression, was largely communal. Sheikh Abdullah's party was initially known as the Muslim Conference, but in 1939 it was renamed the National Conference, marking an important turn from a community-based identity to aspiring to represent all Kashmiris. The party made an open appeal for support from the Kashmir Valley's small but influential Hindu and Sikh minorities. From the late 1930s, Sheikh Abdullah developed a strong bond with two of South Asia's commanding nationalist leaders: Jawaharlal Nehru, who was himself of Kashmiri Hindu ancestry, and Khan Abdul Ghaffar Khan, known as the 'Frontier Gandhi', who like Abdullah was an inspirational, secular- minded leader in an overwhelmingly Muslim region. This was an alliance of progressive nationalists, who courted popular support and were willing to tackle feudal privilege. Mohammad Ali Jinnah's Muslim League and its allies, the political forces which secured the creation in 1947 of the explicitly Muslim nation of Pakistan, had significant support in the Kashmir Valley, but never managed to rival Sheikh Abdullah's mass appeal.

There was another factor encouraging and sustaining Sheikh Abdullah's turn to a more socialist-minded style of politics. Left-leaning intellectuals from Lahore began to congregate in Srinagar.

Some came during the summer; others settled there. As the temper of politics in Kashmir quickened, so did their interest and involvement. In 1941, Sheikh Abdullah himself performed the nikah or Muslim marriage ceremony in Srinagar of his friend, the renowned progressive poet Faiz Ahmed Faiz, and a London communist, Alys George. Her sister Christobel was already married to a prominent Punjabi marxist, M.D. Taseer, who became the principal of Kashmir's most prestigious college of higher education. Her memoir of the Valley includes a group photograph of a remarkable constellation of coming leftist literary talent, among them Faiz and the novelist Mulk Raj Anand, taken in Kashmir in 1938.[9] Most were close to the CPI and several came to be active in the Progressive Writers' Association or the Indian People's Theatre Association, organisations of enormous influence in Indian literature and cinema. The actor and writer Balraj Sahni, a party member, was also an influential figure, and the family home in Srinagar was another gathering place of left cultural figures. 'Since I had come from Bombay, where the Central Office of the Communist Party was,' Sahni wrote, 'the Srinagar comrades used to treat me with a deference, which was out of all proportion.'[10]

Another communist couple began to travel up from Lahore and came to be key players in Kashmiri politics. B.P.L. Bedi was a Punjabi Sikh who as a student at Oxford had met a woman from Derbyshire, Freda Houlston. 'Barely a week after finishing Final Schools', she reminisced, 'we were married in the dark and poky little Oxford Registry Office.'[11] She wore a sari as her wedding dress, and in the autumn of 1934, the Bedis and their four-month-old baby moved to India. They were a striking couple, politically committed and socially outgoing, and to this day warmly remembered by the few survivors of their once large circle of friends. 'In the summer months', reminisced Christobel Bilqees Taseer, 'the Leftists from different parts of India would also be there [in Kashmir], mixing with and influencing the National Conference workers. One particularly popular couple were the Bedis… Both husband and wife were dedicated Marxists.'[12] 'Baba' Bedi was gregarious and forceful – 'very funny character, very happy go lucky type… he had a big smile on his face'.[13] Freda was courageous, clever and her beauty was much commented upon. In the words of her younger son, the film star Kabir Bedi, 'she was blue eyed, white skinned and fighting the British'.[14] They became close friends of Sheikh Abdullah and part of his immediate political circle.

—

Organised CPI activity in the Kashmir Valley appears to date from the late 1930s. Prem Nath Bazaz, who was both a historian of and a participant in Kashmir politics in this era, recorded that two 'Moscow-trained' workers from Lahore spent several weeks in Srinagar in 1937 but achieved little. In the early 1940s, several small socialist-minded discussion groups were set up by students in Kashmir.[15] In this more propitious climate, the CPI made another attempt to recruit. 'In September 1942, Fazal Elahi Qurban, the well known Communist from Lahore organized an anti fascist school in a house boat in Srinagar', according to an Indian intelligence report, 'and the party's influence was slowly being extended.'[16] Pran Nath Jalali, a schoolboy at the time, attended the sessions: 'I ran away from my home to join the first study circle, they called it, which was held in Dal Lake. It was in a boat. We had the first schooling on communist ideology in that doonga [boat].'[17]

Jalali had expected to be taught how to make bombs, but instead learned about topics ranging from evolution to the French Revolution. He recalled about fourteen participants in the classes, most of them students.[18] Among those attending were two future chief ministers of Indian Kashmir and key lieutenants of Sheikh Abdullah. Bakshi Ghulam Mohammad's association with the communist movement was brief. G.M. Sadiq's links were much more long lasting.[19] Small numbers of communists became active particularly within the students, youth and labour wings of the National Conference. 'They did not raise their hand that here we are, communists', Pran Nath Jalali recalled. 'Except that everybody knew. Even Sheikh sahib [Sheikh Abdullah] knew… There was no ban as such. But we were conscious not to run Sheikh sahib on the wrong side because he was very sensitive about any parallel political activity.'

A disproportionate number of these pioneer Kashmiri communists were, like Jalali, Pandits – that is, high caste Kashmiri speaking Hindus, a community which at that time made up less than a tenth of the Valley's population. One Pandit communist, Niranjan Nath Raina, achieved prominence both within the National Conference in Srinagar and in the local trade union movement. 'I admired him because he had great intellect... he was a man of calibre', recalled Mohan Lal Misri; 'he was the number one communist' in the recollection of Mahmooda Ahmed Ali Shah.[20] Raina 'had been indoctrinated with the philosophy of communism while studying in the Allahabad University', recorded Prem Nath Bazaz. 'On his return to his homeland he became the staunchest propagandist of the creed. Through his efforts, the party gained dozens of adherents among the intelligentsia of the Pandits.'[21] Nevertheless, Kashmiri communism was a secular movement which sought to embrace all communities, with secularism at the root of its political purpose.

The most powerful evidence of communist influence within the National Conference came with the party's adoption in September 1944 of the 'Naya Kashmir' (New Kashmir) policy document. According to some of those involved, communist allies of Sheikh Abdullah had urged the National Conference to develop a policy platform. 'In order to get it in a concrete shape', one veteran commented many decades later, 'the National Conference party invited from its members their opinions, articles, suggestions and view-points, all in writing. When a bulk of such material was collected, it was sifted and all good things accepted, compiled and given a proper shape. It was then prepared into a well arranged document with the help of a communist leader, B.L.P. [sic] Bedi who ... mixed his own ideological substance with the material.'[22] Most accounts agree that Bedi was responsible for the greater part of the forty-four-page manifesto, perhaps in collaboration with prominent CPI members in Lahore. Jalali's recollection is that apart from the introduction, there wasn't much writing to do, because the manifesto was 'almost a carbon copy' of documents issued in Soviet Central Asia.[23]

The 'New Kashmir' manifesto has been authoritatively described as 'the most important political document in modern Kashmir's history'.[24] In the introduction, Sheikh Abdullah advocated democracy and responsible government for Kashmir and a planned economy, and made clear where he looked for inspiration:

> In our times, Soviet Russia has demonstrated before our eyes, not merely theoretical but in her actual day to day life and development, that real freedom takes birth only from economic emancipation. The inspiring picture of the regeneration of all the different nationalities and peoples of the U.S.S.R., and their welding together into the united mighty Soviet State that is throwing back its barbarous invaders with deathless heroism, is an unanswerable argument for the building of democracy on the cornerstone of economic equality.

There was certainly no shortage of rhetoric. The preamble to what was in effect a draft constitution asserted the determination of the people of Jammu and Kashmir to 'raise ourselves and our children forever from the abyss of oppression and poverty, degradation and superstition, from medieval darkness and ignorance, into the sunlit valleys of plenty ruled by freedom, science and honest toil, in worthy participation of the historic resurgence of the peoples of the East… to make this our country a darzling [sic] gem upon the snowy bosom of Asia'.[25] The socialist tone was emphasised by the front cover, red in hue, with a Marianne-style depiction of a woman, her head covered, holding the National Conference red flag.

The body of the document was much more earnest, incorporating charters for workers, peasants and women. It advocated equal rights, irrespective of race, religion, nationality or birth. Freedom of speech, press and assembly were to be guaranteed. There was particular emphasis on rights for women, which extended to equal wages and paid leave during pregnancy. The main features of the National Economic Plan were the 'abolition of landlordism' and 'land to the tiller', radical measures in any country but exceptionally so in an underdeveloped and partly feudal principality. All key industries were to be 'managed and owned by the Democratic State of Jammu and Kashmir'. The draft constitution proposed universal suffrage for those aged eighteen and over, though the powers of the National Assembly were to be subject 'to the general control of H.H. the Maharaja Bahadur'. This tolerance of a constitutional monarchy, a deference sharply at odds with the democratic tone of the programme, was further reflected in the decision of the National Conference to present their policy document in person to the maharaja.

'One thing that is difficult to understand is that the programme was not produced in a high tide of mass upsurge', wrote the Kashmiri communist, N.N. Raina. 'On the contrary political activity in 1943–44 had fallen to its lowest ebb… There was an air of unreality about the whole operation.' Yet the 'New Kashmir' programme, Raina argued, pointed the way for the National Conference and allowed it to establish a mass base, and also found a wider audience for communist ideas. 'By the summer of 1945 the number of copies of *People's War*, [a] weekly run by the C.P.I. sold every week [in Kashmir] reached 270', he wrote. 'This was in addition to about 100 permanent subscribers… A few tens were communists by conviction and were National Conference office bearers at various levels.'[26]

—

While 'New Kashmir' countenanced the continuance of princely rule in some form, the memorandum the National Conference submitted to a British cabinet mission to India in early 1946 took a more militant tone. In this, the party took strong exception to the terms of the treaty a century earlier, under which a local warlord acquired the Kashmir Valley. It was the treaty which had established Dogra princely rule over the Valley – and the National Conference now demanded what amounted to its annulment: 'We wish to declare that no sale deed however sacrosanct can condemn more than four million men and women to servitude of an autocrat when will to live under this rule is no longer there', Sheikh Abdullah declared in a telegram sent to the cabinet mission while they were in Srinagar. 'People of Kashmir are determined to mould their own destiny and we appeal to Mission to recognise justice and strength of our cause.'[27]

'Quit Kashmir' was a slogan that resounded around the Valley in the spring of 1946. It was an echo of the Congress's 'Quit India' campaign of a few years earlier. The target of Kashmir's mass agitation, though, was not the British but their own maharaja. The 'Quit Kashmir' movement seems more formidable in retrospect than it did at the time, and provided no immediate threat to princely rule. Yet it strengthened Sheikh Abdullah's political primacy in the Valley, caught the mood which was increasingly hostile to the maharaja and his family, and wrong-footed rival parties.[28] It was arguably the biggest organised political mobilisation the Kashmir Valley had seen – and was the movement that won the attention and applause of Rajani Palme Dutt. The concept of the sovereignty of the people which had been part-expressed in the 'New Kashmir' document was more powerfully achieved on the streets. The maharaja responded to the threat to his rule with repression. Hundreds of National Conference activists were rounded up, and on 20 May 1946, Sheikh Abdullah himself was arrested.

In the face of mass arrests, the communist network helped sustain the larger National Conference as an underground political force. Several leaders of the National Conference, including Sheikh Abdullah's principal lieutenant Bakshi Ghulam Mohammad and the leftist G.M. Sadiq, managed to sidestep arrest and reach Lahore. From there, they sought to organise protests and publish party literature. Ghulam Mohiuddin Kara (or Qarra) – a founder member of the National Conference who recounted that in 1942 he had been 'won over to the Communist cause through the Bedis'[29] – went underground. Kara has been described by a writer not generally sympathetic to the National Conference as the hero of the moment. 'The Government strained every nerve and spent large sums of money to get him arrested but in vain… He did not hide just to prevent his imprisonment but sustained the Movement in Srinagar.'[30] The American photo-journalist Margaret Bourke-White met Kara at the Bedis' home when she visited Kashmir at the close of 1947 and heard stories, legends perhaps, of his underground heroism, and of his affectionate nickname of 'Bulbul-i-Kashmir', the nightingale of Kashmir.[31] Women filled some of the vacuum left by the arrest or flight of male leaders, acting as couriers and also seeking to maintain morale and a sense of purpose. Freda Bedi memorably dressed as a local Muslim woman to enable her to conduct an 'underground messenger service' for the nationalists.[32] Kashmiri women gained a prominence and confidence that they had never before attained or sought. 'When [the] male leadership was put behind the bars or driven underground', wrote Krishna Misri, herself a young political activist in Kashmir in the 1940s, 'the women leaders took charge and gave a new direction to the struggle… However, the leaders addressed no controversial woman-specific issues for they did not want to come across as social rebels.'[33] The leading women activists in Srinagar included the pro-communist Mahmooda Ali Shah, who had graduated from Lahore and was later a pioneer of women's education in Kashmir, as well as Begum Zainab and Sheikh Abdullah's wife, Begum Akbar Jehan.

The Indian communist weekly *People's War* paid little attention to Kashmir, even when the National Conference adopted a socialist policy platform. Its successor *People's Age* made good the omission, championing the 'Quit Kashmir' campaign and lionising Sheikh Abdullah. The CPI's young and popular leader P.C. Joshi described Sheikh Abdullah as 'the wisest and tallest among the State people's leaders'.[34] In August 1947, the paper carried a photograph of a 'giant meeting at Hazratbal [outside Srinagar]... addressed by four underground National Conference workers'. But when the following month, a *People's Age* correspondent reported on a stay of several weeks in Kashmir, the tone was distinctly critical: 'The movement at present is nearly wholly disorganised and among the rank and file workers there is great dissatisfaction and confusion. There is even a danger of disintegration.'[35]

By then the Raj had ended and British India had been partitioned. Nehru had become the first prime minister of independent India, while Jinnah was governor-general of the new nation of Pakistan. Both were preoccupied by the profound loss of life, communal violence, and mass migration that accompanied a hastily executed partition. In the initial post-Raj weeks, the Kashmir Valley was largely unaffected by communal unrest, but there was great confusion about which nation the state would join. In formal terms, the decision rested with the maharaja. He was torn between Pakistan's greater indulgence of princely rulers and the ties of religion which bound him (but only a minority of his citizens) more closely to India.[36] The maharaja dithered and played for time, and Abdullah and many of his supporters were still in jail as India and Pakistan celebrated independence in mid-August 1947.

Sheikh Abdullah was eventually released on 29 September. The rejoicing crowds that paraded through Srinagar were testament to his popularity and political authority. Within days, Abdullah began to make a case for what can only be regarded as a political militia – a startling novelty in Kashmir which had no militia tradition, and indeed where no Valley Kashmiris had been allowed to serve in the maharaja's army. Addressing a public meeting, Abdullah called for volunteers to come forward to establish a 'peace brigade'. Referring to reports of a possible incursion into Kashmir, he advocated 'a volunteer corps to maintain peace and protect "our hearth and homes", irrespective of creed and community'.[37] Whether or not the idea originated with communists, they took on themselves the urgent task of organising the volunteer force.

Two weeks after Sheikh Abdullah called for the establishment of a peace brigade, the invasion of Kashmir he had warned of began. A 'lashkar' or tribal army, ill-disciplined but well armed and numbering several thousand fighters, descended from the tribal agencies bordering Afghanistan. They were pursuing a jihad or holy war – and as well as championing Islam, they were also seeking to claim the Kashmir Valley for Pakistan and (for many the most immediate preoccupation) to seek booty. The extent of Pakistan's complicity in this raid has been hotly debated and disputed. It is clear that the provincial government in Pakistan's North-West frontier aided and encouraged the invasion, as did some in Pakistan's national government and in the army. Aided by Muslim mutineers within the maharaja's forces, the invaders progressed rapidly, capturing Muzaffarabad, advancing along the Jhelum river, and taking the Valley's second town, Baramulla. There the 'lashkar' looted and raped, and caused an international outcry by ransacking a Catholic convent and mission hospital where three Europeans were among those killed. Although the targets were often non-Muslims, the attackers were indiscriminate in their violence and so lost much of the goodwill they might have enjoyed as self-proclaimed liberators from Hindu princely rule.

The fall of Baramulla and word of the atrocities committed there caused alarm in Srinagar, just thirty-five miles away on a good and flat road. The maharaja, prompted by the Indian government, fled at night in a long cavalcade of cars across a mountain pass to the city of Jammu. Many Kashmiris saw this as an act of cowardice. Once in Jammu, Maharaja Hari Singh signed the instrument of accession by which his state became part of India. Sheikh Abdullah was quick to endorse Kashmir's union with India, but he recognised that the most urgent task was to repulse the invaders. With the collapse of the state's army and of much of the maharaja's administration, Srinagar was undefended. The Indian government began an ambitious airlift to provide some defence for the Kashmiri capital, but Srinagar's airstrip was so basic it was impossible to land more than three or four hundred troops a day.

On the day the airlift began, Nehru wrote a private letter endorsing the volunteer force Sheikh Abdullah had envisaged. 'We shall be sending you more arms for distribution to the civil population', he told an Indian officer sent as his personal emissary to Srinagar. 'Chosen young men, Muslim, Hindu and Sikh, should be given rifles and if possible given some simple training. We must do all this on a non-communal basis inviting everyone to joining in defence but taking care of one major factor – to trust none who might give trouble… These armed volunteers can well undertake the defence of, and the duty of keeping order in Srinagar and other towns in the Valley… This would leave our troops for more active work.'[38]

The following day, newspapers reported 'hundreds of "National Conference" volunteers' in the streets. Two days later, 'several scores of them appeared armed for the first time with standard .303 rifles which a spokesman said they had obtained from "friendly sources"'.[39] Sheikh Abdullah reminisced that 'Hindus and Muslims alike were prepared to guard their national honour, having heard about the atrocities inflicted on the innocents by the tribal people… Girls also joined with the Hindu, Muslim and Sikh boys, and all were strictly ordered to guard the non-Muslim households.'[40] N.N. Raina, a prominent Kashmiri communist, gave a sense of the excitement as young Kashmiris enrolled in the militia:

> Within a few hours the whole atmosphere in the Valley changed. Young and old started marching, and offering for guard duties on bridges and in bazaars, banks, telephone and telegraph exchanges… The exhibition ground was used for training and lodging of volunteers, many of whom were from the Srinagar factories, schools and colleges. Gole Bagh was used for training lady volunteers.[41]

He recounted that military veterans and others with relevant experience were brought in to train the volunteers, and cars and motorbikes were requisitioned for their transport.

Although Sheikh Abdullah had been named by the maharaja as emergency administrator rather than head of government, he quickly took the reins of power. The presence on the streets of a volunteer force loyal to him was tangible proof that the old princely order had gone. The militia's task was to protect the Kashmiri capital from the Pakistani invaders, and in so doing it buttressed Kashmir's accession to India. Militia members patrolled the streets of Srinagar, and sought to defend the main points of entry to the city. A journalist who travelled round Srinagar by jeep reported: 'Every inlet to the city had its posse of volunteers, some of whom were armed with guns, others with swords and sticks.'[42] In due course, some militia members accompanied Indian troops, serving as guides and translators and occasionally as combatants. Several members of the militia were killed in the fighting. A few volunteers chose to work undercover in areas that had been captured by the tribesmen. Among these was Maqbool Sherwani, 'an adventurer and a bit showy' in the judgement of his colleague Pran Nath Jalali, who was shot by tribesmen in Baramulla and came to be regarded as a martyred hero of pro-India Kashmiri nationalism.[43]

While there were many non-communists active in the militia and a few in leading positions within it, the predominance of communists and their sympathisers indicates the influence of the left within the National Conference. The leftist G.M. Sadiq was often described as the pioneer and leader of the militia. His sister, Begum Zainab, was the guiding force behind the women's corps. The military commander was Said Ahmed Shah, a Muslim also known by the Hindu-style name Sham-ji. Colleagues recall him as largely non-political in outlook. Rajbans Khanna, a young communist intellectual from Lahore and friend of the Sahnis, took a directing role – and in due course married one of the women's militia, Usha Kashyap. The teenage communist Pran Nath Jalali was the militia's political officer, a post which bore an echo, by design or otherwise, of the leftist International Brigades in the Spanish Civil War a decade earlier. He had the task of promoting literacy and political awareness.

Indian army officers provided a modicum of training, as well as some basic equipment. Photographs survive of groups of young Kashmiri men drilling and parading, and taking part in rifle practice. A children's wing was formed, the Bal Sena, and a group of enthusiastic youngsters was photographed drilling with wooden rifles in the centre of Srinagar. The women's militia was not intended for active service. It was a self-defence corps, intended to give Kashmiri women of all communities the chance to defend their homes and honour should Srinagar be occupied. 'For them it was a matter of life and death', one National Conference leader recalled, 'because women and wealth were the most coveted targets of the invaders.'[44] The women drilled (and on one occasion, were inspected with weapons on display by Nehru) and some learnt how to fire .303 rifles and throw grenades. 'When my instructor shot the first fire, we were so scared we ran away', recalled Krishna Misri, who was fifteen years old when she enrolled in the women's militia.[45] The members also helped with relief work for the thousands of refugees created by the advent of the tribal army and the ensuing panic.

National Conference leaders suggested that as many as 10,000 young Kashmiris enlisted in the militia. This was probably an exaggeration, but many hundreds certainly joined up in what was initially known as the Bachau Fauj (Protection Force). While they contributed to the repulse of the raiders, their military role was not crucial. Their part in maintaining morale and in confirming Sheikh Abdullah's political ascendancy was more emphatic. The tribesmen advanced to the outskirts of Srinagar. The capital was without power, fuel and newspapers and supplies of food and cooking oil were limited. But the attackers had not expected to face the might of the Indian army, supported from the air, and within two weeks of the beginning of the airlift Indian troops had secured Srinagar and repulsed the tribal forces to the edges of the Kashmir Valley. The maharaja was still the nominal ruler of Kashmir, but his state forces were almost non- existent and his authority in the Valley was minimal.

The success of the militia, both in attracting public support and in bolstering the National Conference's public standing, appears to have emboldened communists to act more openly. They argued that the volunteer force, which was largely restricted to Srinagar, should be extended across the state and given an explicit political purpose. 'Our people should feel convinced that they are not fighting merely for the continuance of the old oppressive order but their own freedom', stated an open letter from the communist group in the National Conference written at the end of October 1947, when the Kashmiri capital was still imperilled by the invaders. 'On the basis of this consciousness we should be able to build a patriotic People's Militia which can launch political as well as military offensives to defeat the politico-military offensive of the enemy. We should be able to organise a network of Village Defence Committees, and thousands of Village Militia Units in every corner of the state.'[46]

The communist press echoed the demand for an effective militia and gloried in its reported successes. At the same time as the communists delivered their open message, the *People's Age* declared that Kashmir's 'freedom fight' could not rely simply on the Indian army. It would require 'the mobilization and active participation of the entire following of the National Conference, of the entire common people of Kashmir and Jammu. It will be necessary to arm the entire mass with whatever weapons one can get, to organise a popular guerilla warfare against the raiders.'[47] This call to arms was a new direction for the CPI, which for much of the Second World War supported the allied war effort and was thus opposed to the most formidable of Indian wartime irregular forces, the Japan-aligned Indian National Army. It was, however, not a call for an insurgency against the Indian state, but for a militia which operated in the name of a non-communist party and alongside the Indian army.

The following week, the communist weekly reported on the mobilisation and activities of the Bachao Fauj, which it said, with boundless optimism, numbered 25,000 volunteers. Later in the month, the *People's Age* gave over its front-page to a series of photographs of the militia under the headline: 'Kashmiris Resist'. An accompanying article recounted that 'these kids who rouse their whole mohalla [district] with the spirit of resistance, come every day to the headquarters demanding jobs to do, and, of course, rifles to fight the enemy with'. It also published a letter from Srinagar (apparently written by Usha Kashyap, though her name was not given) giving a sense of the political energy in the air: 'I am writing this letter to you from the Paladium [sic] Cinema which is our headquarters now', she wrote, supposedly to relatives in Bombay. 'Down below at the crossing, thousands of Kashmiris are always mounting guard with their rifles. The whole city is mad with joy… Today four of us girls will be taught the use of rifles. Tomorrow we may be sent to the… front as field-nurses.'[48]

The next issue reported the pushing back of the invaders and the taking by the Indian army of the key town of Baramulla – which meant the lifting of the danger to the Kashmiri capital. The following week, the *People's Age* devoted two pages to photographs of women members of the militia: 'For the first time on the soil of India is there being built an army of women, trained to use the rifle and other modern weapons of war', the paper declared with rhetorical flourish, though it was certainly justified in pointing out the striking innovation of arming and training women volunteers, all the more remarkable in a conservative, mainly Muslim princely state. 'The women in Kashmir are the first in India to build an army of women trained to use the rifle. By their example they have made Indian history, filled our chests with pride, raised our country's banner higher among the great nations of the world.'[49] The prominence in the women's self-defence corps of communist sympathisers, among them Mahmooda Ali Shah, Begum Zainab and Sajida Malik, again underlines the role of the left in leading and directing this citizen's militia.[50]

Alongside the armed militia, a Cultural Front was instituted, with again communists in leading positions – largely to conduct propaganda against the tribal raiders and in favour of Sheikh Abdullah and his radical policy programme. Simple dramas, what would later be called agitprop pieces, were hastily devised and performed: 'We used to go to the front and play the local themes', recalled Usha Kashyap; 'how these raiders, they've come to only kill Hindus, they were doing all sorts, molesting women and all that. And those plays used to be a big, big hit… And my name turned into, instead of Usha, Ayesha, Muslim name. And they loved me.'[51]

'In Battle-Scarred Kashmir A People's Theatre Is Born' read a headline in the *People's Age*.[52] The article reported that the first two dramas had been written and 'are being rapidly rehearsed', both dwelling on the heroism of the militia volunteers. One told the story of Maqbool Sherwani, the motorcycling militia man who had been shot dead by the raiders in Baramulla. The other was entitled 'Sara', portrayed as a 'true story' of a young Kashmiri woman who offered to cook for the raiders when they entered her village but instead informed on them:

> And in a short while, the volunteers of the National Militia were on the spot. They stormed the house, captured the raiders before they knew what to do. The Chief of the raiders tried to take advantage of the confusion to make good his escape from the back of the house. But Sara had her eyes on him. Hardly had he gone a few yards when she shot him with her own revolver.

Usha Kashyap played the lead role in the drama, which had been written by 'a young Kashmiri writer'.

In a later issue of the *People's Age*, Usha Kashyap wrote that the renowned writer K.A. Abbas attended an early performance of 'Sara' in Srinagar. Abbas was not a Kashmiri, but recorded in his autobiography how he was determined to join other progressive cultural figures in Srinagar and, with Nehru's help, got a place on a plane while the emergency was at its height. At Srinagar's airstrip, Abbas was met by a young Kashmiri Pandit, D.P. Dhar – a communist worker, according to the *People's Age* – who later became a political figure of great influence in Delhi. Abbas recalled Dhar as 'a handsome young Kashmiri' who 'carried a rifle slung over his shoulder… who seemed to be doing a dozen things – from training Kashmiri boatmen and farmers into a militia to keep track of the infiltrators who were still prowling about the valley, and looking after the intellectuals who were coming in every day'.

Abbas recalled that an array of leftist writers and artists had assembled in Srinagar. 'The atmosphere reminded one of Spain and the International Brigade where, it was said, writers had come to live their books, and poets had come to die for their poetry!'[53] The International Brigaders in Spain were of course outsiders who fought in solidarity with the Spanish struggle against fascism and Abbas and many others were similarly displaying solidarity with a cause with which they identified strongly but which was not entirely their own. India had not won its independence on the battlefield, but the battle for Kashmir just weeks after independence day became a rallying point for young progressive nationalists. It also became a focus for their creative work in later months and years. Mulk Raj Anand and K.S. Duggal, among others, wrote about the Kashmiri nationalist struggle. Leftist actors and filmmakers worked together to produce in 1949 'Kashmir Toofan Mei' (Storm Over Kashmir), a documentary film about the tribal raid and the popular response to it. K.A. Abbas and Balraj Sahni both played key roles in determining how Kashmir came to be depicted in Indian cinema and culture.[54]

The presence of artistic talent also shaped the visual depiction of the Kashmir movement. Madanjeet Singh, a photographer and painter, was among those who headed to Kashmir, in spite of his looming final exams at Delhi Polytechnic. He had been invited 'to build the National Cultural front in Srinagar to strengthen Kashmir's secular culture and help in resisting the invaders'. He recalled that D.P. Dhar and B.P.L. Bedi were the main patrons of the Cultural Front, and found that several Kashmiri poets and writers – notably the 'coolie poet' Aasi – were also actively engaged in the movement.[55] Some of Madanjeet's photographs of the militia appeared in the communist *People's Age*. When a few months later the Kashmir Bureau of Information put out a well illustrated propaganda pamphlet entitled *Kashmir Defends Democracy*, it was graced by a striking cover designed by Sobha Singh, then a young progressive and much later in life renowned for his portraits of the Sikh gurus. This combined a photograph of the women's defence corps with a dramatic outline in red of a Kashmiri woman lying and taking aim with a rifle (a portrayal of a Kashmiri Muslim milkwoman known as Zuni). In design and iconography, as well as in political message, it was a bold progressive statement.[56]

The guiding role within the militia of communists and their supporters, however, attracted the attention of their rivals. To judge by the account of N.N. Raina, the authorities in Delhi took fright at the extent of communist influence. Early in 1948, Raina asserted, Sheikh Abdullah's deputy, Bakshi Ghulam Mohammad, took control of the militia 'virtually through a coup… and put it under commanders supplied by the Indian Army. Communists were made uncomfortable by various provocations.'[57] Certainly, in the course of 1948, the militia's independence was curtailed and it never became the people's militia that the left had envisaged.

The Popular Front style of politics pursued by communists in Kashmir also fell victim to an abrupt change of line by the Communist Party of India. In December 1947, the central committee turned sharply to the left, denounced as 'opportunism' the policy of seeking to work alongside Congress and influence the Nehru government, and called for struggle against the 'national bourgeois leadership'. Two months later, at its second congress, the CPI removed P.C. Joshi and installed a hardliner, B.T. Ranadive, as party leader. In a key speech, the party's policy of supporting Sheikh Abdullah's National Conference was condemned. The new emphasis was on revolutionary struggle, and particularly on supporting the rural uprising in Telengana in another princely state, Hyderabad.[58] The building of influence within progressive non-communist parties was rejected.

In his early years in power, however, Sheikh Abdullah established a reputation for radicalism. One of his first acts was to rename Srinagar's main square as Lal Chowk (Red Square).[59] The echo of Moscow was unmistakable – and the name has endured to this day. A much more substantial achievement was the execution in the early 1950s of the most far-reaching land reform in modern India, seeing through the most ambitious of the policy proposals in the 'New Kashmir' manifesto. About half of the state's arable land was taken away from large and medium-size landlords within the initial two years of the scheme, creating hundreds of thousands of peasant proprietors. The main beneficiaries were poor Muslim villagers in the Kashmir Valley. Land redistribution secured Sheikh Abdullah's power base for a generation and is seen as his enduring political success.

More generally, Sheikh Abdullah was more successful as a political mobiliser than as a statesman or administrator. There had been little in the way of representative institutions in princely Kashmir, and while Sheikh Abdullah and the National Conference used the rhetoric of democracy they were not by instinct pluralist in their outlook. Once settled in power, Sheikh Abdullah became something of an autocrat and his critics complained of intolerance and repression. Among the communists who initially surrounded Sheikh Abdullah,

B.P.L. Bedi was given a post in charge of propaganda, but after a while there was a parting of the ways. Ghulam Mohiuddin Kara, the hero of the Quit Kashmir movement, broke more decisively and set up his own political party. Pran Nath Jalali found that his growing disillusionment with Sheikh Abdullah's administration, and concern about corruption and abuse of power, was compounded by the indifference of the CPI national leadership. He came to Delhi to talk to communist leaders but found that they were 'busy with their own revolution those days... I came to the conclusion they were not interested in building up a movement [in Kashmir], and the type of movement they wanted, I wasn't interested.'[60]

Sheikh Abdullah's personalised style of governance, and the change of outlook by the CPI, together greatly weakened the influence of communists. At the same time, his radicalism and authoritarianism, and the legacy of his close association with communists, aroused deep misgivings among those inimical to the Soviet Union. Josef Korbel came to South Asia in 1948 as the Czechoslovak member of the five nation UN Commission for India and Pakistan. When a few years later he wrote *Danger in Kashmir*, the peril he had in mind was the sort of Soviet-style communism which had taken root in his home country. He regarded Sheikh Abdullah as 'an opportunist and, worse, a dictator', and expressed the fear 'that Kashmir might eventually become a hub of Communist activities in Southern Asia'.[61]

A similar argument was expressed by local critics of Sheikh Abdullah. In 1952, a pamphlet entitled *Rise of Communism in Kashmir* rehearsed how the left was using Sheikh Abdullah as a 'catspaw' as they prepared to capture power.[62] The following year Sheikh Abdullah was removed from office as Kashmir's prime minister, largely because India's national government came to regard him as unreliable on the issue of the permanence of the state's accession to India. Concerns about communist influence continued to reverberate. An opposition group asserted that G.M. Sadiq, the most high profile communist sympathiser, had great influence in the new state government and that there were several other communist ministers. '[If] no immediate steps are taken to nip the evil', it warned, 'Kashmir may be lost to Communism.'[63]

In 1955, the Soviet leaders Khrushchev and Bulganin travelled to Srinagar during a visit to India. It was a public demonstration of Soviet support for Kashmir's still disputed union with India – the 'Russians are the first great power to have definitely and clearly gone on record as accepting the accession of Kashmir to India as final', Kashmir's constitutional head of state told Nehru.[64] In the following decade, G.M. Sadiq served as chief minister, still pro-Soviet by faction and inclination, but successful above all because he was Delhi's candidate. The steady erosion of Kashmir's autonomy, and Delhi's persistent interference and rigging of elections, prepared the way for the separatist insurgency that erupted in 1989. Some Kashmiris sought independence, others wanted to become part of Islamic Pakistan – but disaffection with Indian rule was evident across the Valley. Over the following two decades, at least 40,000 people, more than one in a hundred of the Valley's adult population, died in the conflict between Pakistan-backed militants and Indian security forces. Over that time, communists have had little visible presence in Kashmir. Many of the youthful communists who enrolled in the volunteer militia remained loyal to the ideology all their lives. Yet at the time of writing (in the summer of 2009), the Communist Party of India (Marxist) has a solitary member of the Jammu and Kashmir state assembly. Sheikh Abdullah's grandson is chief minister of the Indian state of Jammu and Kashmir, at the helm of the National Conference and governing in alliance with Congress. But the strand of militant, pro-India secular nationalism that the Kashmiri communists of the 1940s espoused now has limited resonance. The shifting sands of Kashmiri politics, however, should not be allowed to obscure the substantial role of communists in giving a radical complexion to Kashmiri nationalism in the crucial decade of the 1940s, securing popular support towards ending princely rule and taking up arms in defence of a secular, democratic Kashmir.

NOTES

1. Rajani Palme Dutt, 'Travel Notes No. 5', *Labour Monthly*, 28/10, October 1946, pp319-26. The 'Indian States' refers to the princely states which had not been fully incorporated into British India. I am grateful to

Ajit Bhattacharjea, Sumantra Bose, Suchetana Chattopadhyay and Matthew Worley for their valuable comments on an earlier draft of this article.

2. Gene D. Overstreet and Marshall Windmiller, *Communism in India*, Berkeley: University of California Press, 1959, pp. 240–4.
3. Sheikh Abdulla [sic], 'Not Guilty', *Labour Monthly*, 28/10, October 1946, pp. 311–14.
4. Dutt's life and career is detailed in John Callaghan, *Rajani Palme Dutt: A Study in British Stalinism*, London: Lawrence and Wishart, 1993.
5. Dutt persistently referred to Sheikh Abdullah's party as the People's Conference – apparently confusing the National Conference with another body in which Sheikh Abdullah was prominent, the All-India States People's Conference, which sought to represent the subjects of princely India and was aligned with the Indian National Congress.
6. Overstreet and Windmiller, pp. 241, 244.
7. Of the many modern histories of Kashmir, among the best is Sumantra Bose, *Kashmir: Roots of Conflict, Paths to Peace*, Cambridge, Mass.: Harvard UP, 2003. An engagingly polemical version is Tariq Ali, *The Clash of Fundamentalisms: Crusades, Jihads and Modernity*, London: Verso, 2002, pp. 217–52.
8. Ajit Bhattacharjea, *Sheikh Mohammad Abdullah: Tragic Hero of Kashmir*, New Delhi: Roli, 2008, pp. 29, 42–3, 48.
9. C. Bilqees Taseer, *The Kashmir of Sheikh Muhammad Abdullah*, Lahore: Ferozsons, 1986.
10. Balraj Sahni, *Balraj Sahni: an autobiography*, Delhi: Hind Pocket Books, 1979, p. 143.
11. Freda Bedi, *Behind the Mud Walls*, Lahore: Unity Publishers, [1947], p. 1.
12. Taseer, *The Kashmir of Sheikh Muhammad Abdullah*, p. 38.
13. Pran Nath Jalali interview, Delhi, 11 April 2007. Audio recordings and transcripts of interviews have been deposited in the archive of the School of Oriental and African Studies, London (accession OA3).
14. Kabir Bedi, personal communication, April 2007. Freda Bedi later became a senior Buddhist woman religious. B.P.L. Bedi also turned to religion in later life, in his case to the faith he was born into, Sikhism.
15. Prem Nath Bazaz, *The History of Struggle for Freedom in Kashmir, Cultural and Political*, Srinagar: Gulshan, 2003 (first published c1953), p. 421. Accounts of these small groups can be found in Asifa Jan, *Naya Kashmir: An Appraisal*, Srinagar: Zeba, 2006; N.N. Raina, *Kashmir Politics and Imperialist Manoeuvres, 1846–1980*, New Delhi: Patriot, 1988.
16. Sandeep Bamzai, *Bonfire of Kashmiriyat: Deconstructing the Accession*, New

Delhi: Rupa, 2006, p. 106. The author makes extensive use of official documents in his family's possession assembled by his grandfather, K.N. Bamzai, a Kashmiri Hindu who was a close confidante of Nehru.

17. Pran Nath Jalali interview, Delhi, 30 March 2007.
18. Jan, *Naya Kashmir*, pp. 73–4.
19. According to his son, Sadiq came into contact with communist intellectuals while a student in Lahore in the 1930s and was one of the points of contact with Punjabi communists during the repression of the mid-1940s. Rafiq Sadiq interview in the *Kashmir Sentinel*, February 2003.
20. Mohan Lal Misri interview, Faridabad, 12 June 2007; Mahmooda Ahmed Ali Shah interview, Srinagar, 18 June 2007.
21. Prem Nath Bazaz, p. 422.
22. Maulana Masoodi quoted in Jan, *Naya Kashmir*, p. 78.
23. Pran Nath Jalali interview, Delhi, 30 March 2007.
24. Bose, *Kashmir*, p. 25.
25. *New Kashmir*, New Delhi: Kashmir Bureau of Information, n.d., pp. 7, 12.
26. Raina, *Kashmir Politics*, pp. 121, 125.
27. *Kashmir On Trial*, Lahore: Lion Press, 1947, p. 224.
28. The Quit Kashmir campaign has been described by one historian as 'something of a flop', largely because major disturbances were confined to four towns: Srinagar, Anantnag, Pampur and Sopore – see Ian Copland, 'The Abdullah Factor: Kashmiri Muslims and the crisis of 1947', in D.A. Low (ed.), *The Political Inheritance of Pakistan*, London: Macmillan, 1991, pp. 218–54. This seems a harsh judgement.
29. Taseer, *The Kashmir of Sheikh Muhammad Abdullah*, pp. 174–9.
30. Muhammad Yusuf Saraf, *Kashmiris Fight for Freedom*, Lahore: Ferozsons, vol 1, 1977, p. 686.
31. Margaret Bourke-White, *Halfway to Freedom: A Report on the New India*, New York: Simon and Schuster, 1949, p. 200.
32. Ibid, p. 201.
33. Krishna Misri, 'Kashmiri Women Down the Ages: A Gender Perspective', *Himalayan and Central Asian Studies*, 6/34, 2002, pp. 3–27.
34. *People's Age*, 13 April 1947.
35. *People's Age*, 7 September 1947.
36. For contrasting accounts of the origins of the Kashmir crisis in 1947, see Andrew Whitehead, *A Mission in Kashmir*, New Delhi: Penguin

Viking, 2007; Alastair Lamb, *Incomplete Partition: The Genesis of the Kashmir Dispute, 1947-48*, Hertingfordbury: Roxford Books, 1997; and Prem Shankar Jha, *Kashmir 1947: The Origins of a Dispute*, New Delhi: Oxford University Press, 2003.

37. *Times of India*, 9 October 1947.
38. Nehru to Hiralal Atal, 27 October 1947, *Selected Works of Jawaharlal Nehru*, 2/4, New Delhi: Jawaharlal Nehru Memorial Fund, 1986, pp283-6.
39. *The Times*, 28, 29 and 31 October 1947.
40. Sheikh Mohammad Abdullah, *Flames of the Chinar: An Autobiography*, New Delhi: Penguin Viking, 1993, pp. 93–4.
41. Raina, *Kashmir Politics*, p. 152.
42. *Statesman*, 8 November 1947.
43. For an early telling of the Maqbool Sherwani story, see Bourke-White, *Halfway to Freedom*, pp. 210–11. His death was the inspiration for a novel by Mulk Raj Anand, *Death of a Hero: Epitaph for Maqbool Sherwani*, first published in 1963. The mythologising of his life is discussed in Whitehead, *A Mission in Kashmir*, pp. 212–7.
44. Mir Qasim, *My Life and Times*, Bombay, 1992, p. 37.
45. Krishna Misri (nee Zardoo) interview, Faridabad, 26 May 2007.
46. Raina, *Kashmir Politics*, p. 156.
47. *People's Age*, 2 November 1947.
48. *People's Age*, 23 November 1947.
49. *People's Age*, 7 December 1947.
50. The women's self-defence corps is discussed briefly in Nyla Ali Khan, *Islam, Women and Violence in Kashmir: Between India and Pakistan*, New Delhi: Tulika, 2009, pp. 118–23.
51. Usha Khanna (nee Kashyap), telephone interview, 31 August 2008.
52. *People's Age*, 21 December 1947.
53. Khwaja Ahmad Abbas, *I Am Not an Island: An Experiment in Autobiography*, New Delhi: Vikas, 1977, pp. 304–6.
54. I am grateful to Meenu Gaur for her expert observations about the progressive cultural movement and Kashmir, which is discussed in her coming University of London doctoral thesis.
55. Madanjeet Singh, *The Sasia Story*, Lalitpur, Nepal: UNESCO/Himalmedia, 2006, pp. 48–54. There are also photographs of the Cultural Front and its productions in Usha R. Khanna, *The Making of Samovar*, Worli, India: Spenta Multimedia, [n.d.], pp. 8, 11.
56. *Kashmir Defends Democracy*, Delhi: Kashmir Bureau of Information, [c1948].

57. Raina, *Kashmir Politics*, p. 160.
58. Overstreet and Windmiller, *Communism in India*, pp. 265–74.
59. *Times of India*, 8 November 1947; *Hindustan Times*, 12 November 1947.
60. Jalali interview, 30 March 2007.
61. Josef Korbel, *Danger in Kashmir*, Princeton: Princeton University Press, 1966, pp. 97, 198, 207. The book was first published in 1954.
62. *Rise of Communism in Kashmir*, Delhi: Kashmir Democratic Union, 1952, pp. 31–2. The author, who was probably either Prem Nath Bazaz or an associate, suggested that there was a sharp rift in Kashmiri communism along religious lines, with rival factions lead by N.N. Raina and G.M. Kara.
63. Jagan Nath Sathu, *Red Menace in Kashmir*, Delhi: Kashmir Democratic Union, [c1954].
64. Karan Singh to Nehru, 11 December 1955, in Jawaid Alam (editor), *Jammu and Kashmir 1949–64: Select Correspondence Between Jawaharlal Nehru and Karan Singh*, New Delhi: Penguin Viking, 2006, pp. 182–3.

CHAPTER 8

Engaging Traumatic Histories

The 1947 Partition of India in Collective Memory

SUKESHI KAMRA

Every August, in the days leading up to the 14th and 15th, articles with telling titles such as 'The Ghosts of Partition' (Bangash 2012) and 'The Tragedy of Partition' (Misra 2012) appear in the newspapers of India and Pakistan. Surely, the reminder of the dark underbelly of independence contained in such titles is intended to convince that the story is an intergenerational one, about 'us' as much as about 'them', about the present as much as about the past. Post-partition literary and film culture has been littered with such attempts. It is the subject of a film such as *Khamosh Pani* (2003), a novella such as Joginder Paul's *Sleepwalkers* (1998) and a poem such as Gulzar's 'Toba Tek Singh' (2001). All three offer a present haunted by the unresolved past of partition, as much as Bangash's 2012 piece, which opens with this following attempt at a reminder:

> Every country's Independence Day is a defining moment in its history. The events of the day are the culmination of years of struggle and the day hearkens to a new beginning. The same is true for Pakistan, except that we have yet to move on from our '1947' moment. This is not because historians keep writing about it but that in our collective memory, we still have to reconcile with the events of 1947 and move forward.

The question that lurks in the background Bangash's journalistic piece, as it does behind much partition literature, is, of course, why this is so.

Indeed, we ought to be puzzled. Over the last few decades, Partition Studies has emerged as a field and historiography has made memory a key site of analysis by acknowledging the claim eyewitness testimony has on partition history. There is a significant body of partition literature, and a number of films have appeared in recent years in which 1947 is remembered primarily for partition. We have learned much from these about the depths of human misery, degradation and of the depravity that defined the symbolically charged moment of independence from colonial rule. And still, articles continue to appear every August in the subcontinent, and seem resigned even as they wearily attempt to remind us of this past and its cathecting in the heavily symbolic day of independence. Clearly, in the opinion of many, the 1947 partition is mostly absent from our impressively expansive realm of 'cultural recall', as Mieke Bal (1999) has described the activity by which the past is performatively given the specific shape that it bears in the present, while independence is as clearly overrepresented.[1]

What will turn disengagement into willingness to own this past? How should we go about working through it? What about this past makes us so resistant to moving it (more correctly, speaking of its disturbing elements) out of the private into the public and out of the political into the civic? If Bangash is correct, and it is collective memory that holds the key to a successful civic engagement with traumatic pasts,[2] what would it take to do for collective memory what partition historiography has done for Indian history? After all, the very best in historiography has formulated generative questions about partition, violence in particular. These have made visible the very real dilemmas that accompany representation such as, on the one hand, representing partition violence in terms of particularities and naming agents/perpetrators can legitimise othering as a 'national' mode of engagement with this past; on the other, not representing in terms of particularities and naming agents produces its own kind of subterfuge and, in a sense, makes the question of violence and intent irrelevant: everyone and no one is responsible.[3]

Reflecting on such questions, which are at their most basic level questions of how and why to engage with partition, it struck me, at first, that colonialism does not pose the same kind of problem, requiring eliding, suppressing and so on. Apparently, it does not pose the same kind of threat to our collective identity as does the 1947 partition. Upon reflection, however, I am not so sure that the interrelated pasts (colonialism and partition) are so differently featured in the present. If we do not ask 'why and how should we, as a collective, remember colonialism?', it is likely because here too we have normalised the view of this past that we have inherited. It is a moot point, after all, whether we have made the more threatening/less easily assimilated parts of this part of our story of modern nationhood and social identity a concern, such as the complex structure and affective dimensions to subjugation, the violence of 1857, revolutionary nationalism, and the psychological distortions of colonisation that Frantz Fanon and Ashis Nandy have written about most influentially.

If it is true that we have shied away from confronting the fact of colonialism's routine and extraordinary violences, and it is true that we have been similarly reticent in engaging with partition violence, then the question to ask might be: is the reluctance in both cases unique to the instance or does it speak also of a widespread and historical unwillingness to engage with devastatingly negative themes, such as our participation in histories of violence?[4] In such a reading, for instance, the testimony of survivors – with its many silences as well as an indefinite horizon of victims – is itself best read as symptomatic of the larger condition, of impossibility, of bearing witness to violence and the absence of a tradition to draw on to do so. Conversely, the recent spate of films on 1857 and revolutionary figures of nationalist India (*Rang De Basanti* [2006], *Mangal Pandey: The Rising* [2005] and *Legend of Bhagat Singh* [2002]), which represents an attempt at rehabilitation that skirts dangerously around the issue of violence, rationalising it, mostly, as counter-violence, is a kind of overstatement that acts to compensate for the silence. It is, then, readable also as a reaction to the absence of debate, discussion and careful probing of partition violence in the realm of collective memory.

There is another context that I would like to introduce here as I think it sheds a different kind of light and encourages us to ask another sort of question of our discomfort with partition. Comparisons between Holocaust Studies and Partition Studies are not new, as a 1996 article by Don Miller, which I will cite later, establishes, and, I would note, as the invoking of the Holocaust in 1947–48 India as *the* appropriate inter-text encourages.[5] Besides its paradigmatic status in the world of trauma studies (which comes with its own set of problems), Holocaust studies is where the issue of intergenerational memory has been most fully debated. I am particularly intrigued by the link a scholar such as Andreas Huyssen has drawn between shifting attitudes towards the all-important issue of cultural representation of the Holocaust on the one hand and the requirements, of the past, that the children of survivors have and the claim they make on this past, on the other. He opens his 1997 article on Art Spiegelman's *Maus* with the following observation:

> Since the 1980s, the question is no longer *whether*, but rather *how* to represent the Holocaust in literature, film, and the visual arts. The earlier conviction about the essential unrepresentability of the Holocaust... has lost much of its persuasiveness for later generations who only know of the Holocaust through representations: photographs and films, documentaries, testimonies, historiography and fiction. (Huyssen 1997: 65, emphasis original)

Clearly, in Huyssen's estimation, generations that are best described as indirect witnesses to the Holocaust (it is a crucial part of their emotional, psychological, social and political formation) have laid claim to it. In so doing, they have altered the nature of the debate that dominated Holocaust studies in earlier decades, where the most urgent question, surely, was of the incommensurability of the Holocaust with existing forms of representation on the one hand and the imperative, which some have clearly experienced as an injunction, to document it, on the other. The notion, of the impact and claim traumatic histories have on ensuing generations, is well articulated by Marianne Hirsch (2012), who employed the term 'postmemory' to draw out the vitality of connection generations of indirect witnesses maintain with a catastrophic past such as the

Holocaust. She defines it thus on the website Postmemory.net: '[The term] describes the relationship that the "generation after" bears to the personal, collective, and cultural trauma of those who came before to experiences they "remember" only by means of the stories, images, and behaviors among which they grew up.' The more important point she makes is that the postmemory generation(s) do not bear a derivative or passive relationship with the Holocaust past. In her view, 'these experiences were transmitted to them so deeply and affectively as to seem to constitute memories in their own right', which, she goes on to suggest, means 'postmemory's connection to the past is thus actually mediated not by recall but by imaginative investment, projection, and creation' (ibid.). The impact of 'inherited memories' is of course as much a concern for her – after all, to have such a past as context is to be dominated by and to risk having one's own life stories displaced, evacuated even, by our ancestors (ibid.) as she says.

I find this view, about shifts in perception of (the availability of) the Holocaust (to the present), a useful way of envisioning our relationship with the 1947 partition. It may seem like a simple point, but what is striking is the marginal status of similarly vibrant conversations surrounding partition, as much as the apparent marginalising of intergenerational memory and trauma in our collective recollection. Although we find ourselves in the same position – with the passage of time, partition is a reality mediated by its representations – we have yet to fully engage the question of why representing partition is an imperative. Finally, I find her articulation of the destructive potential of traumatic pasts in the lives of the postmemory generation(s) to be deeply thought-provoking. Are the silence, indifference and disinterest within the familial economy of partition families, and of public culture in general, readable as at once an acknowledgement of the threat the past poses and a fear of being swallowed up by it? At the risk of over-generalising, I think a key difference between the two admittedly very different histories is of the postmemory generation(s), which in the case of partition, works hard at making forgetting the norm, punctured by selective forms of remembrance. This, after all, is Bangash's lament. One of the effects of reluctance to face this past (and probe the ways in which it is ours at more than the political level) has been that when partition is acknowledged in the genres of collective memory (popular culture in particular), it is distanced in time and space from the present, and remains a story about the eyewitness generation, its participation, victimisation, dislocation and trauma. This impression is reaffirmed each and every time a period film, like Deepa Mehta's *Earth* (1998) is made or novel like Bapsi Sidhwa's *Cracking India* (1991) is published, even though the reality is that period pieces are entirely framed by present concerns and are a 'reinterpretation of' the past, not an 'accessing of' it. And, when the story is told as a story of Indian Punjab and Pakistani Punjab (as in *Khamosh Pani* [2003], which is a film I otherwise deeply appreciate for many reasons, including the fact that it features intergenerational trauma), the issue is similarly displaced.

The reluctance to write of painful pasts is, of course, not particular to South Asia. The production of partition in collective memory works here the way the category of remembrance does in general, judging by the claims made by memory theorists such as Wulf Kansteiner. Describing collective memory as something that originates in 'shared communications about the meaning of the past that are anchored in the life-worlds of individuals who partake in the communal life of the respective collective' (Kansteiner 2002: 188), he makes two critical observations: one is about the reason collective memory is so crucial to the functioning of society – it is how the past is made meaningful; the second is about the identifying feature of collective memory – 'low-intensity' (ibid.: 189). What Kansteiner appears to mean is that in collective memory, the past is typically emptied of, or draws attention away from, the contradictions, fissures and conflicts with which events are imbued and contextualised. What remains of this past is what can be 'produced and consumed routinely without causing much disagreement' (ibid.: 190), he writes. In the case of civil war (which partition was), when warring communities are faced with the painful task of rebuilding and re-establishing forms of coexistence afterwards, the 'normal' process by which the past turns into 'low-intensity memory' is particularly charged and difficult, and frequently interrupted by reminders of the 'originary' trauma.[6] I wonder whether the relative absence of partition, as well as the overly visible and settled features of the partition story (other spaces, other times and, as I will later discuss, the emphasis placed on victims), when it is acknowledged, are choices that reflect our ongoing need to produce the all-important low-intensity memory: they produce a partition story (and discourse) that, on the face of it, is the space of a relatively sanguine, non-conflictual remembrance.

Of course, such a need has had its own effects, as I have mentioned earlier: an emphasis on partition and the generation that was a direct witness to it (other space, other time) has meant that what continues to frame partition for us is the forms in which this generation has chosen to remember or not remember the past. This fact has not gone unnoticed. In an article titled 'Against Silence and Forgetting', Jonathan Greenberg (2008: 261) asks: 'To what extent has the memory of 1947 remained "arrested and fixed" for the subcontinent's hinge generation?' And while he, quite appropriately, expresses appreciation of the recuperative work done by postmemory generation scholars such as Sudhir Kakar, Urvashi Butalia and Dipesh Chakrabarty for its having 'provided space for a more honest and expansive version of their society's collective memory' (ibid.: 267–68), the point remains that the predominant affective connections of the first generation with this past still represents a lure that partition scholarship has not succeeded in dislodging. In fact, it sometimes traffics in it as well. Take nostalgia for a pre-partition past, for instance – which is perfectly appropriately encountered in eyewitness memories and in much first-generation partition literature and testimony[7] – is also commonly encountered in popular memory and, sometimes, in disciplinary history.

I offer one example of the complicated function nostalgia has come to acquire today, even in academic discourse. In Neeti Nair's *Changing Homelands: Hindu Politics and the Partition of India* (2011), the summative comment of the last chapter reiterates what is by now a familiar theme of partition historiography: that drawing in the world of memory into the world of history poses problems even as it is crucial in its countering/mediating of history.

> The sheer diversity of narratives proffered by my interviewees suggests that memories, in some small measure, can afford the ground on which to combat the teleology of official nationalist

> histories. And a judicious equipoise between archival sources and memories can draw out the complexity of an event like Partition and its consequences for personal, ordinary lives. (ibid.: 254)

Having effectively reduced memory/testimony to a function, the chapter takes refuge (or so it appears to me) in the familiar partition tropes of first-generation lament and nostalgia for a pre-partition past. She cites lines from a poem by Agha Shahid Ali ('Farewell'): 'Your history gets in the way of my memory/I am everything you lost. You can't forgive me.../your memory gets in the way of my memory' (quoted in ibid.: 253). Framing the lines of poetry is the following statement:

> Memories are neither fragments unaffected by events at the centre, nor are they frozen in time; they are forged in the thick of everyday life, nurtured selectively, carefully, and often quite unimaginatively. This is expressed so hauntingly, by Agha Shahid Ali in *Farewell*, the poem with which I began the book. (ibid.)

As the first and final word on the subject, such an act of ventriloquism keeps attention focused on the generation that was directly impacted as the proper subject of partition historiography; and it normalises nostalgia and lament as the proper affective anchor of subsequent generations.

A similar problem attaches to the admittedly valuable (primarily scholarly) attempt to engage with eyewitness memory. The collecting and archiving of eyewitness accounts is an activity that is not exactly new (G.D. Khosla's *Stern Reckoning*, for instance, was published in 1989). However, Urvashi Butalia, and Ritu Menon and Kamla Bhasin's work in the field in the mid- to late-1990s – at the same time as Gyanendra Pandey was actively questioning the limits of partition historiography and Veena Das was conducting ethnographic work with Punjabi families dispossessed by partition – has had the very important effect of focusing attention on the gendered and classed victims of partition violence and displacement, on their shaping of the past in testimonies in ways that fit with cultural dictates and social injunctions, and so on. However, this 'turn' in Indian historiography, as we might call it, which finally broke the silence surrounding the victims of partition, has had the effect of allowing us to think and write the partition story as one about the making of victims. And, as Slavoj Zizek has repeatedly warned, identification of traumatic histories with their victims, while of unquestioned value and merit, comes with its own dangers. 'The overpowering horror of violent acts and empathy with the victims inexorably function as a lure which prevents us from thinking' (Zizek 2008: 4) and trap us in 'moral outrage' (ibid.: 6). Indeed, it is difficult to set aside what is probably the most devastating fact about violence – its turning of human beings into victims who, in addition to being victims in the classic sense of the term, are so for having being tainted by history, compromised by their own acts of subterfuge, evasion, violations, compromising of values as much as practices and, quite simply, for being part of a rupture in which the structures that frame the 'normal' are radically destroyed. I would like to suggest here that, possibly even more than moral outrage, we have let nostalgia and lament become end points of our engagement with the 1947 partition, allowing uncomfortable questions, including the important one about intergenerational trauma and memory, to recede from view.

How else can we think and relate the story of the 1947 partition? What are some other frames within which we can place partition, violence in particular, thus opening up to potentially different answers (other than communalism, for instance, which much partition scholarship continues to work to dislodge)? And how does the issue of intergenerational memory as well as the erasure of partition in general from decades of public culture inflect/mediate this story? Is it also a story of the postmemory generation, and what is the latter's story? It goes without saying that we have not exhausted all of the frames within which partition violence, in its many forms, can be unpacked, so to speak. It also goes without saying that we have yet to accept the frames that will make intergenerational memory a subject in its own right, frames that we encounter in Joginder Paul's phantasmagoric Karachi of *Sleepwalkers* and in the return of the traumatic past of the 1947 partition, with predictably catastrophic results, in *Khamosh Pani*. In the remainder of this essay, I will return to the issue of partition, and its most troubling feature – violence – which makes it such a stigmatic history, and conclude with a discussion of the interlinked issue of intergenerational memory. To discuss this last, I will turn to the work of Art Spiegelman for the simple reason that I find it to be an exceptionally powerful example of intergenerational memory at work.

Better described as a life-long project, Spiegelman's work is meticulously researched, is always sensitive to the contradictions of the personal (remembrance/memory) and the political (history/narrative), and traverses many boundaries – between history and biography, multiple pasts and presents, mass culture and literature, collective and individual memory, narration and reflection. The subject that is transformed by the specific choices of genre, vocabulary and forms of remembrance Spiegelman makes, all of which produce an incredibly dense engagement with the catastrophic past, is the Holocaust. The latter is the out-of-time and yet intensely historical moment in family history that defies domestication, remaining a profound alterity that taints them, and their family history, with alterity. In the concrete world of the graphic novels, *Maus I* (1986) and *Maus II* (1991), the coexistence of an invisible rupturing history, such as the Holocaust, and of the seemingly banal world of the everyday is the very backbone of the story it relates. Here, the Holocaust bleeds into the past and into the future, which is in itself a moment of multiple histories of three generations and is, thus, at once a discrete history and an everyday experience for an American Jewish family, removed in time and space from the original scene of trauma. Appearing first in 1972 as a short comic strip, called *Maus*, an initial idea that was subsequently brokered, you might say, by interviews he recorded with his father in the 1970s, in 1978 Spiegelman began work on the graphic novel that would put him on the Holocaust studies map.

REFRAMING PARTITION VIOLENCE

The implications of expanding the frames of reference by which to understand what happened in 1946–47 are critical: we might be well placed to undo some of the harmful myths of partition violence – a dominant one being that it remains the responsibility of the other/Punjab and is best described as other/madness – that effect a foreclosure on the possibility of a wider enquiry. In fact, arguably, the reluctance of many to speak of partition violence owes much to the fear of reinforcing such views, which speaks to the paucity that defines the field with which partition violence is circumscribed and within which it gains meaning. We could ask, for instance, how partition violence fits in with the long history of subcontinental philosophies that have wrestled with the subject of violence and with yet others that have produced mechanisms for containing violence within the Indian social order.[8] Or we could ask what partition violence would look like if we extended to (our understanding of) it the category of situational violence. It is the latter that I will explore at some length here. The category serves to draw attention to the behavioural response of normally peaceful citizens in times of civilisational breakdown, such as civil war, and encourages us to seek explanation for mass violence in conditions that obtain at such times – such as extreme fear and panic. As I see it, the category does not presume a causal link exists between fissures, conflicts and pressures that are part of everyday living on the one hand and civil war on the other – that the former produces the latter. Instead, it allows us to entertain the possibility that emphasis is better placed on conditions – that collapse the distinction between political and personal in particular – and produce fresh idioms of conflict.

There is more than enough evidence, even if the process of remembering in testimonials is by nature unstable, that unimaginable levels of anxiety, panic, shock and unprecedented fear were the experience of communities, especially those that found themselves in the vicinity of the rumoured borders. In the first half of 1947, the bewilderment and desperation of individuals, caught between rumour and press reports, is best recorded by Butalia in *The Other Side of Silence* (1998). She writes:

> In the months leading up to Partition, and indeed, after the announcement of the Plan in June 1947, the offices of the All India Congress Committee (AICC) received large numbers of letters from people wanting to know what was happening. What will become of us, they asked. We believe India is to be partitioned: where will we go? *How* will we go? What will happen to our jobs? If we have to move, will we get our old jobs back in the new homeland? What will happen to our homes, our lands, if we have to move? (ibid.: 53, emphasis?)

This on-the-ground reality, of impending loss of livelihood at one end and loss of embedded histories at the other, and the bewilderment at its happening at all, was complicated by other deeply threatening circumstances with which individuals and communities were faced. These circumstances are ones we have come to associate with civil wars: the sense of a terrifying exposure to circumstances beyond one's control and the rupturing of state as well as community, and the shock of living with danger as the new reality. Danger was that much more devastating because of its location within communities as much as outside them. Clearly, even in 1947, at some level, there was a kind of confidence that neighbourliness, which had withstood centuries of daily low-level conflict and periodically intense intercommunity conflict, could be counted on even if the political process could not as the countdown to partition began. If time-honoured, deeply-embedded definitions failed, so too did the startlingly new, as Manto so memorably captures in *Siyah Hashiye* (1948). Refugee camps were not the safe havens they were intended to be, nor were the mass migrations organised by the two governments. Indeed, incertitude, indeterminacy and ambivalence attached to markers of identity, including name, physiognomy, clothing and speech habits. At any moment, each and all could betray one to violence and death. Equally, each and all were turned in to weapons of brutality in the hands of individuals, many of whom no doubt found themselves at once victim and perpetrator.

The fact that situational violence has some explanatory force is, I think, supported by survivor testimony, which seeks to articulate just how out of place, out of time and out of language partition was for those caught in the sudden onslaught of violence. Phrases that are commonly encountered in testimonies identify the time itself as both cause and effect – 'the times were such' (*Seminar* 1994: 19), 'it was that kind of time' (ibid.), 'at that time, the time was like that' (ibid.), and 'that was a strange kind of time' (ibid.: 21). While it is always possible that such speech masks complicity, it is also possible that it is an attempt to articulate that which defies comprehension – the irruption of the uncanny in the everyday. The idiom of the uncanny, which best describes the affective state of discovering the strange in the familiar, the outsider within, is I think developed in phrases such as these; and what they aim to describe even as they admit failure to do so is the quality of the uncanny itself. To extend the notion of the uncanny to the experience of survivors of catastrophic histories is not without precedent. In an attempt to understand the distortion of subjectivity that marks holocaust survivors, van Alphen (1999:30) writes:

> They had difficulty in experiencing the events they were part of, because the language at their disposal offered them only two possibilities. As speaking subjects they must ascribe to themselves the role of either subject or object in relation to the events. But the situation of the Holocaust was such that this kind of distancing from the action was not possible. One took part in a history that did not provide unambiguous roles of subject or object.

Instead, what Nazi death camp inmates found themselves confronted with was an 'ambiguous actantial position' (ibid.: 28). They were 'neither subject nor object of the events' or 'both at the same time' (ibid.). Closer to home, Ashis Nandy and Veena Das have explored the existential dilemma that was the condition of those who were within the field of violence in 1947 and arrived at a similar conclusion. In 'Violence, Victimhood, and the Language of Silence', they conclude their discussion of partition violence with the comment that Manto has 'created the form through which the deafening silence accompanying the trauma of being simultaneously the subject, object, and instrument of violence could be represented' (Das and Nandy 1986: 194). This, it seems to me, is the quality of the uncanny, which survivors 'own' when they confess to their inability to articulate what precisely was and is the partition experience. It might also inform testimonies in which perpetrators admit to participation in violence. Here are a couple of other examples: 'I still cannot understand what happened to me and other youngsters of my age at the time… we were swept away by this wild wave of hatred' (Butalia 1998: 56); and 'I cannot explain it, but one day our entire village took off to a nearby Muslim village on a killing spree. We simply went mad' (ibid.). It seems to me that, taken at face value, such claims to the truth of partition violence on the part of perpetrators can be read as a confession of a profound experience that can only be spoken of as a contradiction, and, as such, outside the boundaries of comprehension. Their response to the judgement of future generations, which they clearly expect, can be only this – that the condition that is theirs is simultaneously one of seeking comprehension of the past and confronting the limits of the past's availability.

To apply the category of situational violence, then, has some merit. It has the advantage of explaining why so many participated, were compromised; and it draws attention to the multiple contexts of violence, participation and victimisation. The most difficult knowledge has to be the fact that the term 'perpetrator' acquired an expansive, ambivalent and indeterminate terrain of meaning. At one end it meant turning informant – reporting neighbours, refusing shelter (possibly in the name of survival) – and at the other end, participating in gang-rapes of women, ritual mutilation and dismemberment, and genocidal rage and murder. Bringing such an approach to bear on partition might also shed light on our discomfort with such stories and their tellers. Because of their occupation of the breakdown of the given system of signification, their being subject, object and instrument of violence at the same time, survivors are an embodiment and disturbing reminder of the tenuousness of identity that depends entirely on the naturalised distinction of the categories of subject and object.[9] They are tainted by history, compromised in a way that 'the rest' were not, in itself a distinction that was in large part enabled by powerful technologies of reading that were pressed into service by the leadership in 1947.[10]

Since we have not explored the potential offered by situational violence to confront the partition, partition-as-subject remains essentialised and othered. If the narrative of colonisation depended much on stereotypes of the uncivilised native, narrative of nationhood similarly depends on the successful, daily performance of a rational body politic unpolluted by the irrationality and inexplicability of partition violence. Its binary other is, of course, the irrational Punjabi (this takes in Muslim, Hindu and Sikh) and, to a lesser extent, the Bengali of partition, shrouded in tropes of irrationality.[11] And yet the fact that many claim that the 'times were such' should give us pause. In such phrases there is an acknowledgement of the inability, or refusal, of those who have been made to bear the burden of responsibility of partition violence to map the nation fully on to the human.

PARTITION AND POSTMEMORY

The questions about the postmemory generation's relationship with partition, which appear to me, have required asking, are clearly also those that have occurred to others. In 2013, an experiment in cross-border, collaborative, multi-genre, graphic storytelling that announces its aim is to 'restory' partition was published by Yoda Press with the support of the Goethe Institut.[12] Entitled *This Side That Side*, its interventionist aim and intent is announced in a prefatory essay by Vishwajyoti Ghosh, who describes himself as the 'curator' of the collection. He cautions:

> Restorying Partition can never be easy. If one wants to avoid the usual revival of Mass Memory, one has to look beyond those maps lodged in our nervous systems that make nervous headlines on our televisions. To listen to the subsequent generations and the grandchildren and how they have negotiated maps that never got drawn. (Ghosh 2013: 12)

The last sentence draws attention to the aporia where a populated postmemory should be. A collection such as this draws attention to the need to be mindful of the gap between traumatic histories and their representation ('Restorying Partition can never be easy'), of the intergenerational shadow of partition ('how they have negotiated maps that never got drawn') and proves invaluable for its offsetting of the various narratives that appear to close the gap, offering the kind of security (to readers) that the kinds of narrations included in *This Side That Side* do not, and rightly so. The problem posed by literature that appears to close the gap between trauma and its representation is well summed up by Neeti Nair (2011: 218) when she complains that contemporary literature that does engage with partition tends to include it in a 'laundry list of genocidal conflict'. I am not sure whether she has Kamila Shamsie's *Burnt Shadows* (2010) in mind, but it certainly comes to mind. And while Nair may be overstating the case, I think it is true to say that the current interest in global catastrophic histories, some past, some abiding and some that are in the making, presents us with another kind of lure: the temptation to find continuities between (usually underrepresented) histories of barbarism. In Shamsie's novel, the atomic bombing of

Nagasaki and the 1947 partition of India are front and centre of a story that traces a continuity between these catastrophic histories of the 1940s and the more contemporary one of terrorist camps in Afganistan and 9/11. So I would like to raise the issue of intergenerational memory if not intergenerational trauma – both of which we encounter in the case of black slavery, for instance, in addition to the Holocaust, most memorably in literature such as Toni Morrison's *Beloved* (1987).

I would like to take the liberty of speaking about a story that I think is a masterful exploration of all of the questions that societies faced with traumatic pasts ask: Whose past is it? Why not forget? Why make a virtue out of remembrance? How should one remember? How should one represent? Who should speak? And so on. The story is told in two volumes, *Maus I* (1986) and *Maus II* (1991), and it is the multi-generational story of a family whose living and dying takes place within the long shadow cast by Auschwitz. For the writer, Art Spiegelman, it appears to be a lifetime's project, always unfinished. Based on a series of conversations that Spiegelman had with his father in the 1970s in Rego Park in New York, *Maus I* and *Maus II* attempt to reconstruct the pre-Nazi past of his Polish parents and the Holocaust experience. In the comics, only his father, Vladek, is featured, since his mother, Anja, committed suicide in 1958 and his father burned her wartime dairies, both of which haunt the text, not the Holocaust, which is fully a subject of the narrative of the comics. The story first appeared as fragmented comic strips of frenzied pencil drawings in his 1977 work, *Breakdowns.* Entitled 'Maushaus', the graphic fragment drew its central narrative mechanism from the Nazi past and featured a fictional Spiegelman who considers how to model himself as the artist-as-a-young-man (the nod to James Joyce is wrought with significance). As one might imagine, the central questions he feels compelled to ask are of the story that is his to tell (he wonders about the possibility of writing the story of black America, for instance), how to render catastrophic history into art, that too popular art, and of the claims of the past on the present and vice versa. To both show and understand the relationship of catastrophic history to the artist, discover art as therapy, to refuse to be any longer a fugitive from this history, to imagine a mode of telling that would be commensurate with it are collectively the contours and theme of the project. History, with a capital H, is intertext and archive from this earliest sketch, and it informs the very powerful visual allegory in which the graphic novels are embedded – of Jews as mice. In *Breakdowns*, Spiegelman explains his choice of allegory: 'Then Hitler's notion of the Jews as vermin offered a metaphor closer to home' ('Rego Park, nyc 1971', np), and the Holocaust, he accepts, is the story that is his to tell. The image that accompanies this early text acts contrapuntally to the high seriousness, and sombreness, which Spiegelman introduces here, and is as devastating precisely for its jarring reminder of the deeply dehumanising vocabulary of Nazism. The fictional Spiegelman walks nonchalantly, a modern day Pied Piper, smoking, while a retinue of mice follows him. As much as the graphic draws from the narratives of both Nazism and the Pied Piper to simultaneously project the allegorised Jewish people as the despised subhuman of Hitler's remark and the terrifying rodent of the Pied Piper folktale, it invisibly invokes a third and as yet unwritten story – in which the artist-as-a-young-man pays the debt that is owed to history, which nips at his heels. The story appears again in a much more jagged, archival form in *Metamaus* (2011), a collage of graphics drawn from earlier works, transcripts of the taped interviews with Vladek, and transcripts of interviews in which Spiegelman reflects on the choice of subject ('Why the Holocaust' is the title of this section), choice of genre ('Why Comic') and choice of Maus ('Why Mice'). These are questions with which he was bombarded once *Maus I* and *Maus II* were published, and choices for which he was severely critiqued.

Embedded in *Maus I* and *Maus II* is the story of the artist-as-a-young-(Jewish-)man. It informs the world, of the family and its multiple pasts, that Spiegelman recreates. We are never allowed, even for a moment, to disappear into the story of the Holocaust, which Vladek reveals in bits and pieces. The context – a series of difficult interviews – is always hovering in the background, when it is not in the foreground, as is the personal and domestic life of vexed relations, ill health and dysfunctional relationships. Vladek's second marriage is in tatters, he himself is suffering from heart problems, is informed by behaviours that identify him as the traumatised victim of the Holocaust at odds with the 'normal' of American life; it is also a present in which the fictional Spiegelman records the work of engaging with his father and with his father's past, the frequent breakdown in (his) resolve to persist in 'storying' the past, navigating between his judgement of his father (for his own participation in violence, for instance, for being victim and perpetrator at the same time) and the sense that the past is an alterity he, Spiegelman, cannot begin to understand. And the story does not end there. It spins out into the post-publication life of *Maus I*, which was clearly a traumatising experience for Spiegelman. This too becomes part of a narrative in which traumas of different intensities and meanings (mother's suicide, the father's destruction of her wartime diary, Spigelman's rage against the past and his father, the Holocaust) swirl and interweave. In *Maus II*, we see the fictional Spiegelman standing at a lectern surrounded by a mass of dead, emaciated, bodies on the floor. The scene is recognisably that which the first photographs taken by journalists such as D.F. Karaka of Nazi extermination camps, marked indelibly in global memory.

If there is one thing that Spiegelman's project teaches us, it is of the work involved in handling a past that opens up a gap between the eyewitness generation and the postmemory one. I am struck by the cognisance the text, in *Maus I* and *Maus II*, displays of this fact. Much of it, after all, is a conversation which the fictional Spiegelman dreads, while treating it as necessary 'work' if he is to be the (Jewish) artist-as-a-young-man. In his visual narrative, the reworked past, interviews and the figure of the father (Vladek) retain the feel of testimony, which accords Vladek's Holocaust years their unquestioned claim on Holocaust historiography. At the same time, the fact that the text makes interviews part of the story told positions the fictional Spiegelman as the interlocutor – the postmemory generation querying and retaining independence from the story of the father. This disjuncture informs the very structure of the narrative. Its effect is to layer subjective (Vladek's account) over nominally objective (Spiegelman consistently questions his father's remembrance based on his own research into this history), to leave the Holocaust past somewhat opaque to the present, and to leave open-ended both the story of the father and the story of the son (which is sometimes in the foreground and sometimes in the background).

I offer Spiegelman's work not because I think we should treat it as paradigmatic, but because I think it is a brilliant example of a text that refuses a shallow or careless, or moralising, sentimental use of the past. At the same time, it refuses to aestheticise the past. In *Metamaus*, Spiegelman describes his relationship with absolute clarity and certain knowledge of what the project, so long in the making, meant to him. It was a working through the 'obligation to the dead' – 'I'd incurred an obligation to the dead' (Spiegelman 2011: 80) – and the debt was paid and determinedly non-oracular: 'All I know in the post-*Maus* moment was that there could be no *Maus III*. The war ended, the story was over, my father died.... I didn't want to become the Elie Wiesel of comic books and become the conscience and voice of a second generation' (ibid.). The last word, though, should go to his daughter, Nadja, the third generation to bear witness to this story. In response to a question about why *Maus* was so 'hard' for her (she had just said that Maus was 'hard' for her to read, not 'difficult') she had this to say:

> My grandparents were this secret that I didn't know anything about. My dad never talked about his parents, and I knew that it was for a reason. I sensed that he had shut the difficult things into this book, and that it was all in there waiting for me whenever I was ready. (ibid.: 84)

The distinction to which she draws our attention is one that we would do well to keep in mind when thinking of partition's post-history—partition is not so much difficult as it is hard to face.

NOTES

1. In her words, cultural recall is 'not merely something of which you happen to be a bearer but something you actually perform, even if, in many instances, such acts are not consciously or willfully contrived' (Bal 1999: vii). The definition serves to remind us of the fact that collective remembrance is subject to the same forces as material culture: it is produced, reproduced and performed in everyday public culture (as is nationalism, of course).

2. The definition of collective memory that Geoffrey Hartman provides in *The Longest Shadow* (1996), in contradistinction to 'public memory', is the one I am drawing on in this essay. This latter is dominated by the media whereas the former is, in Bal's summary of Hartman, 'bound up with community' (Bal, xvii, note 1).
3. In a chapter on the Indian press in 1947, in *Bearing Witness*, I had written of D.F. Karaka's critique in his 1950 autobiography of state censorship and control of vocabulary, which effectively turned civil war in Punjab into 'disturbances'. It is pertinent to the point being made here and I will restate:

> Writing in 1950, Dosoo Farmjee Karaka, notes: 'what was virtually a war of extermination between the Hindus and the Sikhs on one side and the Moslems on the other – an undeclared civil war, as the Captain had called it – our editors called 'disturbances' (*Betrayal in India* 46). The policy of leaving out the names of warring communities in reports of such 'disturbances' led to reports that were 'as unintelligible as possible' (*Betrayal in India* 51) and enabled a claim of ignorance of the horrifying history unfolding in the Punjab on the part of the Indian public. (Kamra 2002: 10)

4. I would like to acknowledge that generalisations such as these automatically fall into the error of overstating the case. They do, however, serve the useful function of focusing attention on the dominant features of the social and cultural narratives that built up around the 1947 partition starting in the 1950s.
5. I am thinking of D.F. Karaka for instance, who remembers in his autobiographical *Betrayal in India* (1950: 46):

> I knew this stench. I had smelt it first at Belsen when the Allied forces liberated that Nazi concentration camp. We said then that all Germans were guilty of that crime. The Germans wept and said they did not know. We said that ignorance of those horrors was no excuse. We called the Germans swine. [np] much the same charge would be levelled against our own people, I thought, if the curtain was not lifted on the happenings in the two Punjabs.

6. This, in India, is the narrative by which intercommunity savagery is digested as communal outbreaks in popular political memory, which, in turn, we are encouraged to regard as a primarily political and law enforcement problem.
7. See Kamra (2002: chapters 2 and 3) for a discussion of nostalgia in the works and testimony of the eyewitness generation.

8. In 'Violence, Victimhood, and the Language of Silence', Das and Nandy (1986) remark that *ahimsa* (non-violence) is a concept that is quite literally handcuffed to *himsa* (violence), even in terminological terms. They suggest that specific languages of violence – 'sacrifice, feud, and vivisection' (ibid.: 181) – provide 'legitimation to many kinds of violence in Indian society today' (ibid.).
9. It is interesting to note that in India there is little attempt to pursue forms of official state memory when it comes to the 1947 partition – there are no archives, museums and commemoration/remembrance day when it comes to partition. Gyan Pandey with (in Miller 1996) pointed this out in his earliest work on the subject. In one work, comparing national attitudes toward colossal loss, such as the losses of the world wars and, in the case of India, partition, he writes: 'The experience... is commemorated... through the erection of major national monuments; there is, not unsurprisingly, no equivalent for Partition in India' (quoted in Miller 1996: 197).
10. Zizek, in *Welcome to the Desert of the Real* (2002) mentions Agamben's countering of the view that the Nazi project banked on the fact that the final solution would be considered so unbelievable as to discredit survivors and their testimonies: 'Agamben's counterargument is: true, it is not possible to bear witness to the ultimate horror of Auschwitz – but what if *this impossibility itself is embodied in a survivor*?' (ibid.: 140, emphasis in original). It is in this sense that our desire to forget the partition, for its violence in particular, is impossible. For, partition violence is embodied in the survivors, their uneasiness about their past, which one senses in many of the testimonials collected by Butalia (1998).
11. Once again, this is not to say that such tropes are not applicable. But it is to be mindful of the use made of them to, for instance, delegitimise or make irrelevant the desire to find explanations. This, Huyssen (2000) has warned, is the unfortunate result of Adorno's famous pronouncement on art after Auschwitz, which has been absorbed into larger debates about representability itself. He writes, in a footnote, 'Much of the recent poststructuralist discourse of the sublime in relation to Holocaust representations does exactly what Adorno feared: it pulls the genocide into the realm of epistemology and aesthetics, instrumentalizing it for a late modernist aesthetic of non-representability' (ibid.: 69, note 12).
12. I am indebted to Urvashi Butalia for directing me towards this collection.

REFERENCES

Bal, Mieke. 1999. 'Introduction', in Mieke Bal, Jonathan Crewe and Leo Spitzer (eds), *Acts of Memory: Cultural Recall in the Present*, pp. vii–xvii. Hanover, NH: University of New England Press.

Bangash, Yaquub Khan. 2012. 'The Ghosts of Partition', *Express Tribune*, 14 August.

Butalia, Urvashi. 1998. *The Other Side of Silence: Voices from the Partition of India*. New Delhi: Viking.

Das, Veena and Ashis Nandy. 1986. 'Violence, Victimhood, and the Language of Silence', in Veena Das (ed.), *The Word and the World: Fantasy, Symbol and Record*, pp. 177–98. New Delhi: Sage Publications.

Ghosh, Vishwajyoti. 2013. 'Curator's Note' in Vishwajyoti Ghosh (curator), *This Side That Side. Restorying Partition*, pp. 11–12. New Delhi: Yoda Press.

Greenberg, Jonathan D. 2008. 'Against Silence and Forgetting', in Anjali Gera Roy and Nandi Bhatia (eds), *Partitioned Lives: Narratives of Home, Displacement, and Resettlement*, pp. 255–73. New Delhi: Dorling Kindersley.

Gulzar. 2001. 'Toba Tek Singh', in Ravikant and Tarun K. Saint (eds), *Translating Partition*, p. vii, New Delhi: Katha.

Hartman, Geoffrey. 1996. *The Longest Shadow: In the Aftermath of the Holocaust*. Bloomington and Indianapolis, IN: Indiana University Press.

Hirsch, Marianne. 2012. 'Postmemory.net'. http://www.postmemory.net (accessed on 13 December 2013).

Huyssen, Andreas. 2000. 'Of Mice and Mimesis: Reading Spiegelman with Adorno'. *New German Critique,* 81(Autumn): 65–82.

Kamra, Sukeshi. 2002. *Bearing Witness: Partition, Independence, End of the Raj*. Calgary: University of Calgary Press.

Kansteiner, Wulf. 2002. 'Finding Meaning in Memory: A Methodological Critique of Collective Memory Studies', *History and Theory*, 41(2): 179–97.

Karaka, Dosoo Farmjee. 1950. *Betrayal in India*. London: Victor Gollancz.

Khamosh Pani. 2003. Directed by Sabiha Sumar.

Khosla, Gopal Das. 1989. *Stern Reckoning: A Survey of the Events Leading up to and Following the Partition of India*. New Delhi: Oxford University Press.

Legend of Bhagat Singh. 2002. Directed by Rajkumar Santoshi.

Mangal Pandey: The Rising. 2005. Directed by Ketan Mehta.

Manto, Saadat Hasan. 1948. *Siyah Hashiye*. Black Margins: Sa'adat Hasan Manto Stories, Delhi: Katha, 2000.

Earth. 1998. Directed by Deepa Mehta.

Miller, Don. 1996. 'Mosque, Temple and Crypt', in John McGuire, Peter Reeves and Howard Brasted (eds), *Politics of Violence: From Ayodhya to Behrampada*, pp.193–206. New Delhi: Sage Publications.

Misra, Salil. 2012. 'The Tragedy of Partition', *Deccan Herald*, 12 August.

Morrison, Toni. 1987. *Beloved*. New York: Alfred Knopf.

Nair, Neeti. 2011. *Changing Homelands: Hindu Politics and the Partition of India*. Cambridge, MA: Harvard University Press.

Paul, Joginder. 1998. *The Sleepwalkers* (translated by Sunil Trivedi and Sukrita Paul Kumar; edited by Keerti Ramachandra), pp.11–110. New Delhi: Katha.

Rang De Basanti. 2006. Directed by Rakeysh Omprakash Mehra.

Seminar.1994. Number 420.

Shamsie, Kamila. 2010. *Burnt Shadows*. London: Bloomsbury.

Sidhwa, Bapsi. 1991. *Cracking India*. Minneapolis, MN: Milkweed Editions.

Spiegelman, Art. 1986. *Maus I: A Survivor's Tale; My Father Bleeds History*. New York: Pantheon Books.

———. 1991. *Maus II: My Parents Survived Hell and Moved to the Suburbs*. New York: Pantheon.

———. 2008. *Breakdowns: A Portrait of the Artist as a Young %@&*!*. New York: Pantheon Books (first published in 1977).

———. 2011. *Metamaus: A Look Inside a Modern Classic, Maus*. New York and Toronto: Pantheon.

van Alphen, Ernst. 1999. 'Symptoms of Discursivity: Experience, Memory, and Trauma', in Mieke Bal, Jonathan Crewe, and Leo Spitzer (eds.), *Acts of Memory: Cultural Recall in the Present*, pp.24–38. Hanover, NH: University Press of New England.

Zizek, Slavoz. 2002. *Welcome to the Desert of the Real*. London and New York: Verso.

———. 2008. *Violence: Six Sideways Reflections*. New York: Picador.

CHAPTER 9

Revisioning and 'Restorying' Partition

Modes of Testimony

TARUN K. SAINT

The problem of finding a mode of representation to adequately bear witness to the event of the 1947 partition and its traumatic after-effects has been addressed in different ways by visual artists and writers across three generations. Whether one thinks of responses to partition-era violence and migration by artists like Satish Gujral and S.L. Parashar (amongst admittedly few others), or literary representations by writers of fiction on both sides of the border, especially since the appearance of Sa'adat Hasan Manto's remarkable work, the ethical imperative to responsibly engage with a cataclysmic event of unprecedented scale and magnitude has been in evidence. The difficulty of breaking the silence surrounding the excesses of 1947 has been reflected on since then by literary critics, social scientists and feminist historians. I have examined the critical debates pertaining to trauma, memory and representation with reference to partition literature in greater detail elsewhere (Saint 2010: esp. 1–60).

The publication of *This Side, That Side: Restorying Partition* in 2013, an anthology of graphic narratives curated by Vishwajyoti Ghosh, was especially welcome as a creative initiative that included a new and perhaps unique collaborative dimension. For the graphic novel, with its interplay between the visual and the textual, has repeatedly broken new ground in South Asia, especially since the publication of

Ghosh's own *Delhi Calm* (2010), a novel in graphic form set at the time of the Emergency, and Vyam et al.'s *Bhimayana* (2011), a retelling of Ambedkar's life story in graphic form. The following observations stem from an exchange of ideas at the book launch, as well as a later, more careful reading of the volume as a significant contribution to partition discourse.[1] In this essay, I seek to contextualise this volume with reference to earlier responses by writers, who were in many cases primary witnesses to the event. Furthermore, I hope to elucidate both parallels and contrasts between modes of testimony devised by contributors to this anthology and in previous writings with select examples from a range of responses, varying from the perceptive and empathetic to the sensational and banal.

The rupture of partition, which took the form of a limit event that in many respects boggled the imagination, posed serious difficulties with respect to the question of witnessing (Saint 2010: esp. 38–56.). Near-genocidal violence, ethnic cleansing (especially in Punjab), and the unprecedented targeting of women and children took place on a scale never seen in the subcontinent before. The ferocity and ruthlessness of reprisal killings, followed by extensive interruption of mourning rituals and a curious absence of remorse in the public domain (with some exceptions in the Gandhian or socialist vein, which in several instances took on a ritualised and predictable form with the passage of time), entailed a curtailment of the space for witnessing. The widespread numbing and silence that ensued was, ironically enough, only one side of the picture. For the circulation of irresponsible and communally charged narratives about violence, especially sexual violence, constituted the dark discursive underbelly that marred the prospect of ethical engagement with memories of pain and suffering.[2]

The generation of writers who survived the ghastly mutual attrition of 1947–48 also underwent psychological shock and attendant trauma in varying degrees, whether as refugees or migrants themselves (Sa'adat Hasan Manto, Khadija Mastur, Intizar Husain, Bhisham Sahni, Krishna Baldev Vaid and Khushwant Singh), for instance, or as witnesses (Abdullah Hussein and Rahi Masoom Raza). Many of these writers consciously came to terms with 'popular' memories encrusted with frozen affects such as narcissistic rage and self-loathing in their work. Manto's early testimonial narratives, especially *Siyah Hashye* (translated as *Black Margins*) constituted a breakthrough, as often atypical instances of literary witnessing in abbreviated form. For example, in 'Jelly' (Manto 2003a), the situation in an unnamed city, where an ice vendor has been stabbed to death, is represented from the vantage point of a child. The child notices congealed blood on the road, and exclaims, 'Look, Mummy, jelly!' (ibid.: 187). The horror of organised attacks on the street is captured in this vignette through the emphasis on the discrepancy between the child's innocent perception and the gross reality of violent death. Indeed, the further irony is that such murders were becoming routine at the time in everyday life in cities across north India. The grotesque image of blood as jelly conveys to the reader not only the shock of viewing such a spectacle, but also the ominous likelihood of the pervasive deadening of sensitivity and misrecognition of the after effects of violence.

Manto's major short stories, as well as important stories by Amrita Pritam, Ashfaq Ahmad, Mohan Rakesh, Ismat Chughtai, Intizar Husain, Attia Hosain and others, were responsive in nuanced ways to the immediate aftermath of collective violence and displacement. These narratives on the whole abjured the tendency to dwell on the wounds of one's community and the losses of a particular family or group. In effect, as fictive testimony, these works underlined the need for both truth telling as well as empathy for the suffering of victims from the 'other' community. A language of resistance to the dominant tendencies towards either erasing the history of pain and loss or, on the other hand, appropriation of such experiences (while recasting their significance in the idiom of martyrdom and sacrifice) comes to the fore in these narratives. The identitarian thrust in nationalist and communitarian myth making is undercut in the important stories through the deployment of devices such as irony and satire, as well as modes of empathic unsettlement (LaCapra 2001: 78–79). Perhaps the most significant of the short stories written after the event are Manto's 'Toba Tek Singh' (2003c) and 'Khol Do' ('Open It!' [2003b]), Ashfaq Ahmad's 'Gadariya' ('The Shepherd' [1998]), Intizar Husain's 'Bin Likhi Razmiya' ('An Unwritten Epic' [1998]), Mohan Rakesh's 'Malbe ka Malik' ('His Heap of Rubble'

[1995]), Bhisham Sahni's 'Amritsar Aa Gaya Hai' ('We Have Arrived in Amritsar' [1995]), Rajinder Singh Bedi's 'Lajwanti' (1995), and Ismat Chughtai's 'Jadein' ('Roots' [1995]), besides Amrita Pritam's novella *Pinjar* (*The Skeleton* [1987]).[3] These narratives achieve an intensity of focus in their pared-down retellings, steering clear of the pitfalls of long-windedness and prolixity that at times afflicted early novelistic renditions of the event, which often slipped into a banal mode of historical narration or an overemphasis on redemption and transcendence.

Perhaps of equal importance with respect to the effort to responsibly come to terms with the partition catastrophe are some of the memoirs that appeared in its wake. Anis Kidwai's *In Freedom's Shade* (2011) and Kamlaben Patel's *Torn from the Roots* (2006) are testimonial narratives of a different kind, drawn from personal experience, yet taking on a greater significance due to references to very public involvements in the aftermath of widespread abductions of women on both sides of the border. The recovery and rehabilitation of these women was a messy and difficult exercise, tangled in processes of state formation and re-establishment of 'national' honour. Both Kidwai (her hard-hitting literary memoir appeared in print long after being composed) and Patel played a critical role in the effort to provide humanitarian assistance to such women after the signing of the treaty between the two nations to ensure the return of abducted women to their families. In both narratives (perhaps to a greater extent in Kidwai's account), some of the ambiguities and ambivalences pertaining to the exercise of rehabilitation came to the fore. Political memoirs such as Maulana Azad's *India Wins Freedom* (2003), Ram Manohar Lohia's *Guilty Men of India's Partition* (2009), as well as reminiscences such as Shaista Suhrawardy Ikramullah's *From Purdah to Parliament* (1998) and Jahan Ara Shahnawaz's *Father and Daughter: A Political Autobiography* (2002) illuminated the personality conflicts and ideological differences in the realm of high politics that contributed to the widening of the rift between communities. However, the unsparing revelations about sexual violence and its social and psychological effects (as witnessed by Kidwai and Patel), and the sensitivity with which these are discussed, cause these two major testimonial narratives to stand out.

Later, in fictional representations of the event in the 1960s, 1970s and 1980s, we find a renewed focus on the long-term damage wrought by partition on forms of syncretism and the pluralistic sensibility of yore. The recrudescence of identity politics and the renewed demand to prove unquestioned loyalty to the nation and community indicated the persistence of earlier conflicts that partition was supposed to resolve. Micro-narratives about local communities and the situation of minority groups came to the fore as writers sought to work through the traumatic memories of 1947. In the process, they delved deeper, dredging out cultural memories of syncretic ideals and idioms of resistance to narratives advocating exclusivism and hatred. These retellings were not always cast in a romanticised mould, though an elegiac tone can be discerned in many. As retrospective narratives, there is more of reflection here, an attempt at grounding the retrieval of memory in the context of the present. Important novels such as Qurrutulain Hyder's *Ag ka Darya* (*River of Fire* [1998]), Attia Hosain's *Sunlight on a Broken Column* (1994), Rahi Masoom Raza's *Adha Gaon* (*The Feuding Families of Village Gangauli/Half a Village* [1994]), Abdullah Hussein's *Udas Naslein* (*The Weary Generations* [1999]), Intizar Husain's *Basti* (1999) and Bhisham Sahni's *Tamas* (2001) are marked by a strong sense of historical consciousness and self-awareness about the tricks subjective memory can play. Such emphasis on the complexity of temporal flows and the workings of the mirror box of memory is certainly accentuated further in novels as Anita Desai's *Clear Light of Day* (2001) and Krishna Baldev Vaid's *Guzara Hua Zamana* (*The Broken Mirror* [1994]).[4]

To illustrate the kind of creative openings into the abyss of the past afforded by second-generation writing, let us turn to Gurdev Singh Ropana's Punjabi short story 'Sheesha' ('The Mirror' [2012]). This story represents the destabilisation of a sense of an ethical baseline during the near-genocidal violence that took place in 1947–48 from a vantage point three and a half decades after the event. To begin with, the narrator, a prominent Punjabi writer, invites Dennis, a French scholar of 20th-century Punjabi literature, to accompany him on a visit to his native village, Ropana. When they arrive, the cremation rites of a well-known scoundrel named Boorha are being performed. It seems that Boorha had died a painless death, more befitting someone who lived a life of *punn* (good deeds), in contrast to another man named Dharam Singh, a pious individual who had nonetheless died in pain. Boorha's son Keharu attributes his father's painless demise to a single act of *punn* he had performed in his lifetime.

During the years of partition, said Keharu, a large caravan of Muslim refugees was passing through the area, when they were ambushed. The men were butchered, the women kidnapped. After the massacre, fearing an epidemic, the locals began clearing the corpses, upon which they found several infants amongst the bodies. Some were adopted, but at least 30 remained whom no one wished to take to an orphanage. It was then that Boorha volunteered to send them to salvation, since, according to him, nobody was waiting to greet them with sweets in Pakistan. Keharu, himself a child at the time, describes how they were taken to a canal and decapitated by Boorha. The French scholar asks if this was done with a sword and when Keharu confirms that each child was killed with a single stroke, Dennis's face turns white and he throws up shortly afterwards.

As they walk home, the narrator notices Dennis' reserve and the disappearance of his sense of curiosity. The traumatic effect of summoning this memory manifests itself that night when the visiting scholar is overheard by the narrator talking to himself in French, wondering how after 35 years this could still be regarded as a good deed. Dennis himself has a three-month old daughter, perhaps the reason for his intense disquiet. He repeatedly looks at his face in the mirror, seeking to reaffirm his sense of being human. When the narrator asks if he is all right, Dennis replies that this compulsion to keep looking at his reflection is something he cannot understand, and that he is unwell. He poses a query to the narrator with respect to an earlier story written by him about the episode of the caravans, titled 'Hawa'. He asks why his host had not mentioned the incident of the babies being killed in that story. The narrator can only reply that he must have forgotten about it. 'The Mirror' ends with Dennis leaving the next morning, despite the narrator's attempts to persuade him to stay on.

As a second-generation instance of fictive testimony, 'The

Mirror' effectively captures such inversion of ethical norms in areas of the Punjab in the wake of 1947, where even the merciless slaughter of innocents could be described as *punn* (a good deed). Ishtiaq Ahmed's (2011) exhaustive study of ethnic cleansing in the Punjab region on both sides of the border confirms the extent and intensity of reciprocal forms of violence. However, here the grotesque perversion of religious ideas like *punn* in localities where the enemy community was wiped out is depicted with a searching sense of self-irony, as the narrator (modelled on the author himself) is subjected to questioning his own failure to record such instances of inhumanity in his own work. It is through the figure of the visiting scholar as secondary witness and his troubled attempt to come to terms with societal indifference to moral and ethical debasement in latter-day Punjab that the true horror of what happened in 1947 becomes evident. It is the outsider who has greater empathy for these children; Dennis perceives the grievous breach in ethical coordinates that must underpin a humane society.

The memory of the macabre killing of infants is summoned up at the death of the perpetrator, who, ironically enough, dies without any pain and is regarded as someone who performed a necessary good deed at a critical moment, an instance of the lasting impact of ethical dysfunctionality and the culture of impunity that came into being during partition. The absence of affects such as contrition, remorse or self-disgust amongst community members becomes clear, in contrast to the secondary trauma experienced by Dennis. His quest for self-recognition in the mirror is perhaps indicative of his apprehension as regards being sucked into the cauldron of cynicism and indifference in the village, still marked by the imprint of dehumanisation.[5] Gurdev Singh Ropana's short story is one of the few to address the 'normalisation' of pathological forms of violent behaviour and the bizarre elevation of perpetrators in some contexts to the stature of doers of good deeds, even as nihilistic justifications of collective violence gained credence.

Since 1984, a host of significant publications on partition began to appear, partly as a result of the sense that the subcontinent was still haunted by ghosts of the partition era.[6] This spectral persistence of memories of extreme violence was apparent as partition was invoked or echoed during later episodes of collective violence such as 1984, 1992–93 and 2002. During this period, and after, important anthologies of short stories in translation and in English by Alok Bhalla (1994), Cowasjee and Duggal (1995), Mushirul Hasan (1995), M.U. Memon (1998), Debjani Sengupta (2003) and Rita Kothari (2009) amplified our understanding of the varied themes and problems negotiated by writers of short fiction. More recently, a fourth volume of Bhalla's pioneering anthology redressed the balance with a renewed focus on writings in translation from Bengali, Sindhi, Punjabi and other languages, while rediscovering important Urdu stories by Manto, Intizar Husain, Joginder Paul, Qurrutulain Hyder and others (including Paul's later Mantoesque narrative 'Dera Baba Nanak', in Bhalla [2012]). Writers with no direct memory of the event, such as Kamila Shamsie (*Burnt Shadows* [2009]), Sorayya Khan (*Five Queen's Road* [2009]) and Amit Majmudar (*Partitions* [2011]) have also sought to represent partition and its afterlife, not always in equally nuanced fashion. A work for young adults, *A Beautiful Lie* by Irfan Master (2011), has attempted to retell the story of 1947 for young adults and a new generation of readers. A longer discussion would be required to do justice to this array of recent writings, some of which do reach back to the past in distinctive and innovative ways.

As an instance of an important story that does achieve complex testimonial effects, let me turn to Shashi Deshpande's poignant story 'Independence Day', written in 1997, fifty years after the partition (Deshpande 2003). The hyphenated nature of the experience of 1947 comes to the fore in this story about the retrieval of memory. Set in Bangalore, the narrative encompasses the experience of Sindhis who migrated to south India after forced displacement. The trauma experienced by the community is captured retrospectively, through the vantage point of a proxy witness. The narrator recalls an episode from her childhood when she was chosen to perform the role of Bharat Mata (Mother India) at a school ceremony to commemorate independence. Before this, she was dressed up as Mother India and taken to meet some Sindhi refugees who had been given shelter at the house next door. However, rather than provide solace, the sight of the child in her costume brings back for a Sindhi woman the wrenching memory of the loss of her daughter during the violence of partition. She begins keening in a grotesque and uncontrollable way. The next day, while on stage at the school function, the child is unable to see the audience in front of her. For the uncanny apparition of the mother lamenting her lost daughter superimposes itself before her instead. This story thus bears witness to the duality of the experience of independence–partition. Fifty years later, the narrator struggles to come to terms with this spectral memory, as a proxy witness to suffering and loss after horrific atrocities. As the narrator says, memories are records—they refuse to remain within covers. Indeed, they may choose to spring out at you at any time. What stands out in this tale is the interruption of nationalist commemoration by the memory of mourning (often otherwise truncated during large-scale dislocations and forced migration) (ibid.; also see Saint 2010: 307).

We see a certain degree of self-consciousness about the workings of memory and the pressure it exerts upon the present in this story. While such meta-awareness about the status of fiction as testimony to splintered recollections of the past is not unique, it is the extreme difficulty of achieving resolution of such traumatic memories at the personal and public levels that is foregrounded in Deshpande's story. Indeed, the invocation and consolidation of nationalist and communitarian narratives about partition continues apace on both sides of the border. The performative hostility of the flag-lowering ceremony at the Wagah border (anticipated brilliantly by Fikr Taunsvi in his satire 'The Wagah Canal' [2012]) may be a symptom of entrenched views and polarised attitudes rooted in the moment of separation. Despite the efforts of groups such as the Pakistan–India Peoples' Forum for Peace and Democracy, not enough headway has been made with respect to the peace process and the task of 'bridging' partition, except at the individual level or amongst dedicated groups.[7] The reverberations of earlier conflicts and tensions and the rupture of partition resound till today. After-images and residual traces of the event can be traced in many domains of society and culture. In recent times, social media (besides the domain of print culture) has become the site for the virtual replaying of historical memories of hostility and blood-letting. Hate-speech and incendiary rhetoric take on a peculiar intensity in such exchanges. The continuing virulence of intercommunity antipathy and increased intolerance of difference seem symptoms of unresolved knots and tangles in the collective psyche. The dangers of selective appropriation and memorialisation of the past become even more apparent at moments of intensification of communal/sectarian violence.

It is in this context that the efforts of the 42 contributors to the 2013 volume curated by Vishwajyoti Ghosh become especially significant, as an initiative to reinvent the possibility of dialogue across borders. The collaborative dimension brought in here is unusual, as writers and graphic artists from Pakistan, India and Bangladesh came to terms with the legacy of division in distinctive ways. I was reminded of Manto's poignant query as regards whether the literature of the subcontinent too would be partitioned, after the political and geographical demarcation was complete (cited in Asaduddin 2003: 29). While earlier anthologies have sought to reverse the partitioning of consciousness implicit in the redefinition of canons of literature along national lines by juxtaposing writings from both sides of the Radcliffe line, the joining of hands in the shaping of such collaborative work here is perhaps unique, especially in the context of some narratives, with the writer and graphic artist interacting in virtual space ('blind dates', as described by the curator) while creating these graphic narratives. In the curator's note, Ghosh (2013) alludes to the subcontinental Rashomon effect that came to the fore as a result, with different perspectives on the event emerging, as in the case of Akira Kurosawa's film *Rashômon* (1950). *This Side, That Side: Restorying Partition* encompasses genres such as reportage, the memoir, the modern fable, the short story and poetry in graphic form. The interplay between the visual and the textual, between memory and fiction, and between imagination and historical reality has generated some compelling narratives in this volume.

I remember speculating some years ago whether a graphic novel like Art Spiegelman's *Maus* (1986, 1991) might be attempted about partition. While such a novel is still to appear, to an extent *This Side, That Side* has answered the question. As Ghosh admits (2013: 12), it was his desire to write a graphic novel on partition (which did not eventually materialise) that led to the genesis of this project.

Even so, little direct influence of Spiegelman's graphic narrative is apparent here, indicating a different set of stylistic and historical concerns. It would be interesting to see, nonetheless, if Spiegelman's self-reflexive wit and frame-breaking techniques do get incorporated in future graphic narratives on partition. Such innovative techniques enabled Spiegelman to reckon with the trauma of the Final Solution as experienced by his father from a post-memorial standpoint. As a Holocaust survivor's son, Spiegelman's recreation of memories of the event and its afterlife in the form of the personalised beast fable pushed the boundaries of representation further than perhaps had ever been achieved in this form, bringing up the question of the limits to representation of extreme events in narrative form. Such questions do arise in the context of *This Side, That Side* as well, inevitably. This project, however (three years in the making, including several workshops with contributors), has largely steered clear of the traps of either trivialisation of the issues pertaining to partition era violence or of aestheticisation of such violence. Critical questions relating to identitarian recovery of memory predicated on communitarian and nationalistic agendas have beset many a well-intentioned foray into the quagmire of partition history. Again, the best narratives here steer clear of victim-centred storytelling or the rhetoric of blame. As an instance, Salman Rashid's and Mohit Suneja's 'I Too Have Seen Lahore' (ibid.: 207–20) depicts a survivor's memory of collective violence on the Punjab border with sensitivity. The story is told from the point of view of the second generation – the son of a migrant from Jalandhar, now based in Lahore, visits the city to locate his parents' erstwhile home. While this theme had been explored earlier in stories such as Mohan Rakesh's 'His Heap of Rubble', here the story takes a different turn as the migrant's son fails to locate his parents' former residence, instead meeting a Sikh who claims that he too has seen Lahore. The Sikh then shares his childhood experience with the visitor from Lahore: he and his family fled Lahore by train in 1947. This survivor narrates the story of his own narrow escape from death during a time of massacres of refugees, especially in trains and in the fields of Punjab. When they were approaching the bridge leading across the Ravi, the driver of the train, a Muslim, declined to proceed further, given that

Muslims were being butchered in east Punjab. On both sides of the train, mobs of assailants awaited the dismounting of passengers, ostensibly to take revenge for the killing of Muslims headed for Pakistan. Then, a Sikh leader of the Bajwa clan of Klasswala stepped down from his carriage and requested that the refugees be allowed to proceed on foot unharmed. Something inexplicably human came to the fore at this moment and they were allowed to pass. Ironically, as these people moved further into East Punjab, they saw the results of massacres of Muslim refugees, including many bodies at Dera Nanak. However, instead of any weighing of the scales, what comes to the fore here is the possibility of resistance to the logic of reprisal killings. This admittedly rare instance of cessation of violence is recorded in an instance of secondary witnessing, as the visitor from Lahore (whose own family history is displaced as a locus of concern) bears witness to the possibility of the cycle of retributive genocide being interrupted via the Sikh survivor's story. Mohit Suneja's illustrations add a level of further meaning in their sensitive evocation of expressions of different characters, as well as the horror of the moment of prospective violence.

The Bangladeshi poet Kaiser Haq brings his poetic sensibility to bear in 'Border', visualised by Hemant Puri (ibid.: 43–50). The second-person mode of narration introduces the idea of a romantic quest for an unnamed woman, who happens to be located across a border. The narrator underlines the ironies of being in the border zone, a knife that slices the earth without the earth knowing, severing and joining at the same instant. Families split asunder by the border (in an instance of wry humour) eat under one flag and defecate under another, humming a different national tune. Finally, the addressee of this poetic narrative lies down under the livid moon on that fateful line, and raises the universal flag of flaglessness, even as the dawn explodes into a salute amidst bird anthems. In this cryptic piece, Haq offers an allegorical critique of identitarian definitions inherited from the partition era, visualising a notion of the self that transcends flags, anthems and other such markers of national identity. 'Border' is an instance of poetic witnessing of the damaging effects of divisive politics, even as it attempts reclamation of alternative self-definitions and the space of in-betweenness through such existentialist gestures, and comprehensive negation of the notion of borders being impermeable.

Mahmood Farooqui's translation and reprise of Intizar Husain's 'A Letter from India' (1994) (illustrated by Fariha Rehman in Ghosh 2013: 69–82) draws upon his own adaptation of this piece while performing 'Dastan-e Taqseem-e Hind', a collage of writings on partition. The agonising dilemmas attendant on displacement, especially for divided Muslim families—brought to light in detail by historian Vazira Zamindar (2007: esp. 1–18)—come to the fore in this narrative. The narrator is from Ghazipur, part of a Muslim family divided at the time of partition. The discovery of a letter written 25 years after partition, when Pakistan itself was divided, by Qurban Ali, an Indian Muslim, to a relative in Karachi leads to a recovery of buried memories. There are allusions to the disintegration of ties after migration, gaps in communication and mutual understanding in the wake of 1947, as well as to the loss family members both in India and in Pakistan. This epistle acquires greater poignancy when the narrator, after reading it, attempts to call his far-flung relatives across the border and is reminded of the risks with respect to dialling that particular country code. He decides never to dial that number again, a consequence of the lasting hostility between the nation-states after separation and the paranoia of the state as regards possible fifth-columnists, which had its effects on the lives of those once part of such extended families. The genre of the graphic *dastan* that this piece inaugurates (at the launch, during the performance of the 'Dastan-e Taqseem-e Hind', graphic images from the volume were displayed in the background) seems to hold out promise in rearticulating such lost fragments of historical and cultural memory.

'Tamasha-e-Tetwal', by Arif Ayaz Parrey and Wassim Hallal (Ghosh 2013: 113–28), captures the fractured reality of the situation at the Line of Control at Tetwal in Kashmir effectively. The narrative ushers in the perspective of the journalist sent to investigate the story of a death on the border, where he discovers that both nations have aimed loudspeakers at each other, incessantly broadcasting propaganda. He is told that in the resultant cacophony, the art of whispering has been lost, something the local community will never forgive. Despite geopolitical tensions, there is still the possibility of exchanges across the river in the Tetwal valley, as bags of mushrooms are thrown across from the Pakistani side (where they are supposedly tastier). The inter-textual echoes of Manto's well-known story, 'Tetwal ka Kutta' ('The Dog of Tetwal' [2001]), were of especial interest to this reader (the story begins with the visual image of a dog, and allusions are made to characters from Manto's story such as Jamadar Harnam Singh). Manto's critique of jingoistic nationalism and the descent into dehumanised behaviour of those assigned to defend the boundary is still pertinent, and such ironic inter-texts add a further layer of meaning to this tale about happenings in contemporary Tetwal.

'A Good Education' by Vishwajyoti Ghosh (ibid.: 149–62), based on the Bengali memoir *Aranyalipi* (*The Forest Chronicles*) by Ghosh's grandmother Amiya Sen, delineates the vicissitudes of refugee life in the forest of Dandakaranya and in refugee centres in Delhi with telling irony. This mainly epistolary narrative captures with sensitivity the reality of displacement and its dehumanising effects from the point of view of a woman social worker assigned to assist those displaced from Bengal to camps in Dandakaranya in Madhya Pradesh. This account is interleaved with memories of Ghosh's own childhood, spent in part amongst such refugee children, occupying a special position (as the grandson of the social worker) as their 'prince'. The situation of refugee women in the Mana camp who are willing to relinquish their children to the care of relief workers at the Kasturba Niketan Centre (operating under the Ministry of Rehabilitation) in Lajpat Nagar in Delhi due to straitened circumstances and limited prospects is an indicator of the erosion of kinship ties brought about by forced dislocation. The social worker eventually finds herself wondering about her own family's identity, when her husband seeks to discourage her grandson from spending too much time with such 'refugee kids' at the Kasturba Niketan Centre in Delhi. The disclosure that the young graphic-novelist-to-be was sent eventually to Bluebells School heightens the ironic contrast with the situation of the displaced children.

'The Taboo' by Malini Gupta and Dyuti Mittal (Ghosh 2013: 235–48) is marked by a keen awareness about the continuing afterlife of partition. Written after a visit to Cooperstown in West Bengal by a microfinance officer engaged in developmental work, setting up women's savings and credit groups, the story reveals the lasting stigma attached to former transit camps that became permanent colonies – such as Cooperstown itself. The short cut to Cooperstown taken by the narrator opens up a window to the ways in which a group of people could become cut off from society, their place of residence taboo to prospective visitors. The story of Lily, a former inhabitant and colony girl who has become the owner of a garage, testifies to the indomitable will to survive that brought her clear of the miasmic situation in Cooperstown that resulted from the rehabilitation process, despite the collapse of her own marriage. The graphic illustrations in this narrative bring out the labyrinthine intricacies of this process brilliantly.

Priya Sen and Deewana's 'The Last Circus' (ibid.: 275–82) introduces an unusual perspective, that of Dasharath, a former trapeze artist whose real name was Don Emanuelle Stanislaw. Although his family was from Manila, he was born in a circus in Lahore in 1947. The authors meet him in Bangalore, 66 years after he migrated from Lahore. The Mantoesque line 'And then the circus was partitioned' leads up to the description of Dasharath crossing the border by elephant, even as his two brothers remain behind. The fantastical and real collide in this account of a survivor who still dreams of his brothers and their magical closing act on the trapeze in the final moments of the show. The movement of the grand old circus onwards to future destinations acquires a special meaning for the viewers of this show. Indeed, the divided circus becomes a metaphor for the topsy-turvy-ness ushered in by partition, affecting not just the major communities, but also the destiny of many from ethnic groups and off-beat professions.

Finally, let me note the prevalence of postmemory (a form of memory of a traumatic event that is transmitted to the next generation, in Marianne Hirsch's [1997: 22–23] terms) in several of the narratives in this anthology, including '90 Upper Mall' by Ahmad Rafey Alam and Martand Khosla (Ghosh 2013: 177–90). In this personal account, we are introduced to Alam, the author, who while studying law in Britain meets Martand Khosla, a student of architecture from India. As their friendship grows, they discover that

Alam's family actually live in Lahore, in a house once occupied by the Khosla family (which included the well-known judge G.D. Khosla, author of *Stern Reckoning* [2002], one of the first attempts at a history of partition based on interviews primarily with refugees from West Punjab). The students exchange notes and attempt to fill gaps in collective memory; there is less of a sense here of the predominance of frozen and residual affects such as bitterness and narcissistic rage. Rather, in this story about the reclamation of memory, we learn more about the forced migration of two families, the Khoslas and the Alams, and how the Alams were eventually allocated the house at 90 Upper Mall in Lahore in 1959, leading to the coincidence of these two students meeting in London. For Alam, the absurdity and arbitrariness of partition becomes clear through this disclosure. Rather than remaining subject to inherited prejudice, the retelling of this story leads to dissolution of the usual rhetoric about violence and loss associated with partition. The photographs included act as snapshots of a different history of the self, which might run counter to official history, with its baggage of blame and recrimination.

More could be written about the wide range of contributions to the volume; my own focus has been on the pieces that I found most striking. Tabish Khair and Priya Kuriyan's 'An Old Fable' (Ghosh 2013: 15–30) tends to fall back on well-worn and received ideas about divide and rule, and British culpability for partition, albeit in a satirical and fabulist mode. In a similar vein, the allegorical intent in Irfan Master and Prabha Mallya's 'Fault Lines' (ibid.: 31–42) seems rather forced, with Tagore's ghost popping up like a deus ex machina to provide a ray of hope to two prisoners in no man's land. While Khademul Islam and Sarbajit Singh's well-drawn 'The Exit Plan' (ibid.: 83–98) includes a moving account of the departure of Bangladeshis from Karachi in 1971, the links with the context of 1947 were not self-evident, except insofar as 1971 can be regarded as the second partition in the history of the subcontinent. I have often wondered about the paucity of counter-factual narratives tracing alternative trajectories leading up to the event of 1947 in the domain of fiction; alternative histories as fictional counterparts to a desire for closure seem not yet to have appeared as a sub-genre of partition literature, in comparison with many such narratives about the Final Solution.

The closest to this possibility in this volume is Mehreen Murtaza's 'Bastards of Utopia' (ibid.: 293–300), which, though visually arresting, did not really address the specificities of the partition moment. The piece seemed to belong to another anthology, even as we await the arrival of such reimaginings and counter-factual reconstructions of the overdetermined history of partition.

I hope this essay will further the ongoing conversation about this volume, as well as its context, in which graphic artists, writers, literary critics, as well as historians and psychologists might participate. The visual and stylistic elements included in some of the experimental pieces such as Orijit Sen's 'Making Faces (ibid.: 327–36), which effectively dismantles the fixing of ethnic and religious stereotypes in the form of visual images, certainly require a more elaborate discussion than has been possible here. Indeed, it is the new kind of reflection prompted by the interplay between the texts and illustrations/images that is the most significant aspect of the volume to this reader. The networking that preceded publication, including workshops and exchanges of ideas across cyberspace (some collaborators apparently never met at all), has ensured that a plurality of perspectives emerged, some abstract, others satirical. There is even a direct plea for the possibility of people to people contact, especially for divided Muslim families ('Milne Do!' by Beena Sarwar and Prasanna Dhandarphale [ibid.: 311–16]) – Sarwar is a founding member of the Pakistan–India Peoples' Forum for Peace and Democracy, formed in 1994). Such encounters across the contested terrain of historical (and official) memory, which might allow for a differential relaying of the traces of historical trauma and perhaps the creative dissipation of frozen affects, are of inestimable importance. One hopes this volume is a harbinger of creative initiatives that may push the boundaries of fictive testimony further in times to come.

NOTES

1. A previous presentation on early narratives about partition at the 'Partition: The Long Shadow' series of lectures coordinated by Urvashi Butalia became the basis for my initial synoptic discussion of first and second generation responses to the partition debacle.

2. See Amrit Rai's 'Kichar' (translated as 'Filth' [1994]) for an account of the proliferation of such stories.
3. This list of short stories on partition is selective, of course. I have critically analysed these stories in detail in an earlier study. See Saint (2010: esp. 240–93).
4. For a longer discussion of these novels, see Saint (2010: 115–239).
5. The intense soul searching that followed the end of the Vichy regime (and the phase of collaboration with the Nazis) in France comes to mind, though this context is not explicitly invoked in the story.
6. Studies by Urvashi Butalia (1998), Ritu Menon and Kamla Bhasin (1998), Veena Das (1995, 2007), Gyanendra Pandey (2001), Mushirul Hasan (1993, 1995, 2001) and Vazira Zamindar (2007), among others, excavated in different ways hitherto untold histories of the era, including those of abducted women and children, as well as the fraught situation of divided Muslim families. Ayesha Jalal's 2013 biography of Manto cast new light on the history of partition, drawing on the resources of memory and the family archive, besides generating a fresh perspective on Manto's work.
7. See Kothari and Mian (2010) for various essays describing a variety of initiatives by activists, artists and common folk at the grassroots level.

REFERENCES

Ahmad, Ashfaq. 1998. 'The Shepherd', in Muhammad Umar Memon (trans. and ed.), *An Epic Unwritten: The Penguin Book of Partition Stories from Urdu*, pp.30–86. New Delhi: Penguin.

Ahmed, Ishtiaq. 2011. *The Punjab Bloodied, Partitioned and Cleansed: Unravelling the 1947 Tragedy through Secret British Reports and Eyewitness Accounts*. New Delhi: Rupa.

Asaduddin, M. 2003. 'Introduction', in Muhammad Umar Memon (ed.), *Black Margins: Stories*, pp.9-43. New Delhi: Katha.

Azad, Maulana Abul Kalam. 2003. *India Wins Freedom*. New Delhi: Orient Longman (first published in 1959).

Bedi, Rajinder Singh. 1995. 'Lajwanti', in Mushirul Hasan (ed.), *India Partitioned*, Vol. I, pp.179–91. New Delhi: Roli Books.

Bhalla, Alok (ed.). 1994. *Stories about the Partition of India*, Vols I, II, III. New Delhi: Indus.

——— (ed.). 2012. *Stories about the Partition of India*, Vol. IV. New Delhi: Manohar.

Butalia, Urvashi. 1998. *The Other Side of Silence: Voices from the Partition of India.* New Delhi: Penguin.

Chughtai, Ismat. 1995. 'Roots', in Mushirul Hasan (ed.), *India Partitioned*, Vol. I, pp. 279–89. New Delhi: Roli Books.

Cowasjee, Saros and K.S. Duggal (eds). 1995. *Orphans of the Storm: Stories on the Partition of India.* New Delhi: UBS.

Das, Veena. 1995. *Critical Events: An Anthropological Perspective on Contemporary India.* 1995. New Delhi: Oxford University Press.

———. 2007. *Life and Words: Violence and the Descent into the Ordinary*. New Delhi: Oxford University Press.

Desai, Anita. 2001. *Clear Light of Day*. London: Vintage (first published in 1980).

Deshpande, Shashi. 2003. 'Independence Day', in *Collected Stories*, Vol. I, pp. 121–31. New Delhi: Penguin.

Ghosh, Vishwajyoti. 2010. *Delhi Calm*. New Delhi: HarperCollins.

——— (curator). 2013. *This Side That Side: Restorying Partition.* New Delhi: Yoda Press.

Hasan, Mushirul (ed.). 1993. *India's Partition: Process, Strategy and Mobilization.* New Delhi: Oxford University Press.

——— (ed.). 1995. *India Partitioned*, Vols I, II. New Delhi: Roli Books.

———. 2001. *Legacy of a Divided Nation: India's Muslims since Independence.* New Delhi: Oxford University Press.

Hirsch, Marianne. 1997. *Family Frames: Photography, Narrative, and Postmemory.* Cambridge, MA: Harvard University Press.

Hosain, Attia. 1994. *Sunlight on a Broken Column.* New Delhi: Penguin (first published in 1961).

Husain, Intizar. 1994. 'A Letter from India', in Alok Bhalla (ed.), *Stories about the Partition of India*, Vol. I, pp. 79–90. New Delhi: Indus.

———. 1998. 'An Unwritten Epic', in Muhammad Umar Memon (trans. and ed.), *An Epic Unwritten: The Penguin Book of Partition Stories from Urdu*, pp. 153–78. New Delhi: Penguin.

———. 1999. *Basti* (Frances Pritchett, trans.). New Delhi: HarperCollins.

Hussein, Abdullah. 1999. *The Weary Generations.* New Delhi: HarperCollins.

Hyder, Qurratulain. 1998. *River of Fire.* New Delhi: Kali for Women.

Ikramullah, Shaista Suhrawardy. 1998. *From Purdah to Parliament.* Karachi: Oxford University Press (first published in 1963).

Jalal, Ayesha. 2013. *The Pity of Partition: Manto's Life, Times, and Work across the India-Pakistan Divide.* New Delhi: HarperCollins.

Khan, Sorayya. 2009. *Five Queen's Road.* New Delhi: Penguin.

Khosla, G.D. 2002. *Stern Reckoning: A Survey of the Events Leading up to and Following the Partition of India* (in Mushirul Hasan, ed., *The Partition Omnibus*). New Delhi: Oxford University Press.

Kidwai, Anis. 2011. *In Freedom's Shade* (Ayesha Kidwai, trans.). New Delhi: Penguin.

Kothari, Rita (ed.). 2009. *Unbordered Memories: Sindhi Stories of Partition*. New Delhi: Penguin.

Kothari, Smitu and Zia Mian (eds). 2010. *Bridging Partition: People's Initiatives for Peace between India and Pakistan*. New Delhi: Orient Blackswan.

Rashômon. 1950. Directed by Akira Kurosawa.

LaCapra, Dominick. 2001. *Writing History, Writing Trauma*. Baltimore, MD: Johns Hopkins University Press.

Lohia, Ram Manohar. 2009. *Guilty Men of India's Partition*. New Delhi: Rupa (first published in 1961).

Majmudar, Amit. 2011. *Partitions*. Oxford: Oneworld.

Manto, Sa'adat Hasan. 2001. 'The Dog of Tetwal' in Ravikant and Tarun K. Saint (trans and eds), *Translating Partition*, pp. 94–103. New Delhi: Katha.

———. 2003a. 'Jelly', in Muhammad Umar Memon (ed.), *Black Margins: Stories*, p. 187. New Delhi: Katha.

———. 2003b. 'Open It!' in Muhammad Umar Memon (ed.), *Black Margins: Stories*, pp. 200–203.

———. 2003c. 'Toba Tek Singh', in Muhammad Umar Memon (ed.), *Black Margins: Stories*, pp. 212–20. New Delhi: Katha.

Master, Irfan. 2011. *A Beautiful Lie*. London: Bloomsbury.

Memon, Muhammad Umar (ed.). 1998. *An Epic Unwritten: The Penguin Book of Partition Stories from Urdu*. New Delhi: Penguin.

Menon, Ritu and Kamla Bhasin. 1998. *Borders and Boundaries: Women in India's Partition*. New Delhi: Kali for Women.

Pandey, Gyanendra. 2001. *Remembering Partition*. Cambridge: Cambridge University Press.

Patel, Kamla. 2006. *Torn from the Roots: A Partition Memoir* (Uma Randeria, trans.). New Delhi: Women Unlimited.

Pritam, Amrita. 1987. 'The Skeleton', in *The Skeleton and That Man* (Khushwant Singh, trans.). New Delhi: Sterling.

Rai, Amrit. 1994. 'Filth', in Alok Bhalla (ed.), *Stories about the Partition of India*, pp. 111–18.

Rakesh, Mohan. 1995. 'His Heap of Rubble', in Mushirul Hasan (ed.), *India Partitioned: The Other Face of Freedom*, Vol. I, pp. 238–48. New Delhi: Roli Books.

Raza (Reza), Rahi Masoom. 1994. *The Feuding Families of Village Gangauli/ Half a Village* (Gillian Wright, trans.). New Delhi: Penguin.

Ropana, Gurdev Singh. 2012. 'The Mirror', in Alok Bhalla (ed.), *Stories about the Partition of India*, Vol. IV, pp. 123–28. New Delhi: Manohar.

Sahni, Bhisham. 1995. 'We Have Arrived in Amritsar' in Mushirul Hasan (ed.), *India Partitioned: The Other Face of Freedom*, Vol. I, pp. 114–26. New Delhi: Roli Books.

———. 2001. *Tamas*. New Delhi: Penguin.

Saint, Tarun K. 2010. *Witnessing Partition: Memory, History, Fiction*. New Delhi: Routledge.

Sengupta, Debjani (ed.). 2003. *Mapmaking: Partition Stories from Two Bengals*. New Delhi: Srishti.

Shahnawaz, Jahan Ara. 2002. *Father and Daughter: A Political Autobiography*. Karachi: Oxford University Press.

Shamsie, Kamila. 2009. *Burnt Shadows*. London: Bloomsbury.

Spiegelman, Art. 1986. *Maus I: A Survivor's Tale; My Father Bleeds History*. New York: Pantheon Books.

———. 1991. *Maus II: My Parents Survived Hell and Moved to the Suburbs*. New York: Pantheon Books.

Taunsvi, Fikr. 2012. 'The Wagah Canal', in Alok Bhalla (ed.), *Stories about the Partition of India*, Vol. IV, pp. 357–64. New Delhi: Manohar.

Vaid, Krishna Baldev. 1994. *The Broken Mirror* (Charles Sparrows, trans.). New Delhi: Penguin.

Vyam, Durgabai, Subhash Vyam, Srividya Natarajan and S. Anand. 2011. *Bhimayana: Incidents in the life of Bhimrao Ramji Ambedkar*. New Delhi: Navayana.

Zamindar, Vazira Fazila-Yacoobali. 2007. *The Long Partition and the Making of South Asia: Refugees, Boundaries, Histories*. New York: Columbia University Press.

FURTHER READING

Gujral, Satish. 2000. *Selected Works 1947–2000*. New Delhi: Lalit Kala Akademi.

———. 2002. 'Crossing the Jhelum', in S. Settar and I.B. Gupta (eds), *Pangs of Partition*, Vol. II, pp. 47–58. New Delhi: Manohar.

Hasan, Mushirul. Ed. *Inventing Boundaries: Gender, Politics and the Partition of India*. 2000. New Delhi: OUP, 2002.

Hasan, Mushirul. Ed. *The Partition Omnibus*. New Delhi: OUP, 2002.

Hasan, Mushirul. *From Pluralism to Separatism: Qasbas in Colonial Awadh*. New Delhi: OUP, 2007.

Hosain, Attia. "Phoenix Fled". *Phoenix Fled*. 1953. By Hosain. Delhi: Rupa, 1993. 9–15.

Hyder, Qurratulain. "The Housing Society". *A Season of Betrayals: A short story and two novellas*. Trans. C.M. Naim. New Delhi: Kali, 1999. 175–266.

Manto, Sa'adat Hasan. *Dastavez*. Eds. Balraj Menra and Sharad Dutt. 1993. New Delhi: Rajkamal, 1998. 5 Vols.

Manto, Sa'adat Hasan. *Selected Stories*. Trans. Aatish Taseer. Noida: Random House, 2008.

Mastur, Khadija. *Inner Courtyard*. Trans. Neelam Hussain. 2000. New Delhi, Kali for Women, 2001.Trans. of *Aangan*. 1952.

Menon, Ritu. Ed. *No Woman's Land: Women from Pakistan, India and Bangladesh write on the Partition of India*. New Delhi: Women Unlimited, 2004.

Pandey, Gyanendra. *Memory, History and the Question of Violence: Reflections on the Reconstruction of Partition*. Calcutta: K.P. Bagchi, 1999.

Panjabi, Kavita. *Old Maps and New: Legacies of the Partition-- A Pakistan Diary*. Calcutta: Seagull, 2005.

Paul, Joginder. *Sleepwalkers*. Trans. Sunil Trivedi and Sukrita Paul Kumar. New Delhi: Katha, 1998. Trans. of *Khwabrau*. 1990.

Ravikant and Tarun K. Saint. Eds. *Translating Partition*. New Delhi: Katha, 2001.

Sen, Amiya. (Unpublished translation, I think). *The Forest Chronicles* (Bhaswati Ghosh, trans.).

Singh, Khushwant. *Train to Pakistan*. 1956. New Delhi: Ravi Dayal, 1986.

CHAPTER 10

A Long Walk Out from Partition

PRAJNA PARAMITA PARASHER

We live so embedded in our history that its very visibility can make it difficult to acknowledge. Stand at any Indian street corner, urban or rural, home or diasporic, and signals from the past are everywhere. Architectural details, signs in food shops, designs floating on passing saris, broken fragments of conversation – these are the scattered ends of what brought us here, often recognizable should one focus but generally lost in the hubbub of automobiles, Calvin Klein, Coca Cola, Pepsi Cola. It is conventional to say that official history is written by the winners, and like most conventions there is truth there. Another kind of memory, unofficial but always crowding forward, is the one of everyday awareness, individual in each separate person yet always just below connection, like suddenly recognizing an unexpected old friend. As we begin to assemble documentation and scholarship on the Partition era, not only is this past slipping from invisibility, but as it emerges, we are looking inward too, to a quicksilver mirror showing what it has made of us through a glimpse of what it has left out.

It is a conundrum of the creation of national myth that we are assembling this more official documentation just as we are losing the last of those who experienced the events of 1947 and can offer personal accounts. S.L. Parasher (1904–1991) was an artist, writer and teacher who lived through this tempestuous period and left a rich archive of material, a personal voice emerging from so many still silenced.

This body of work, some of it formerly private, is in various mediums. From the Partition line-drawings on their common bits of paper to his sculptures through the bright landscapes and portraits of the Shimla days to the murals still standing in Delhi and Chandigarh, he was active for his whole long life. As his public profile became larger, more elaborate in style and dimension, it also became deeper in resonance and less opaque in meaning. Tied both to traditional subcontinent symbolisms and to contemporary movements in world art, these large works incorporate a philosophical dimension impossible to ignore in the viewing. The line drawings of 1947–1949 however seem to have a parallel life of their own, direct, clear, almost snapshots of an era going invisible before his very eyes. Although it can now only be conjecture, hindsight seems to suggest that their very immediacy, and the immediacies of the situation, turned him inward and toward a documentarian's use of art. Realistic, almost photographic, they are also hasty and immediate, an image of multiple traumas, those in front of him and the artist's own in the viewing. The Partition line drawings, brought into the comfortable present, bring along their terrifying acknowledgement of the fragility of life, and a spectre even there of the evanescence of beauty.

LATITUDES OF LOSS

For some years now it has been the mission of the SarNir Foundation to insure that Parasher's works have a permanent home in the national record. From out of the cupboards under the stairs these images assert themselves, memories not lost but displaced, resurfacing now, claiming their place, evidence of a journey that left few tracks on the road.

In the piles of old papers and letters mixed with the sketches, I pull out a post card:

> I, Sardari Lal Parasher son of Pt. Dewan Chand, 51 years, 5 months of age, reside at 'Khud Cottage' Simla – 4, do solemnly affirm that I am a refugee from the West Punjab. I was registered under registration card no. 1181-1-11 dated 20.10.1947 at Connaught Place, New Delhi, which I have lost. (See figure 1)

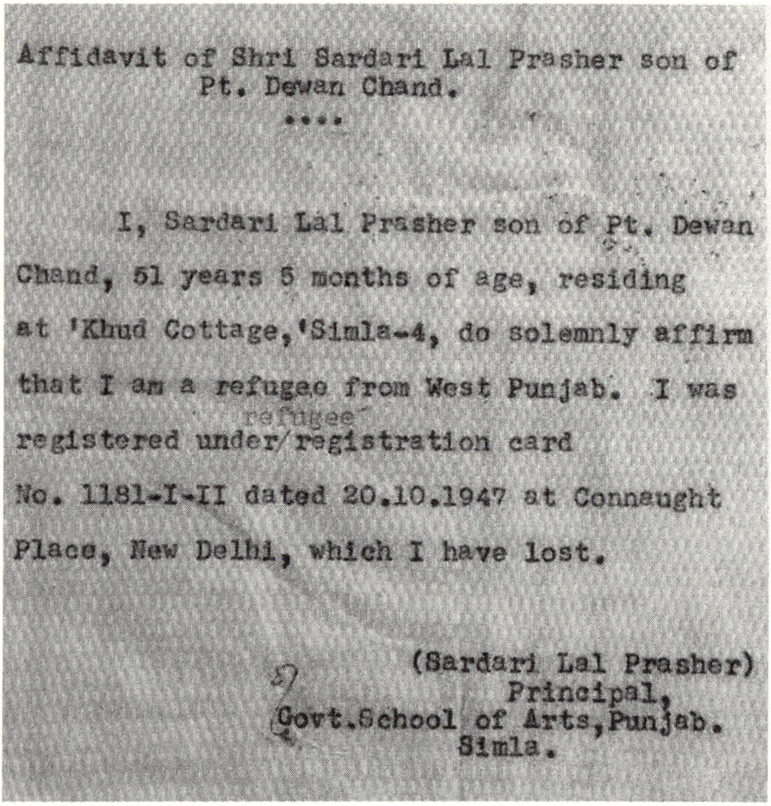

Affidavit of Shri Sardari Lal Prasher son of
Pt. Dewan Chand.
....

I, Sardari Lal Prasher son of Pt. Dewan Chand, 51 years 5 months of age, residing at 'Khud Cottage,' Simla-4, do solemnly affirm that I am a refugee from West Punjab. I was registered under refugee registration card No. 1181-I-II dated 20.10.1947 at Connaught Place, New Delhi, which I have lost.

(Sardari Lal Prasher)
Principal,
Govt.School of Arts, Punjab.
Simla.

Figure 1

Although this was written before I was born, as I sit over this document the thing that torments in the loss of his registration card is the necessary absent space that requires a declaration. It is a felt absence that does not appear. Or does it? Swearing his refugee status, participating in the national realities that had separated him from his father's home, what has he shown us? What my father has left us in his line drawings and art works are his answers; he knew we in our own turn would have to spin outside their ogee into the right questions.[1]

When I was a child, my grandmother, my father's mother, lived with us in Delhi. She stayed upstairs in the *barsati*. I remember her as a presence not quite in rhythm with the rest of the household. My father would go to her room and speak to her every afternoon, but I think we children tried to avoid her whenever possible. In my child's mind, it never occurred to me to try to imagine what her experience must have been. There she was, not in Lahore but in Delhi, citizen of a country and resident of a nation that was mostly unfamiliar and torn away from what she recognized and most of what she must have loved. To be made into a refugee must be hardest on the old, who can't really imagine creating a new life and whose sense of themselves and whatever their lives might mean has been left behind in the road. I am reminded of a scene in the film *Garm Hawa*: at a dramatic point in the narrative the daughter of the evicted Muslim household, Amina, scarches for her grandmother. Dressed for the street in her flowing *burkha*, Amina races up and down staircases of the *haveli* calling out. The blocking allows the camera following her body to trace it through the lineaments of the empty house. She finds her grandmother hiding in the wood room – there with the rest of the abandoned and unable to answer the calls of the next generations.

My grandmother's story will remain one of the lost ones. There is a little trace evidence in her isolation and the fragments of memories carried by her grandchildren, but these bits and scraps are more like chips of incised stone, evidence that a passage happened, but not a readable record of it.[2]

In her representations of the Partition experience, (infrequent as they were) my mother was also separated from the possibility of being an authentic witness to herself. This collapse of witnessing is precisely what is central to the Partition experience. Yet how could I call her life a failure? Twice an émigré, she rebuilt her home repeatedly, managed to keep us well and together through many trying situations her previous experience could never have prepared her for. None of us saw what she saw, and nothing in our way of relating to one another would have allowed her to speak. Is there a way to tell your daughter what it is like to sew a few jewels in your petticoat and close the door on a whole life? To hide in ditches, body spread over the babies? To watch a friend be raped and to be silent? I stand in the safety of the life she gave me and wonder how I could ask.[3]

In holocaust museums in other countries such fragments find a place -- a scrap of child's writing or drawing, poetry on the board wall of an infirmary, a few photographs or feet of film. In our project we have even less to work with. But these line drawings were actually there, and are here still. The need to engage with them is urgent, a responsibility as well as an honour. The making of them could never have been felt as a gift, but that's what they have become. By standing in front of them and seeing through Parasher's pencil some brief image of what is lost in this terrible past we are changing, by only a little, the shape of the present.[4]

Trauma brings with it the need to witness, to speak, to somehow make an impression on the world that records the outrage of the moment. But trauma also stuns, dazing us into silence. Just when there is the most to be expressed we are least up to the task. The traumatized, we might say, carry an impossible history within them or they become themselves the symptom of a history that they cannot entirely possess because it is intimately bound up with the question of truth. Human horrors are a litany of loss, and we have to resign ourselves to the recognition that all we have in the aftermath is the least tracery, like a fossil leaf embedded in a flake of shale. My parents seldom spoke of Partition though I imagine they must have thought of those days frequently. 'You are asking me to remember what I have taken a lifetime to forget,' my mother said when I pressed her. How does one access a forgetting? What does it mean to witness? How does a mute object become a witness?

Precisely in the capacity to emit radioactive waves which other materials don't. Sometimes what moves me most about the Partition line drawings is their immediacy. I look at them and try to imagine what it must have been like in Ambala, not just the simple things like the crowding and the mud and inadequate everything, but how could it have been for them, marooned in a place that was no place, everything they treasured ripped away and the days ahead impossible to trust? In my imagination, almost the only way to access this gone world, the people next door were only strangers, perhaps so unfamiliar as to speak a different dialect. When a woman reached out to stir the pot, it wasn't there; like everything else it was in a place never to be seen again. And when her head turned at a child's cry it

Parasher, at the Baldev Nagar Refugee Camp, Ambala

turned back again, not her child. Also forever lost. We've been told so little – a few anecdotes – my father had to ride on the top of a train to apply for the position of Commandant at the Baldev Nagar Refugee Camp in Ambala.

We've been told he was a good administrator, doing the best he could in a difficult situation. We've been told that when he was troubled, which must have been all the time, he would walk around the camp and draw the refugees. There are so many of these line drawings, as compelling now as at the moment of their creation. Some are on flaking pieces of art paper, but many are on envelopes, invoices, pages torn from ledgers and notebooks. And the lines of the figures! They are drawn in pencil, in charcoal, in ink. Most appear to have been drawn in haste, maybe in fury. My father as I knew him was a calm man, serene even in crisis, but the hand that made these line drawings feels driven, racing to impress onto these happenstance scraps the evidence of the disaster swirling around him. And yet when I say furious, I must also say they radiate love. From the soft covered heads of women leaning toward one another to the isolated man compressed into a single howl of despair the figures draw us toward them, pulling us back through time with the force of their images.

The lines of these drawings ensnare. Sometimes they feel like a spider web; sometimes they feel like barbed wire. There is a demand here like no other of his works. 'In "Cry" the howling man wails that at least in part he knows his voice meets silence. It is the upper half of the man, rendered in heavy dark strokes, hairy chest, rough beard and eyebrows, topknot unravelling, all dark and frantic. The open mouth cries, or shouts or screams – no way to know. But his wrist bangs his forehead and his eyes too are closed. It's the idea, not the wail, caught by the artist; catastrophe still the subject's own.'[5] (GJM) (See figure 7)

Compelled, I witness, my belated empathy so useless it feels perverse. I do not know how to honour this past, these records of it. It has taken a half-century for us to begin to speak of the unspeakable. To whom am I addressing this discourse? My desire, in presenting this reality, these surviving scraps of a past which made us what we are, is to reorganise the other options, the loved, lost options in that black scream – 'All gone' we say over the empty bowls of our lucky, living children. All gone, all those that Partition killed or didn't allow to be born. They are the ones who let us be who we are, here, trying to remember what has been dismembered from us.

VOCABULARY OF SILENCE

Could it be possible that we don't remember pain, not the pain itself? What we remember is that there was pain, and that at the time it was so overwhelming it overrode everything else. More than half a century after Partition, it continues to be with us, a scar on the body politic. Or maybe worse than a scar; for some it is the healed-over stump that reminds us of something now gone. What scant records we have of this dismembering are finding their way into the present, creating new memories in new generations, never the original trauma itself but a gesture toward it, a sign like a place name that suggests what passed here once and is now forever to be recalled as a litany of loss. In 'Small Comfort', most figures are drawn into themselves, centripetal forces holding together what is in every danger of flying to pieces. (See figure 2)

Figure 2: 'Small Comfort'

Even the bullocks, those plodding engines of agrarian life, are drawn into this whirlwind. Their placid bodies look reduced, small in scale compared to the people near them. (See 'From the Road', figure 3)

Living their accustomed lives wherever they find themselves, these beasts are the least touched by circumstance, their familiar peace a counterpoint to the distressed people trying to make sense of what is happening. Interestingly though, it is rare to see a whole animal. There is close to a full view in 'From the Road' and 'Way Station', figures 3 and 4, though the faces, like that of the man,

Figure 3: 'From the Road'

are partially obscured by the angle of sight. Both of these though convey a feeling of repose. They are blanketed and eating, their lot of heavy labour only faintly suggested by the straight lines above them that indicate their usual work.

Figure 4: 'Way Station'

Figure 5, 'In Search of a New Home' is different. Very little of the animal shows, only the hindquarters. What is centred here is not the creature, but the creature's connection. The cart he might be pulling, though he doesn't seem to be hitched to it at this moment, is a tumbled load of people and parcels, every sign of a hasty journey away from home, the place that allowed for the meticulous hand construction of the cart itself. In this, as in most of the sketches, the faces are turned away. It is a posture of mourning, mourning so close to the event that there is not yet any way to engage with it. Balanced atop what of their former lives they were able to bring along, the women turn inward and toward one another, unable to face looking forward or back, locked into the moment, pitiable way station on an unwanted journey into the unknown.

Figure 5: 'In Search of a New Home'

Such turning away is found frequently in these line drawings. Stunned despair shows in many of the huddled bodies who do not engage with the artist and thus neither with us, the viewers. What was in his own overwhelmed heart Parasher only rarely confronts. In 'Cry I and II' – figures 6 and 7 though, an outraged man speaks directly.

Figure 6: 'Cry I'

Figure 7: 'Cry II'

While all these line drawings appear to have been done quickly, the pencil strokes here seem even more urgent. One fist is in the air, as if railing against fate, and the other hand almost out of the frame, possibly reaching toward something already gone. The open mouth is a dark hole in the bearded face, shout coming toward us through the decades, still unanswerable. His hair and garment flow, as if he were leaping or running, but his body and muscular arms also suggest a solidity, as if this man is the only thing left to rely on and he is indeed reliable. Like most of the drawings, it is an isolated figure. This must have been an intentional choice since in a relocation camp there would have been people crowding everywhere. Wrenched from everything they had previously known and deposited amongst strangers, the residents would have felt adrift, perhaps even erased from view. In this figure, though, we are forced to confront the bleak realities of those days. The people who made it as far as the camp knew, however unthinkable, that they were the fortunate survivors. Did they consider themselves lucky? In making it from the past to this place, each would have seen, and escaped, unimaginable horrors, and now inescapably carries those horrors within. Not only were they witnesses to violence, but many would have lost loved ones to it. The possibility of even imagining a future must have been remote. The terrible current moment is all there is.

'Heavy Despair', figure 8 shows what could be the same man, but this time in a different pose. This image is unlike the others in many ways. It is just as hasty and urgent, but this time in watercolour/ink rather than pencil. There is background too, a step or lintel where the figure is seated and the suggestion of both a floor and a wall around him. While these things are available to the viewer, the subject is oblivious to them himself. The strong arms are supporting the bowed head, possibly raking the hair or even more likely, a static figure clearly full of vigour but marooned, unable to make any use of himself, unable to make any impact on the overwhelming events that brought him here. Poignant as this image is, it is counterpointed by others more hopeful. 'Company', figure 9 presents similar men, but this time with a sense of something like community.

Figure 8: 'Heavy Despair'

Figure 9: 'Company'

They sit companionably together talking as mildly as if they were in their home village but the lines of the tent remind us that they are not. The man in the foreground has the familiar strong body, a man in the prime of life and accustomed to work. The one on the left looks more gaunt, possibly elderly or frail. Along with the top knots, these connections and the suggestion of more people in the background give the impression that this is a family, and the men are deciding how best to manage. They are turned toward one another familiarly without either outrage or despair, faces open and receptive. It is said that when people find themselves in temporary situations, the first thing they do is make some kind of demarcation that indicates 'us' and 'ours' as part of the whole, but also separate, individual a point of recognition of that which can be maintained.

Of all the depictions of men, one of the most puzzling is 'Clean Sweep', figure 10, the gnome-like sweeper.

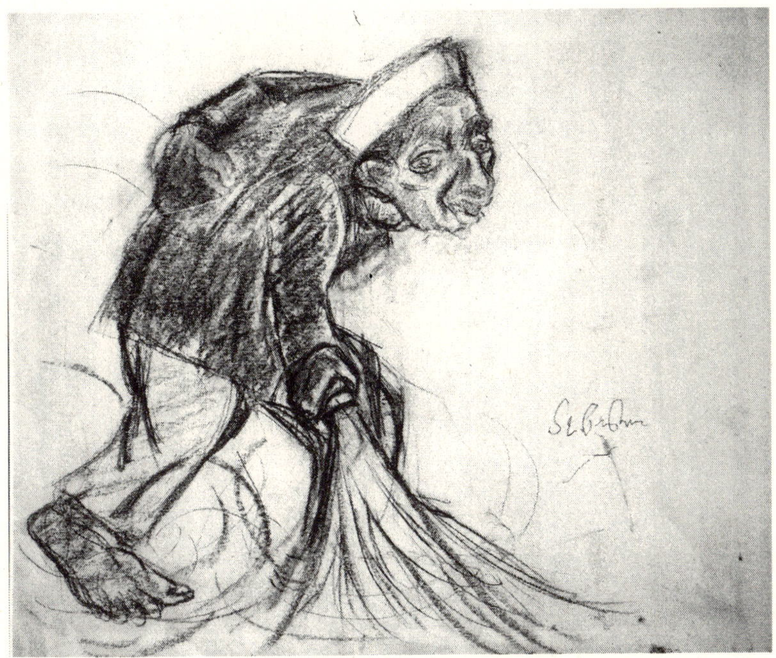

Figure 10: 'Clean Sweep'

With bent-over body and short legs, he is close to caricature, homely pleading face looking up at the artist. There is a resignation here, perhaps that as a sweeper he is in some uncomfortable way less dislocated than others. The right hand goes about its accustomed work here as anywhere else. Years with this tool have made him the same as his task, bent to the shape of necessity. He is suitably brought forth in charcoal, timeless as fate, an image of what felt immutable in a world turned topsy-turvy. It must have felt special in some way to Parasher himself, because he signed this one as he did few others. He could not have guessed when he recorded it that this incarnation of forever would soon slip into the past

The grief embedded in the sweeper's face is unlike that in another signed piece, 'Grief has no Voice', the two old people in figure 11.

Figure 11: 'Grief has no Voice'

They do not look at one another but their very propinquity suggests that they are a couple. She turns away, crabbed hands pulling her *dupatta* over her hair, expression of sorrow turned inward, hopeless. The man is equally hopeless but he faces forward, not looking at anything necessarily because the eyes are shrouded. The mouth is open as if he might be speaking, but nothing in this sealed-off face suggests he expects an answer. It is the stunned expression of one who has looked into disaster and shrivelled with the experience, static in recognition of his own diminishment.

Parasher catches this waiting posture most often in the figures of women – 'Calling Out', 'What Now?' 'Confining Grief', 'Together in Another Place'. See figures 12, 13, 14 and 15.

Figure 12: 'Calling Out'

Figure 13: 'What Now?'

They are usually seated on the ground, wrapped in their salwar kameez and dupattas, often in comforting groups. Their postures would have been utterly familiar, the same as they would have had at home, cooking, caring for a child, doing women's work. There's a little unexpected sorrow in the postscript that the future in divided India would make this way of living, as for the sweeper, a thing of the past for most of them. In *'Together in Another Place',* three lean

Figure 14: 'Confining Grief'

Figure 15: 'Together in Another Place'

close enough to touch, letting their bodies connect as their faces do not.

Many of the women are pictured in similar style. They are so swaddled in their garments that they appear almost as much like children as adults. The love expressed in these curvilinear shapes is complex though. In 'Small Comfort', they are crowded together as if herded there, very likely what they felt, but right in front we see one sturdy hand reach out to console her companion.

Figure 16: 'Waiting Change'

As often, the faces are covered, whether from modesty or despair we cannot tell. We do not know what they have already suffered, and like so much that never gets into the record, some of them must have experienced rape along with the ordinary insults of social breakdowns. What we do see are the bent backs, the vulnerable bare feet. The gentleness in these postures reminds us of their 'choicelessness', their inability to do more than wait. In 'Grief has no Voice', figure 17, we do see a couple of faces, but they are turned inward, closed to us.

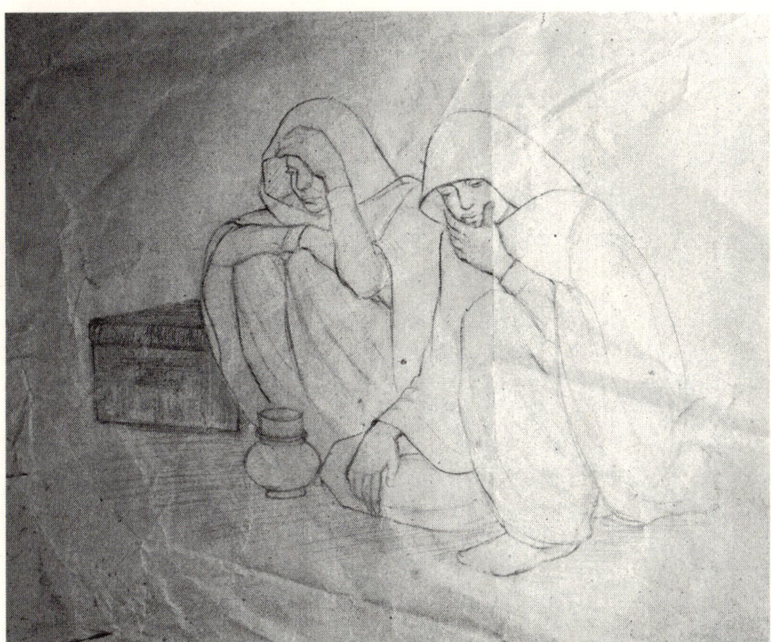

Figure 17: 'Grief has no Voice'

One woman has a water pot, one a box, and these artifacts are held close enough for her to look possessive. Although they are together, they are as isolated in their shock as in the single 'Curled Up', figure 18. Here the curved lines are almost ovoid, a visual image of Plath's 'I rocked shut / As a seashell', a body in such despair that it seals away from the world.

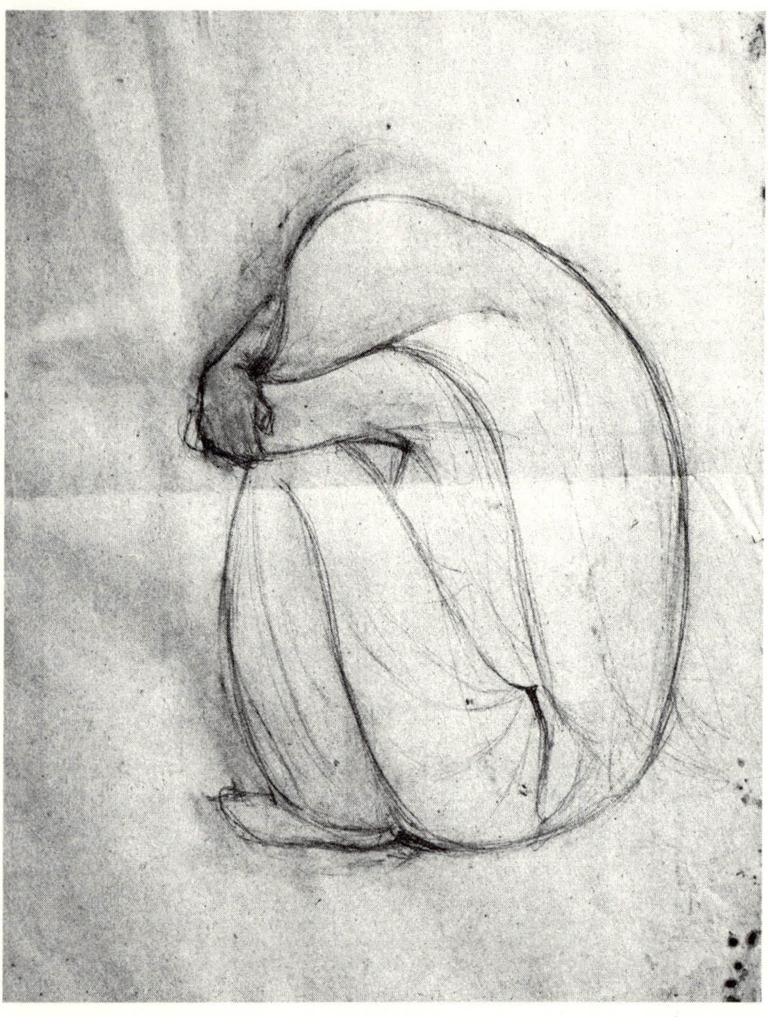

Figure 18: 'Curled Up'

Parasher maintains the softness of these lines whatever the women's posture. 'Anguish', Figure 19, are figures of entreaty, faces open and anguished, although a few are clearly individual portraits.

In 'What Now?' Figure 13, and 'Absence', Figure 25 there is no

Figure 19: 'Anguish'

effort to make the face recognizable. The feelings are. Not only is the whole body expressing urgency, but so are their expressions.

As in 'Calling Out', Figure 12, these are moments captured where the whole focus is winnowed down to a single, forceful request. It's

Figure 20: 'Absence'

not the same as the man in 'Cry I', Figure 6, though. Where he appears to be shaking his fist at the heavens, these women appear to be making a simpler, more immediate request. In that our father was asked to be commandant of the camp soon after his arrival there, this was a posture he may have seen often. I remember his stories of rotten or missing supplies, of inadequate responses, of rain and mud and flies.

Another vivid image of what life must have been like there is in 'Confining Grief', Figure14, where the seated women are in orderly rows as if marshalled together.

Although the faces are only sketched, it is easy to see that they are old and young together, docile and still waiting in front of some marker, a tree or a post or a wall—it is only suggested. Some of the artist's own patience is visible in the way the scene appears as peaceful as cowed. 'Waiting Change', Figure 16 and 'No Place', Figure 22 might be part of the same set of studies. In 'Nothing Safe', Figure 21 though we see some fraying of mood. What seems to have been an affectionate portrayal of a large family ends abruptly with a hectic scribble over one of the figures, as if it all were too impossibly much to try to record.

Beyond their haunting, there is also a photographic quality to these images. Like a photographer, a news photographer, Parasher recognized himself as witness and took on that responsibility too. With all the other things on his mind, this must have been primary: how to do it. As this writer was told at Terezin in 2009, 'We can show you how it looked, but we can't show you how it was, the bugs, the noise, the smell of fear.' Each of these images is a tiny cantonment, sealed like a locket. Here they are now, safe in their antiseptic frames. When they were sketched, it was far different. Overwrought by so much misery, my father said he often couldn't sleep and would roam the camp, drawing on whatever paper could be found. What he captured rises out of the emptied past, triumphant. While he was in some part a recorder, he was a memoirist as well. He, the person, was a resident of the camp, along with his wife and small children. There is enormous love behind the pencil, especially in the patient, huddled women. He knew them of course, the way he knew his own hand. That hand gestures out of the frames and into the room, whisking away time. Recognition of its gesture makes the past mutable.

Figure 21: 'Nothing Safe'

Figure 22: 'No Place'

NOTES

1. Cathy Caruth in *Unclaimed Experience: Trauma, Narrative and History* identifies the facets of the impossibility of telling in the face of trauma.
   a) Each individual position as a witness -- the level of being a witness to oneself within the experience, the level of being a witness to the testimonies of others, and the level of being a witness to the

process of witnessing itself. There is a cadence to violence and to recovery from violence. Apparently enough time has passed that we are now able to approach the subject of Partition, or let it approach us, over the gulf of time and space that it has created. Into the vacuum of our previous silence has fallen the inexpressible grief of those who experienced it, the occasional scraps of their speaking, the theatrical approximations of film recreations, and what records we can rescue, such as Urvashi Butalia's book, (1998) *The Other Side of Silence: Voices from the Partition of India* (New Delhi: Viking Penguin)

b) The Imperative to tell – the need to tell and thus come to know one's story. While there are still some alive who remember Partition and may be persuaded to speak, every year these are fewer. For the rest of us who do not ourselves remember, what we do remember is the way we are its creation. There is never enough – never enough words or the right words, there is never enough time or the right time, and never enough listening or the right listening to articulate the story that cannot be fully captured in thought, memory and speech. We can recognize this, and honour it as a permanent absence, not only the might-have-been, but what-is-instead.

c. The impossibility of telling - the imperative to tell the story of the Partition is inhabited by the impossibility of telling, and therefore, silence about the truth commonly prevails.

3. An event without a witness - during its historical occurrence, an event produces no reliable witnesses. How to understand or conceive of the Partition as a world in which the imagination of the other was no longer possible? Because the event had no witness to its truth, essentially it did not exist and thus signified its own reduction into absence. For the most part, we work out of this, using the imaginary to glue together the shards that are left.

4. Witnessing and restoration - Yet it is essential for the narrative of Partition that could not be articulated, to be told, to be transmitted, to be heard, and hence the importance of endeavours like Parasher's. The responsibility for bearing witness that previously he bore alone encounters today's viewers.

5. Prajna Parasher and Sandy Sterner (eds) *Time, Space, Light, Consciousness.*

6. A long note on the perspective of history: Our decisions in organizing the collection are based on three levels of temporality that Parasher's Partition line drawings depict:

First is that of the personal narrative also illustrated by things our father told us. This is oral as well as visual and revolves in a linear fashion from the beginning of disturbances through the way those large forces impacted personal lives.

Second is that of the collective narrative, the line drawings in this instance, but also in other narratives such as literature, film and drama. These accounts are not linear because they revolve around individual traumatic experiences that could recur and have recurred in other situations again, though of course not to the same people. Third is that of the nation's history narrativized in events of significance such as those found in meta/hegemonic accounts of the history textbooks. The first two (the personal and collective narratives) are necessarily intrinsically entwined and are brought to us in fragments of information loaded in memory. This temporality gives the past a different meaning, one hardly touched upon in the nation's history.

The chronology of Partition in the third type of temporality (i.e. the history textbooks) ignores the small and fragmentary mainly because it is not based on 'proper' sources of information; therefore, official records run parallel to the first two and the three never meet except in the memories of those who experienced them. In literature and the arts attempts are of course made to look at all these as part of a holistic account.

Art history has been less inclined than traditional history to incorporate spatiality. Scholarship disinclined to involve itself in individual concerns is increasingly making way for that straddling of different kinds of spaces. Those who found themselves in relocation camps would be living in:

1) The space of a lost homeland and the longing for a return to it; 2) the transitory space of the refugee camp; 3) the imagined space of the nation state belonging to us but with no specificity to lay claim on. A faceted viewpoint is important to emphasise since when one speaks only of time, language takes over and the simultaneity of space is lost. The whole question of loss is about space and not necessarily of the past; historical memory remains close to us as we remember constantly and it has multiple meanings of belonging, family and cultural embeddedness.

In London and here in Delhi or wherever we have travelled with our father's work we have kept this framework in mind and thought it was a good idea to divide the Partition sketches by time and space. A visit to the Gallery is designed as a return to this journey from home to homelessness. Here are the echoing cries left behind in the black silence after a conflagration, then a series of line drawings that figure women-- the most disturbing of the images in the camps. Women turned inward are the grounding of this experience as they are the grounding of family life. Reflected against their backs the impact of violence and other acts like those suggested by the Sikhs are in high focus and most articulately brought out. This is how we organize them, within a chronological sequence working along the lines of the personal, collective and the nation's narrative accounts. Out of all we have lost rises the importance to look at his works together rather than in separate compartments.

REFERENCES

Caruth, Cary. 1995. *Unclaimed Experience: Trauma, Narrative and History*, Baltimore: Johns Hopkins University Press.

Parasher, Prajna Paramita and Sandy Sterner, 2004. *Time, Space, Light, Consciousness*, New Delhi: SarNir Foundation.

CHAPTER 11

My Religion Is Less Violent than Yours

Myth, History and the Representation of Violence

JYOTIRMAYA SHARMA

On 23 December 1926, Swami Shraddhananda was murdered by Abdul Rashid. Shraddhanand was born Munshiram and acquired the name Shraddhananda after he renounced the world on 12 April, 1917 and became a *sanyasi*.[1] He belonged to the Arya Samaj. In his early forays into public life, he had a lofty disdain for politics because he felt that people in politics, especially Congress politics, did not have a pure and strong character, and were not men of worship/religion. He wanted people in public life to live according to Vedic ideals. Gandhi drew him to politics with the promise of bringing what Gandhi called 'dharmic aims' into the political realm. Though he had married and had a family, he considered *brahmacharya* or celibacy extremely important and as a central principle of the Arya Samaj, advocated it with enthusiasm. His espousal of celibacy was also something that attracted Gandhi's attention.

But soon differences between the two emerged. These were about Gandhi's 'dictatorial' style of functioning but also about the tactics of the civil disobedience movement and the operational details of satyagraha. He found Gandhi's non-cooperation too narrow, and felt it was purely destructive and not constructive. Over the boycott and burning of foreign cloth, their differences further deepened. He also felt that imposing the ideal of non-violence to the entire mass of people was impractical and ought to be restricted and enforced strictly only to members of organizations like the Congress. On closer scrutiny, it would seem that their differences were largely not over doctrinal or conceptual issues, but on questions of practical organization of political mass movements.

Another feature that remained an abiding concern was his campaign for the removal of untouchability, something that he shared with Gandhi, though here too, their differences only grew over the years. His agenda of educating, protecting and socially uplifting the untouchables was also closely connected in his pronouncements and writings with the question of conversion. He felt that the untouchables were becoming Muslims and Christians for non-religious reasons. He felt that conversion to Christianity made the untouchables denationalized and also made them supporters of the Raj. While he wanted to abolish untouchability, he also wanted the re-establishment of the Vedic *varnadharma* by abolition of castes and sub-castes.

He was also an early proponent of Hindu-Muslim unity, something that would dramatically change later. After a riot in Delhi in 1919, wearing the ochre robes of a *sanyasi*, he even preached from the Jama Masjid. In the early 1920s, he was part of the Khilafat deputation to the Viceroy. Between 1920 and 1922, he transformed from being pro-Khilafat to entertaining deep distrust of Muslims at all levels. Initially, he supported Khilafat because he was a staunch votary of religious freedom. In this newfound, though short-lived, unity between Hindus and Muslims, Shraddhananda saw an opportunity to push his agenda of ending slaughter of cows on the part of the Muslims. He soon clashed with Gandhi on several issues connected with Khilafat, the Moplah rebellion and also the attitude of Muslim Congressmen towards the depressed classes. By 1921-22, he was arguing that for Muslims, 'Islam comes first and Mother India second'. This impelled him towards *sangathan*, an effort to bring about Hindu unity.[2]

In the period after 1922, as his disenchantment with Muslims grew stronger, he unfolded an initiative called *shuddhi*, which took the form of reconversion of converted Muslims and Christians back to Hinduism. For him, *shuddhi* was an integral part of the move to bring about *sangathan*. He advocated a radical distancing of Hindus from all things to do with Muslims, including not participating in Muslim festivals, not venerating Muslim saints and visiting Muslim shrines. *Shuddhi* and *sangathan* further vitiated the relations between Hindus and Muslims. All this led to much criticism, including a scathing indictment of Shraddhananda, his mentor, Swami Dayananda and the Arya Samaj by Gandhi. Shraddhananda rejected the claim that Hindu-Muslim unity had been impaired by *shuddhi* and *sangathan*; it was the hostility and the crookedness of the Muslims that brought it about. He wrote vigorously against Muslims and Islam, calling Islam 'blind faith', and in 1924 arranged for the translation of Joseph von Hammer's *History of the Assassins* to which he wrote an introduction. His intent was to show that certain Christian and Muslim sects had used assassination as part of their tradition and that this was not an aberration: it was a natural consequence of their 'blind faith'.

—

Gandhi reacted to the murder in a tribute published in *Young India* on 30 December 1926. (*CWMG*, Vol. 37: 455-57) Titled 'Shraddhanandji – The Martyr', Gandhi begins by recalling Swami Shraddhanand's visit to the Satyagraha Ashram at Sabarmati six months before his assassination. Shraddhanand had spoken to Gandhi about threats to his life during this visit. Gandhi terms the assassination as nothing 'untoward'. Reformers, he argues, have always a price on their head and, therefore, there was nothing 'untoward' in either receiving threats or these threats being carried out. He calls Shraddhanand a reformer, a man of action, a 'living belief', 'bravery personified', a man who never 'quailed before danger' and one who suffered for his beliefs. At the very outset, Gandhi does two things: he places reformers in a unique category by attributing special virtues and character traits to them, but by doing so, he normalizes the act of the assassin, the very fact of the murder.

When Shraddhanand was murdered, he was ill and confined to his sick-bed. Gandhi also slips in the fact that his physician was Dr Ansari, a Muslim, who was 'giving him all the loving attention he was capable of giving.' Despite being on a sick-bed, Shraddhanand, Gandhi asserts, had died the death of a warrior, for a 'warrior loves to die, not on a sick-bed, but on the battlefield.' Gandhi pushes the argument further: he was no ordinary warrior. He was chosen by God to die a martyr's death. He was no ordinary martyr either: after all, despite his illness, he agreed to meet his future assassin in order to hold a religious discourse on Islam. Implying that Shraddhanand was a religious martyr, Gandhi speculates about Shradhhanand's last words while being felled by the assassin's bullets and comes to the conclusion that he would have forgiven his assassin 'who knew not that he was doing anything wrong.' Having invoked Christ's words on the cross, Gandhi then cites the *Bhagvadgita* ideal of an individual dying fighting a righteous war: 'Happy the warrior who achieves such a blessed death.' Lapsing into a long discourse on death, Gandhi considers death at any given point of time 'blessed' and more so for a warrior who dies for a cause. In his case, death is twice blessed because the cause for which righteous warriors and religious martyrs die is truth. Death is no fiend, but a friend. Death helps us against ourselves, gives us new hopes, and releases us from agony. Like sleep, death is a 'sweet restorer.' The death of martyrs like Shraddhanand was not an occasion to be mourned; his glorious death had to be envied. Shraddhanand lived the life of a hero and died a hero, concludes Gandhi. Significantly, Gandhi acknowledges that Shraddhanand had not sought martyrdom and hence unsought martyrdom was even a greater joy and a reason to celebrate.

Next, Gandhi turns his attention to the murderer, Abdul Rashid. For him, Rashid's act was a 'foul deed' done by an individual who 'bears a Muslim name'. He was 'an erring, misguided brother' and asks Muslims, as a community, not to 'gloat over the errors of the least of our fellows.' Similarly, he asks Hindus 'not to ascribe the crime of an individual to a whole community.' He even goes to the extent of pleading that Hindus ought not to consider the murder as a wrong 'done by a Mussalman against a Hindu, but of an erring brother against a hero.' Gandhi says he wanted to plead on behalf of the assassin, even though he did not know Abdul Rashid. Even more dramatically, Gandhi refuses even to be interested in the reasons that impelled Abdul Rashid to kill Shraddhanand. For Gandhi, the assassin was possessed by a 'hot fever' that made him murder Shraddhanand. In fact, the 'erring, misguided brother' had tempered the joy of Shraddhanand's death to an extent because it had come in the hands of an erring, misguided, possessed and febrile individual. In saying so, he absolves Abdul Rashid from any direct responsibility and control over his actions; the 'foul deed' of the 'erring brother' is, instead blamed on the media for spreading the 'contagion of lies and calumnies.' It is the newspaperman who injects the virus of secret and insidious propaganda into the unsuspecting and receptive minds of the educated and semi-educated class of people and it is with them that the responsibility for the assassin being possessed by a 'hot fever' lay.

But this is not all. The narrative switches constantly between assertions, generalizations and themes that can best be described as contradictory and confusing. Though at one point Shraddhanand's assassination was the 'foul deed' of an individual 'who bears a Muslim name', Gandhi also simultaneously claims that he considered himself a friend of all Muslims. In the very next sentence, he calls Muslims, not just his friends, but his 'blood-brothers', establishing a bond where their wrongs are his wrongs and he shares their joys and sorrows in equal measure. What was described as the foul deed of an individual now assumes the character of a tragedy of national importance, an 'evil that is eating into the vitals of the nation', where Hindus and Muslims are called upon to exercise the choice of eliminating evil and error. Almost suddenly, Gandhi finds both Hindus and Muslims collectively culpable of Shraddhanand's murder: 'We are both on our trial'. Having so addressed both communities, he begins to address each of them separately. Understandably, the arguments are couched within the discourse of the intractable problem of Hindu-Muslim unity.

Resentful of Shraddhanand's murder, Gandhi fears that Hindus might harbour the spirit of retaliation. He asks them to exercise self-restraint and forgiveness, and for both he invokes elements from within the Hindu religious tradition. For self-restraint, he recommends the *Upanishads* and in the case of forgiveness, he asks them to emulate Yudhisthira, one of the principal characters in the epic *Mahabharata*. Lack of self-restraint and forgiveness would vitiate efforts for Hindu-Muslim unity and would result in ascribing the crime of an individual to a whole community. Turning to the Muslims, he begins by warning them of the ordeal they will have to pass through as a result of the murder. What follows the warning is clearly an orientalist caricature, historically inaccurate and politically contentious. Gandhi agrees with the general impression that Muslims 'are too free with the knife and the pistol.' He immediately retracts and clarifies that the sword was 'no emblem of Islam' and almost immediately adds that Islam was born in an environment where the sword was and still 'remains the supreme law.' Keeping intact the 19th century distinction between religion as cult and religion as moral action, he considers the message of Jesus Christ and of Prophet Mohammad as embodying a 'reflecting faith', but their message was lost because the environment was not ready to receive it. If Muslims secretly endorsed Shraddhanand's murder, Gandhi warns, it would bring upon them a calamity of universal proportions. He wants them to unequivocally condemn 'the atrocity' and issues them an ultimatum: 'The sword is yet too much in evidence among Mussalmans. It must be sheathed if Islam is to be what it means – peace.... Reliance upon the sword is wholly inconsistent with reliance upon God.'

Two ideas stand out in this short essay. The first is a generalization that figures early in the narrative. Error does not become obvious and open to scrutiny – the word Gandhi uses is patent – till it becomes atrocious. Once it becomes atrocious, Gandhi continues, it is disgraced, and, once disgraced, it dies. Closely tied to this is the striking last paragraph where Gandhi extols the greatness of Shraddhanand and hopes that 'his blood may wash our guilt, cleanse our hearts and cement these two mighty divisions of the human family.'

As stated at the end of this piece, Gandhi promises a more personal portrait of Shraddhanand in the next issue of *Young India*. The piece appears on 6 January 1927. (*CWMG*, Vol. 38: 13–16) Two important themes emerge from this essay. Differences between Shraddhanand and Gandhi over *shuddhi* is the first significant point. Gandhi's rejects the idea of *shuddhi* as proposed and practised by Shraddhanand and voices his general misgivings about conversion. He believes that a liberal study of world religions would radically alter the ways in which faiths emphasized form rather than substance while proselytizing people. Conversion based on mutual indictment could only lead to hatred and violence. Shraddhanand advocated *shuddhi*, or reconversion to Hinduism, of converted Muslims and Christians and paid with his life for his beliefs. But his assassination, Gandhi suggests, could become an opportunity for Hindus and Muslims to understand that self-purification constituted the real and deeper meaning of *shuddhi*. A second significant point is Gandhi's attempt to clarify Shraddhanand's stand on Muslims. He argues that though Shraddhanand distrusted some Muslims, he was no hater of Muslims. In fact, what seems as his hatred of Muslims was only his mission to make Hindus brave and equip them to defend themselves and their honour.

On 20 January 1927 (ibid.: 85–88), Gandhi revisits the theme of the Shraddhanand murder in *Young India*. In a piece titled 'A Candid Critic', he begins by reproducing a letter by a reader. The reader wonders if Gandhi really was a saint as he had compromised the all-important relation between a saint and truth. Gandhi, the anonymous reader charges, had not condemned the 'sword of Islam' adequately and not drawn the correct inference about the act of an individual tainting the entire community. He had further supressed the truth by calling Islam a religion of peace and was unduly harsh on the Arya Samaj for its activities related to *shuddhi*. He objects to Gandhi only calling Muslims his blood-brothers. If Gandhi was a saint and a truth-teller, he would be fearless and answer his questions. Gandhi's reply reiterates that the murderer was hardly responsible, both as an individual and as representative of his faith. Religions, Gandhi elaborates, are always pure and aspire for peace. The pure, lofty and original core of religions is transformed into religious violence due to misinterpretation and irreligious propaganda of their followers. Therefore, he condemns the murder but not the murderer.

Turning to the question of religions, Gandhi suggests that religious scriptures are products of historical contexts and are hardly universally applicable forever. Religions, then, constantly evolve and evolve for the better. For these reasons alone, no final interpretation of any prophet's message is possible. Saying so, he returns to discussing individual faiths and their fidelity to peace:

> But I do regard Islam to be a religion of peace in the same sense as Christianity, Buddhism and Hinduism are. No doubt there are *differences in degree*, but the object of these religions is peace. I know

> the passages that can be quoted from the Koran to the contrary. But so is it possible to quote passages from the Vedas to the contrary. What is the meaning of imprecations pronounced against the Anaryas? Of course these passages bear today a different meaning but at one time they did wear a dreadful aspect. What is the meaning of the treatment of untouchables by us Hindus? Let not the pot call the kettle black. The fact is that we are all growing. I have given my opinion that the followers of Islam are too free with the sword. But that is not due to the teaching of the Koran. This is due in my opinion to the environment in which Islam was born. Christianity has a bloody record against it, not because Jesus was found wanting, but because the environment in which it spread was not responsive to his lofty teaching. (ibid: 85-88)

Having emphasized the need for religions to evolve and to constantly reinterpret themselves in the light of the present context, Gandhi begins concluding his reply by insisting that the seat of religion was in the heart. To this end, that is, of locating religion in the heart, he comes up with an unconventional solution. He is emphatic that Hindus, Muslims and Christians can write the interpretations of their respective faiths in one way alone, and that is, 'with our own crimson blood.'

—

Gandhi's reply to the anonymous reader elicits a sharp response from Vinayak Damodar Savarkar, the pre-eminent Hindu nationalist thinker. For Savarkar, the question of which faith is more peace-loving than the other is easily resolved through a 'cursory' look at history. In the light of this 'cursory' look at history, Savarkar terms Gandhi's assertion about Islam an 'audacious testimony'. For him, this 'audacious testimony' reflected Gandhi's ignorance of history. Armed with history as the arbiter of all contentious issues, Savarkar isolates Gandhi's assertion that the seat of religion lies in the heart and pours scorn on it. In prose dripping with sarcasm, he subjects Gandhi's statement to historical scrutiny through a set of carefully chosen rhetorical devices. The 'cursory' history that unfolds is a story of Islamic violence (not Muslim violence) and Hindu compassion towards the victims of this violence. He rejects Gandhi's assertion that Islam's fondness for the sword was to be understood in terms of 'the errors of unfavourable circumstances'. The history of Islam for him is an illness that requires correct diagnosis and only a degree of objectivity in reading Islamic history would help in correctly diagnosing the illness and recommending a cure. Gandhi is blamed squarely for his criticism of the Arya Samaj and for ignoring Muslim aggression and other mala fide intentions against the Hindus. Through the prism of the same 'cursory' history, Savarkar finds the Hindu past devoid of any violence. It was this love of non-violence that had not stood them in good stead. Savarkar exhorts Hindus to become violent in the future, adding that all forms of Hindu violence will always, of course, be dharmic or righteous.

—

The three pieces written by Gandhi after Shraddhanand's murder and Savarkar's reaction to the last essay raise three distinct lines of inquiry. The first relates to our understanding of Gandhi's representation of violence, but, more significantly, his formulation of non-violence. The second question interrogates Gandhi's understanding of Hindus and Muslims and their respective religions. Both questions assume a critical importance because the post-Partition narratives have sought to divide our understanding of history into a world divided between men of light and men of darkness. The non-violent Gandhi is often pitted against Hindu nationalists as enthusiastic advocates of violence. Rather, it is useful to see the ideas of this entire period as a heady mixture of European modernity, orientalism, ideas of reform and restatement of society and religion forming the foundational basis for much of what masquerades as the decisive versions of nationalism. These premises and assumptions are often shared by the Hindu nationalists and the secular nationalists alike. If there is a difference, it is in the politics, and, in the practice of this politics. Finally, the contradictions that emerge from Gandhi's reaction to Shraddhanand's murder are to be seen as part of the suggested answers to the question of representation of violence and to Gandhi's understanding of Hinduism and Islam.

Looking at the narratives above, there are a number of themes that jostle for attention: the tendency of reducing all questions to questions of religion; martyrdom and the status of a warrior felled on the battlefield; questions of individual and collective guilt; the legitimacy of a righteous war; self-purification. If one were to just select a few striking elements from within the three narratives illustrated above, there must be a way of making sense of his likening Shraddhanand's murder as nothing untoward, his celebration of death and portraying it as martyrdom in the cause of a religious war. For finding answers to these questions, we must return to Gandhi's commentary on the *Bhagvadgita*, a text that is part of the larger epic, the *Mahabharata.* At the very outset, Gandhi refuses to acknowledge the *Gita*, or, indeed the *Mahabharata*, as historical texts. History was only a guise and physical warfare only a poetic metaphor to describe the perpetual internal duel in the battlefield of the human body between right and wrong. While the people described in the *Mahabharata* and the *Gita* may be historical, the author of the epic uses them only to drive home a religious point. In fact, Gandhi interprets the crucial second chapter of the *Gita*, where the argument regarding the immortality of the soul and the dispensability of the human body is articulated, as one where the real focus is the way in which a perfected man is known. Detachment, allegiance to truth, distaste of falsehood and non-violence is the theme of the *Gita* as indeed of the entire epic. He acknowledges that non-violence had been a 'primary duty' even before the *Gita* was composed; indeed, the *Gita* may not have been written to establish the primacy of non-violence. Rather, not questing after the fruit of one's action was the central message of the *Gita*, because desire for the fruit of one's action lies at the roots of untruth and violence.

The warlike illustration in the *Gita* is further explained. Gandhi concedes that at the time of the writing of the text, while people believed in non-violence, war might not have been discredited and was certainly not taboo. Hence, few would have noticed the contradiction between the desirability of non-violence and the fact of war. Moreover, words change and so do the meaning of words. The poem makes it its business to argue that non-violence was impossible to attain without the renunciation of the fruit of action. That is the real meaning, then, of sacrifice in the *Gita.* It is not sacrifice of animals nor is it the ritual sacrifice of the Vedic kind.

Continuous concentration on God to the exclusion of all else is the sacrifice that the *Gita* preaches, concludes Gandhi. In assuming that by merely denying the historicity of the war and expunging the violent bits in favour of what seems a lofty metaphysics, he would be able somehow to alter the context and the longevity of the social structures that circumscribe the *Gita*'s unambiguous legitimizing of fratricidal violence and murder. Indeed, the message of the tenability of fratricidal violence remains to this day the widely accepted and popular, if not incontrovertible, reading of the text.

Turning to Gandhi's understanding of differences in faiths, the inevitable starting point for him is the need for understanding and clarifying. In the face of conflict between two faiths, comparison leads to understanding. Understanding is the way forward towards clarifying the contentious issue; together, understanding and clarifying provide solutions to religious strife. All faiths are true after comparison and all religions are paths to the same God. (*CWMG*, Vol 4: 242-47) After this initial generalisation, Gandhi asserts that there is little to distinguish between Hindus and Indians: '[T]he ways and manners of the Hindus and other Indians are all but identical' (ibid.: 234). Except devout Hindus, not all Hindus might believe in the divine origins of the Vedas but share common features such as belief in Brahman, quest for moksha, ethics driven by even-mindedness and humility, and temporal affairs driven entirely by caste. Gandhi makes no attempt here to relate the spiritual, ethical and temporal realms. Moreover the question of belief supercedes the much more contentious question of temporal affairs and the role of caste. He turns to Buddhism next. He sees Buddhism as a reaction to Hinduism's growing enchantment with the outward forms of religion and the Buddha as someone who merely 'suggested' reforms within a unified entity called Hindusim. Reminiscent of the standard nineteenth and early twentieth century views, Gandhi rejects the idea that the Buddha founded a new or different religion; indeed, Hinduism and Buddhism were one and the same and had identical fundamental principles. (ibid: 244) The separate identity of Buddhism was the work of the Buddha's followers who came after him to fashion a distinctive faith. All Buddhism's virtues of peace, debate, discussion, persuasion and non-violence are subsumed and annexed as the strengths of Hinduism or what Gandhi calls 'the distinctive beauty of Hinduism'. (ibid.)

Next, Gandhi turns to what he calls the profound influence of Islam on Hinduism. At the outset, he offers a general assessment of Islam, one that is again strikingly similar to that of a nineteenth century figure like Swami Vivekananda: 'Zeal or passion, then, is a great speciality, a mighty force, of Islam. It has been the cause of many good deeds, and sometimes of bad ones too'. (ibid.) A history of Islam in India follows: 'A thousand years ago the army of Ghazni invaded India in order to spread Islam. Hindu idols were broken and the invasion advanced as far as Somnath'. (ibid.: 244-45) Zeal, passion, proselytizing, breaking idols – that is the initial picture of Islam. Did Islam do any good? Gandhi asserts that while violence was used, Muslim saints were also preaching the real merits of Islam. What were these? The Muslim saints taught the Islamic principle that all those who embraced Islam were equals. Was it a good thing? Gandhi says it made a favourable impression on the lower classes/castes and hundreds of thousands of Hindus converted to Islam. This caused a 'great commotion in the whole [Hindu] community'. (ibid.: 245) Kabir tried to bring a synthesis between Hindus and Muslims. What was the foundation of this synthesis? Gandhi says that it was Kabir's belief that according to Hindu philosophy, there could be no distinction between a Hindu and a Muslim. Kabir's teaching did not have much of an impact and his followers were reduced to being a distinct sect. Influenced by Kabir, Guru Nanak too tried to bring Hindus and Muslims together. But Nanak's Sikhism was premised on the belief that along with efforts to bring about unity between Hindus and Muslims, Hinduism had to be defended against Islam, and, if necessary, with the help of the sword.

Gandhi's portrait of Buddhism and Islam shares several common features: the frequent threats to Hinduism, the ability of Hinduism to withstand these threats, the distinctive beauty of Hinduism to absorb foreign currents. In sharp contrast, other faiths challenge, convert, desecrate, unleash violence and cause commotion. In the case of Islam, it appeals only to the lower classes. In this portrait of encounter with other faiths, Hinduism and Hindus are superior, but also innocent victims. Just as one begins to see a pattern in his understanding of religions in relation to Hinduism, Gandhi makes an assertion that renders his views on religion at once ambiguous and paradoxical:

> The result of all this is that, despite the prevalence of Hinduism and Islam as the two principal religions of India today, both the communities live together in peace and amity and are considerate enough not to hurt one another's feelings save for the bitterness caused by political machinations and excitement. There is very little difference between a Hindu yogi and a Muslim fakir. (ibid.)

Put differently, in the spiritual realm the two principal religions are similar but in the temporal realm they tend to hurt each other. A few sentences later, Gandhi finds the Christians alighting in Goa at a time when 'Islam and Hinduism were vying with each other'. (ibid.)

What did the Christians do after reaching India? Like the Muslims, they 'set about converting Hindus to Christianity'. (ibid.) and in doing so used force and persuasion in the same way as Muslims had done in the past. The Christian clergy, like Muslim fakirs too were kind-hearted and generous and their appeal lay with the lower classes of Hindu society. Over a period of time, says Gandhi, the Western civilization and Christianity got conflated and Christianity began to find disfavour among the Hindus. Gandhi concedes that Christian priests not only imparted education of a high quality in India but also pointed out to some glaring defects in Hinduism. This influenced reformers and reformist organizations in India and had a considerable impact of Hinduism as well. The Theosophists too told the Hindus and Muslims of the evils of Western civilization.

Having summarized the religions of India, Gandhi proceeds to highlight the tenets of Hinduism. While most of it reflects a popular 19th century view that combines neo-Vedanta along with arbitrarily chosen set of concepts and categories from a host of schools, sects and popular beliefs. He admits to a plurality of schools and sects, but perceives them as resulting from a difference not in doctrine but from variations in secular practices. For Gandhi, what is important is his belief in a beleaguered, assaulted, attacked, victimized, and, yet, triumphant Hinduism:

> Thus, we have seen how there have been three assaults on Hinduism, coming from Buddhism, Islam and then Christianity, but how on the whole it came out of them unscathed. It tried to imbibe whatever was good in each of these religions. (ibid: 246)

Did this view, held in 1905, alter in later years? Writing in *Young India* on 24 April 1924, Gandhi argues that 'it is the good fortune or the misfortune of Hinduism that it has no official creed.' (*CWMG*, Vol. 27: 292) He proceeds to define the Hindu creed for himself: 'I should simply say: search after Truth through non-violent means.' (ibid.)It is crucial to note that truth and non-violence have been defined as Gandhi's *Hindu* creed. Having so defined his religious credo as a Hindu, Gandhi summarizes his version and understanding of Hinduism:

> A man may not believe even in God and still call himself a Hindu. Hinduism is a relentless pursuit after truth and, if today it has become moribund, inactive, irresponsive to growth, it is because we are fatigued, and as soon as the fatigue is over, Hinduism will burst forth upon the world with a brilliance perhaps unknown before. Of course, therefore, Hinduism is the most tolerant of all religions. Its creed is all-embracing. But to claim that is to claim superiority for the Hindu creed over all other creeds of the world. (ibid.)

Gandhi's thesis is one that he shared with almost all 19th century reformers of religion and as also later-day Hindu nationalists. With every assertion of Hindu superiority, there is also in Gandhi the relentless exhortation of all religions preaching mutual respect, love, kindness and co-existence.

While the texts cited till now might emerge from responses to actual political situations, they tend to be biased towards greater generalizations, instances where Gandhi is called upon to clarify doctrinal issues connected with Hinduism. In contrast, the essay titled 'To Hindus',[3] written in August 1920, places Gandhi in the midst of the Khilafat issue and the question of Hindu-Muslim unity. (*CWMG*, Vol. 21: 209–10) He begins by clearly stating the political agenda: India's good lay in unity between Hindus and Muslims. Starkly put, three-fourths of India could never hope to enjoy freedom while remaining hostile to the one-fourth. Equally impossible was the extermination of seven crore Muslims. (ibid.: 209) Having barely stated the political position on the Hindu-Muslim question, Gandhi returns to examining the Hindu-Muslim question in religious and emotive terms. He rejects the idea that Hinduism enjoyed the protection of British rule. Calling it a humiliating suggestion, he feels that twenty-three crore Hindus ought to be strong enough to defend themselves against Muslims. If they were unable to do so, either the Hindu religion was false or those who believed in it lacked courage and were wicked. Gandhi also dismisses the idea of the British maintaining an artificial peace between the Hindus and the Muslims. Instead, he would prefer that Hindus and Muslims 'settled their accounts by means of the sword.' (ibid.)

In transforming a political problem into a religious problem, Gandhi makes a number of assumptions. He legitimizes the idea that Hindus and Hinduism needed protection and defending against Muslims and Islam. But he also implants the idea that there were scores that still needed settling between Hindus and Muslims. Winning Muslim hearts was crucial also to ensure protecting cows, protecting Hindu temples and protecting Hindu women. A friendly approach to the Muslims and winning their hearts was the substitute for settling scores and living with them as brothers. Gandhi deftly conflates the political and the religious agendas. On the one hand he clearly delineates the need for Hindu-Muslim unity being imperative for India's good, and on the other, he clearly spells out what he perceives to be the Muslim threat. While he emphasises that Khilafat was the opportunity that 'will not come again for a hundred years', (ibid.) he also continues to harp on the fundamental reasons for Hindu distrust of Muslims. He says: 'To be sure, you will find in history cases of injustice done by Muslims.' (ibid.) The case for Hindu-Muslim unity is presented again in religious terms. The religion of the Muslims is noble and Muslims are a noble people. Despite injustices committed against the Hindus in the past, Islam was a religion that respected other people's faith and had compassion. Muslims also knew how to repay an obligation.

This idea of the Muslim propensity to repay an obligation is extended further. Gandhi asks the Hindus to work for unity unconditionally. Muslims required a change of heart and this cannot be accomplished keeping in mind 'a shop-keeper's calculations'. (ibid. 210) Hindu religion teaches one to expect no reward for good deeds and also preaches that trust always produces good. What is the obligation that Muslims would eventually repay? The question is never directly answered. But Gandhi asks the question about a possible scenario where, despite Hindu attempts to forge unity and forget the injustices meted out to them in the past, Muslims betrayed Hindu generosity. Gandhi's answer unravels the complexities inherent in the nationalist discourse. It also calls into question the excessive use of religion in order to grapple with political and social issues.

The Gandhian framework was clear. Muslims had committed injustices in the past. Essentially, Islam was a religion of peace, tolerance and compassion. But it posed a threat to Hindus and the good of India lay in forging Hindu-Muslim unity. Hindu generosity ought to be unconditional and would bind Muslims in their debt. Since Muslims knew how to repay an obligation, they would be compelled to change their hearts and work towards unity. In the eventuality of Muslims betraying these generous Hindu overtures, the Hindus would still have to deal with the constant and uninterrupted Muslim threat. Here Gandhi suggests that in the likelihood of a betrayal, Hindus will not be cowards and will have the strength to protect their religion. In fact, in helping Muslims, Hindus will acquire the strength to defend and protect their own religion. Why? Through supporting Muslims in the context of Khilafat, 'in the process, Hindus will have to display the great qualities of determination, courage, truthfulness, capacity for self-sacrifice, unity, organizing ability, etc.' (ibid.) The argument that weak Hindus, in helping Muslims, would gain strength is dropped with alacrity as soon as it is formulated. Hindus ought to help Muslims because it was their duty to help them in a cause that was just and the means to attain their goals were just too. In performing this highest duty, every Hindu would be 'saving India and protecting his religion.'[4] Neither consideration of reward nor fear of betrayal ought to enter the minds of the Hindus in discharging their duty towards their Muslim neighbours. It was nothing short of a yajna, where everything had to be sacrificed. Whether or not Hindus make this sacrifice, they at least ought to understand the 'true meaning of this war'. (ibid.) Which war? Gandhi does not tell us.

In reading these narratives, simple binaries rarely help. Contradictions assail and seemingly dissonant voices confuse. Intellectually lazy portraits of one set of thinkers and leaders as heroes and another similar set as villains does not takes us too far. Questions of violence and non-violence too have to be traced to the invoking of tradition, and, within tradition, the centrality of religious symbols and metaphors. A modest beginning has to be an attitude that is more sceptical about our own tradition, questioning self-assumed identities and interrogating the voice and authority of traditionally privileged individuals, icons and texts. Put differently, there is a tension between an entrenched nationalism that seeks to selectively deify individuals versus the demands of an empirically rigorous and analytically unconventional interpretation. The only way to forge a dialogue between these two seemingly antagonistic positions is to delineate themes, concepts and categories that require further interrogation. The task of writing the histories of modern India can sometimes just be to chronicle contradictions and no more.

NOTES

1. A fairly good biography of Swami Shraddhanand is that of J.T.F. Jordens. See, J.T.F. Jordens (1981). Also see Fischer-Tiné (2000).
2. For examples of differences over a number of issues between Gandhi and Shraddhanand, see, *The Collected Works of Mahatma Gandhi* (henceforth, *CWMG*), Vol. 28, pp. 43–62; pp. 96–99; pp. 138–140; Vol. 29, pp. 141–145.
3. *CWMG,* Vol. 21, pp. 209–210.
4. Ibid., p. 210.

REFERENCES

Fischer-Tiné, Harald. 2000.'Kindly Elders of the Hindu Biradri: The Ārya Samāj's Struggle for Influence and Its Effect on Hindu–Muslim Relations, 1880–1925', in Antony Copley (ed.), *Gurus and Their Followers: New Religious Reform Movements in Colonial India*, New Delhi: Oxford University Press.

Jordens, J.T.F. 1981.*Swami Shraddhanand: His Life and Causes.* New Delhi: Oxford University Press.

The Collected Works of Mahatma Gandhi. 1999. New Delhi: Publications Division Government of India, 98 volumes (ebooks). http://www.gandhiashramsevagram.org/mkgandhi/cwmg/cwmg.html (accessed on 30 April 2014).

CHAPTER 12

Bad Times and Sad Moods*

ALOK SARIN, SARAH GHANI AND SANJEEV JAIN

Abrupt and sudden dislocation, loss of social rootedness and exposure to social unrest have all been identified as causes of trauma. It is now also widely accepted that such trauma can make people more susceptible to developing physical and mental health problems. There has been considerable documentation of the long-lasting effects of politically motivated violence, on both victims (Schick et al. 2013; Sharon et al. 2009) and perpetrators (Bayntun 2005). The partition of India in 1947 was accompanied by large-scale migrations, violence and the breakdown of established civic life in large parts of the region. While this can be seen as part of the general shifting of populations in the post-World War II reorganisation of 'national boundaries' in Europe, its effects on the newly decolonised regions in Asia and Africa were vastly different. These emerging states did not have the adequate administrative or medical infrastructure to cope with this unprecedented transmigration, especially since this was attended by horrific acts of violence, looting and sexual assault.

While the Holocaust, the disintegration of Yugoslavia (Kunitz 2004) and violence in Africa have been associated with high rates

* This work was supported in part by a grant from the Wellcome Trust, 'Turning the Pages' (096493/Z/11/Z). The immense help of Prof. Pratima Murthy, Prof. P.S.V.N. Sharma and Dr P. Radhika is gratefully acknowledged, as is the participation of all the respondents to the questionnaire, with whom we plan to have further conversations.

of trauma and disease, other events such as the reunification of Germany (Achberger, Linden and Benkert 1999) do not seem to have resulted in any major impact on mental health. There is, however, very little literature in the medical field on the impact of political violence on mental health parameters in the 'developing' countries of the Third World.

In the specific context of India, partition was accompanied by significant difficulties of both mental and general health. There was widespread violence, the death of about half a million people (estimates vary widely), and significant physical and sexual assault, arson and looting as well as the destruction of property (Brass 2003). It was against this backdrop that the largest transmigration of people in human history took place, and it is estimated that upwards of 15 million were moved across the new borders in traumatic and tumultuous circumstances (Kamtekar 1995; Khwaja, Mian and Bharadwaj 2008). The available infrastructure to either control the violence, or support the migration and 'resettlement' of the refugees was woefully inadequate; the magnitude of the phenomenon had clearly been underestimated, and apparently 'unexpected' (Shone 1947). There is considerable documentation of the migration and translocation, as well as the acts of brutal and inhuman violence in which both major religious communities were equally victims and perpetrators. The likelihood that this would cause psychological impact in the short and the long term seems obvious (Portney 2003). Intriguingly, however, there is little documentation or exploration of this kind of psychological impact – something that seems strange for what was clearly a phenomenon of some magnitude.

Over the past decades, there has been increasing awareness of the 'silence' regarding this event (Butalia 1998), and awareness of its long-lasting psychological consequences has also grown. In the absence of any public acknowledgement of the trauma, or an understanding of its reasons and how it can be addressed, most individuals and families have coped as best as they could. The absence of any discussions about these events, and their impact on health, has led to a spiral of silence, so that the impact of subsequent political violence on social parameters (including health services) or psychological health is also largely absent from the public gaze. The human cost of these is, thus, not understood, and no interventions are planned.

In recent times, however, we have seen a growing awareness of the 'inter-generational transmission of trauma' (Portney 2003). While most of the available literature on this focuses on victims of the Holocaust, it stands to reason that other traumatic experiences, like that of the violence linked to partition, would be just as likely to lead to such intergenerational transmission of trauma. There are important differences to note though: unlike the violence of the Holocaust, violence during partition was not restricted to a particular community or class. Both of the large subcontinental communities were perhaps equally victims and perpetrators in acts of brutality.

Adequate descriptions and first-person accounts of the events during partition are now publicly available. One might, therefore, ask: had psychiatric and counselling services been available at the time, would the nature of trauma and emotional distress have been recognised? While it is certainly important to consider what kinds of models of intervention would be considered, if they had been available, it is perhaps also appropriate to start conversations on how a larger awareness of these issues would have influenced subsequent historicity.

Apart from this, we also need to explore the frameworks that mental health professionals would use to assess the impact of political violence and communal conflict, specifically on the recognition, intervention and 'understanding' of the symptoms described by individuals.

OBJECTIVES AND METHODOLOGY

The main objective of this essay is to interrogate the understanding of mental health professionals regarding the psychological aspects of communal conflict. To this end, we attempt to see whether experts read into narratives of communal conflict a mental health issue, whether they think this constitutes mental disorder, and to see what interventions, if any, they would have deemed appropriate. We also hope, by this enquiry, to begin some conversations on how psychological trauma and communal conflict are related.

We developed 15 vignettes (see Appendix 1) from first-person accounts of people who have experienced political violence. The majority of these are abstracted from publicly available first-person accounts (1947 Partition Archive 2013; Butalia 1998) of people from India and Pakistan who experienced partition, and also Indians and Pakistanis in the United States who migrated there afterwards. We also included five first-person accounts from the Hutu–Tutsi riots in Rwanda (Cultures of Resistance 2011; Rwandan Stories 2013), which were characterised by both political and religious violence. We have anonymised these and removed all reference to time, context and geography. Each vignette had four identical questions about the diagnosis, treatment and therapy (both medical treatments and psychotherapy), and did not include any information about the social or political background of the people.

An outline of the proposed study was circulated to a mailing list of psychiatrists and other mental health professionals, comprising around 450 members, asking their willingness to participate. Fifteen practitioners responded, and they were then mailed the full questionnaire including the case vignettes and the queries. Of these, a total of 13 completed the questionnaire.

The enquiry is intended as a first step in constructing a dialogue with mental health professionals to explore thinking about mental health issues around communal strife and political violence. In this essay, we analyse the responses to the questionnaire and discuss these.

RESPONSES AND RESULTS

The respondents were requested to reflect on the following:

1. Whether they would consider a psychiatric diagnosis in a particular case, and if yes, offer one?
2. What sort of intervention would they offer?
3. Would they offer pharmacotherapy (intervention with medication) or psychotherapy (intervention with 'talk therapies'), or a combination?
4. What kind of therapy would be suitable (brief dynamic,

interpersonal, cognitive behaviour therapy [CBT], client-centred or some other)?

We found that the almost all mental health professionals felt the people in the vignettes were suffering from psychological problems and that they required professional help. Nearly 80 per cent said the people were suffering from post-traumatic stress disorder (PTSD). The rest felt that they had adjustment disorder, depression, major depressive disorder and agoraphobia. A few (two) did not feel like giving a diagnosis. The vast majority (90 per cent) felt that a combination of psychotherapy and pharmacotherapy would work best. The others suggested that either only psychotherapy or family therapy would work, or that only pharmacotherapy would work. A few (two) also felt that a specific treatment called eye movement desensitisation and reprocessing (EMDR) and emotional relieving under barbiturate anesthesia should be used (a form of abreaction or catharsis under medication). More than two-thirds of the professionals felt that among therapies, CBT would work best. The rest felt that interpersonal therapy, supportive therapy, EMDR, client-centred and group therapy would work.

DISCUSSION

It is interesting that a majority of mental health professionals saw in these vignettes of trauma, diagnosable and potentially 'treatable' psychiatric disorders. There was near unanimity on this score. Most offered specific interventions. This in itself throws up several questions that we think need to be further explored.

The Recognition of Disorder and the Thinking of Diagnosis

Most of the respondents were of the opinion that the individuals described were suffering from mental health issues that could benefit from intervention. These diagnoses ranged from PTSD to adjustment disorder and depression. In this, they were following current diagnostic trends, as the symptoms and behaviours described, that fall within the ambit of mood and behavioural disorders as defined by diagnostic systems like DSM-5 and ICD-10 (American Psychiatric Association 2013; WHO 2007). However, this raises larger epidemiological questions of the validity of construct and prevalence. These accounts, in themselves, represent a minuscule fraction of those who lived the experience, as do also the number of mental health professionals who responded to the survey. While it may not be methodologically appropriate to extrapolate from these limited numbers, it is quite apparent that the symptoms and idioms of distress were expressed and recognised. Thus, it can be estimated that a significant proportion of those who experienced these events did, and may continue to have, mental health issues.

The fact that trauma caused psychological distress is obvious. It is only when we begin to ask whether this distress, which is the 'understandable' response to trauma, constitutes disorder, that questions begin to emerge. Interlinked with these are the nature, severity and duration of the distress that the trauma causes, as also aspects of the trauma itself. There is some work that seems to differentiate between trauma caused by natural and 'man-made' factors. In a study of individuals 20 years after exposure to political violence, almost half had anxiety symptoms, a third had depressive symptoms, while 20 per cent met the full criteria for PTSD (Eisenman et al. 2003; Sabin et al. 2003). Such long-term sequelae have rarely been investigated in response to 'natural disasters', though persistent effects were noted among tourists (Kraemer et al. 2009) and resident populations up to three years after the tsunami of 2004 and for many years after the Chernobyl disaster. Detailed analyses that compare resilience or coping strategies following these disparate kinds of stress have not been commented upon, although a convergence to cause even greater occurrence of PTSD, following 'man-made' trauma has been noted (Catani et al. 2008).

The second question is about the psychiatric conceptualisation of trauma. It has long been known that the categories of adjustment disorder and PTSD are among the common diagnoses made in psychiatric practice. It has also been recognised that the present diagnostic categorisation of PTSDs is, at best, both limited and preliminary. The World Health Organization's attempt to differentiate between PTSD and a related but distinct category of an enduring personality change after a catastrophic experience (classified as F62.0)—which some of these subjects clearly seem to have described—is a move to understand the nuancing of the different ways in which difficult situations influence people (Maercker 2013). While this may not necessarily be the best platform for a detailed exploration of the concepts of psychiatric diagnoses, it is obvious that the dialogue with social science is an essential ingredient for informing this debate.

A related issue is the trans-generational transmission of the effects of this. Many studies have commented on psychological issues among the children of those who experienced the Holocaust (Portney 2003). We have not specifically addressed this here, but if those estimates were extrapolated to the South Asian situation, where several million went through a traumatic experience, the figures may be quite large. Thus, we feel that the ways in which such events impact our lives – not only in terms of numbers of people, but also how social relations, the processes of psychological myth making and societal stereotyping are affected, needs to be thought about.

Professional Silences

These are issues that mainstream psychiatry seldom addresses. So professional forums and psychiatric publication is largely silent on this. In a sense, this is may be why, despite the invitation to 450 members, 15 evinced interest, and only 13 participated. An interesting question that arises is the possible reasons for these professional silences. Various explanations have been offered.

Is this insensitivity to 'psychological' processes? With the growth of the biomedical gaze in science, it may perhaps be a reason, though when these rather cataclysmic events occurred half a century ago, both biomedical and psychological gazes were perhaps equally important, at least in the developed world. However, the medical profession in India at that point was preoccupied with infective and somatic disease, and social and psychological antecedents of disease and distress were not commonly debated. These issues were not prominent in the wider political discourse either. So this may be part of the explanation for this neglect, although, perhaps, not a sufficient one.

Is this an aspect of the rather inadequately informed 'colonial' mindset that has characterised psychiatric thinking? The inner life of the individual, which is often the subject of scrutiny in contemporary psychology (psychoanalysis, existentialism/humanism, cognitive neuroscience) was not considered relevant to the specific person under colonial rule. Thus, communitarian identities (martial race, tribal, caste, or regional – Arab, Pashtun, Tamil, Bengali – and finally religious identities) were thought sufficient to explain both subjective experiences as well as the overt behaviours of individuals. A shared, common experience of distress and trauma to social events, thus, could not be envisaged. While this remains a possibility, we feel that this is certainly an area that needs to be further explored.

Is this part of a 'psychological blindness'? Psychiatry, while a medical discipline, is the most socially rooted and dependent of all the medical specialties. In India, as also in other parts of the world, the rules under which psychiatry operates have often been identified with political processes. This ranges from the attitudes to the 'African mind', to the neglect of psychotherapy in India (Jain and Sarin 2000), to the actual abuse of psychiatric terminology (Kecmanović 2002; Weine 1999). So it may perhaps not have been only individuals suffering from the consequences of trauma, but, indeed, society. The subsequent silences across the board may be a reflection of this.

The consequences of this inattention could, however, have been quite significant. The non-recognition of the biggest 'elephant in the room (partition-linked violence)' also led to the under-recognition of the traumas and the consequences it engendered in subsequent decades. The spirals of violence that have followed, due to the persistence of ethnicity, religious, linguistic and caste-based politics, were never addressed as causing a definite personal and health impact, which would then need interventions. In any case, health, especially mental health, was never viewed as an organic correlate of social health, and the system could thus afford to ignore the psychological impact of this partitioning of minds and hearts.

Interventions

The third question is that, regardless of diagnostic category, if obvious distress is seen as causally related to traumatic events, what is the best intervention that can be offered? The answer would very likely depend on whom the question is addressed to. It is clear to us that the interventions will have to include measures of rehabilitation and social support, without which psychological intervention becomes meaningless. If, for the purpose of this discussion, we were to focus on mental health interventions, the nature and variability of the interventions offered is itself interesting. Across the board, psychological therapies clearly find a more central place, with a choice between cognitive behaviour therapy, interpersonal therapies and family therapies. These, we feel, probably reflect the individual predilections of the professionals in question. It is also interesting that only a few (medically trained professionals) suggested pharmacotherapy.

There is considerable debate about the nature of interventions. These arise from the observations of differences in rates of PTSD across ethnic groups, and the influence of family and social factors. It has been suggested that the social and psychological consequences of violence be anticipated, especially when there is likely to be community destruction or displacement (Norris 2009). Some authors highlight inherent community coping strategies, while others highlight the provision of services. In the context of partition, the nature of the 'community' was redefined along partisan lines and the services of assistance (medical and social) were dismembered, thus making any help near impossible. These processes, in a sense, continue, with the rather extreme example of accusations of doctors of one community being inimical to the other (Varshney 2001), being potent tinder to escalate violence. The converse, that medical and mental health services are avowedly non-partisan, is neither emphasised nor, apparently, taken for granted.

The fourth question is related to the queries raised by some people to whom the questionnaire was sent. The fact that awareness of the particular events and contexts is necessary for a more complete understanding of individual distress is quite evident.

Thus, an understanding of the individual story, with its sociocultural rootedness, what is called 'pre-morbid' functioning, the nature of the traumatic event, the availability of different forms of support, and the duration of the persisting 'symptom', are probably important. However, there is little in the education and training, or research, in the Indian mental health services that addresses the historical origins, interactions or consequences of political events on psychological health. Attempts to understand the specific nature of each individual event/personal account could thus transmute into a limited 'local' understanding, leaving the larger social (universal) context unaddressed.

In summary, we feel that there is a need to evaluate the psychological aftermath of partition. This would allow us to better understand the nature of the trauma and its consequences, and also encourage debate about the interface between individual mental health (well-being and sense of autonomy) vis-à-vis historical, social and political processes. Psychiatric services, as the primary resource for both help and debate, need to address these issues.

APPENDIX I

Vignettes

Vignette 1

A 45-year old man has a sense of despair, chronic feelings of frustration, anger, hatred and emotional detachment. He saw his best friend being killed, and this moved him to the core. He didn't understand what was happening and why. His family, seeing his condition sent him away to a relative's home, but his symptoms and behaviour only got worse. He began having recurring nightmares and flashbacks. The loss of his friend, and the shift from home, affected him so much that he became emotionally detached from his family.

Vignette 2

A 30-year old man developed symptoms of sadness, feelings of hopelessness and despair. Many members of his family had been killed right in front of him. He and his siblings managed to escape the killings. He expressed emotions of hurt regarding the whole situation. He is constantly reminded of the event and this has made him lose hope. He feels he is useless as he couldn't do anything at the time and feels he will not be able to do anything now.

Vignette 3

A female of 38 years developed symptoms of depression, insomnia and recurrent nightmares. Her home had been ransacked so they moved to a safe place for a while, but were not happy there. She felt like an alien, though they were in a safe place. So the family came back to their earlier home but it was now occupied by another family. Her father filed a case and fought in the court, and got the house back. Now that they were back in their home and she was glad, but kept feeling that she might lose the house again. She used to wake up with the same nightmares everyday.

Vignette 4

A 41-year old man developed symptoms of feelings of despair, loss of self esteem and flashbacks. He had lost his ancestral fertile land and soon after that his father was killed. The subject, though young, had to travel a lot in search of jobs as he has two younger sisters and carried the responsibility of getting them married. He lost faith in his ability; he didn't know how he could manage to get his sisters married. He had to work very hard to manage all these issues throughout his life. He had flashbacks of the past, his happy childhood and wished that it could come back. He didn't want to move on.

Vignette 5

A 32-year old woman developed feelings of sadness, nightmares and difficulty in sleeping. Her home was attacked and the family was forced to take shelter in a different place. Though the new neighbours didn't harm her and her family physically, but they didn't accept them, and treated them as outsiders. Hence she and her family came back to their home but it was completely empty. They had to start afresh. She keeps on reliving the past and gets hurt every time she thinks about it. Her nightmares are mostly of getting attacked again.

Vignette 6

A 37-year old woman became suspicious to the extent of developing paranoia, she had difficulty in emoting and was unable to sleep comfortably. She is a widow living with her son and daughter, and works as a domestic help in the neighbours' homes. She and her family were attacked and to add to her misery a neighbour of hers was shot in front of her. Being witness to this, the family fled to another place. When they lodged a complaint with the police, the police in turn looted them and burnt their house down. They faced many problems in the new place. So they left and came to their old locality only to find it in a horrible condition. Going through so many traumas has made her emotionally numb. She does not know whom to trust.

Vignette 7

A 40-year woman developed symptoms of emotional detachment, paranoia, and feelings of despair. She saw a young girl being burnt alive in front of her house. Seeing this, her family took shelter in a relative's house. She couldn't sleep at all in fear that it would happen to her or her loved ones. Her family eventually settled in a different city but she refused to go with them. She insisted on staying in the same place and since then she has never left her home.

Vignette 8

A 34-year old woman has chronic feelings of suspicion, a fear of the future, feelings of hopelessness and disturbed sleep. Her entire family had been brutally killed, and their home burned down. She managed to escape with her infant son, and found shelter. Her son gradually lost his vision and couldn't work. She is always on the edge as she feels that she will be found and attacked again. She is even scared of the future as she does not know what it holds.

Vignette 9

A 35-year old woman has developed symptoms of depression, paranoia, insomnia, and a sense of hopelessness. She was married at the age of fifteen. She lost her husband very early. But even after losing her husband, she continued to stay with her in- laws. Her father wanted her to remarry but she refused to do so. It later happened that they were attacked and injured and their house was ransacked. They were forced to move to a new place and settle there. She longed to go back to her home but couldn't. This event affected her so much that she always lived in a state of fear that it would happen again. And because of this she never ventured out on her own.

Vignette 10

A 23-year old boy developed symptoms of paranoia, feelings of sadness, and recurring nightmares. His entire family was killed. He somehow managed to escape and took shelter in his neighbour's house. After many months of hiding he left town and stayed with his distant relatives. Though he is continuing his studies now, he is still haunted by memories of that time. He is not able to move on as he feels that it can happen to him anytime anywhere.

Vignette 11

A 35-year old man has developed feelings of guilt, sadness and hopelessness. Hundreds of people, including him, hid in a community centre to avoid getting killed. But unfortunately their hiding place was discovered and many people were brutally killed in front of him. He was hurt but he and seven others survived. He keeps wishing he had died along with his family and friends. He feels guilty for not being able to do anything and has lost interest in living.

Vignette 12

A 28-year old female has developed symptoms of depression, paranoia and she has recurrent flashbacks. She had come home from her hostel for a holiday. Her parents sent her to hide as their relatives and neighbours had been attacked and they wanted her to be safe. She hid in a neighbour's bathroom for almost three months with no contact to the outside world except a radio. When she finally came out, her entire family, relatives, her friends and neighbours had all been killed. She lost everything. She is always on edge, feeling that it is going to happen all over again.

Vignette 13

A 31-year old female developed feelings of guilt and blame and has horrible nightmares. She saw her neighbours being attacked and she knew that her house would be next. So out of fear she ran to her backyard and climbed the tree and hid there. She heard her family members screaming. They brought her family out and burnt them alive. She witnessed the whole thing but couldn't do anything. She blames herself for this. Every night she wakes up with the screams of her family. She can't shut out the screams no matter how hard she tries.

Vignette 14

A 21-year old girl developed symptoms of depression, recurrent nightmares and feelings of despair. She hid in a school along with thousands of people in different classrooms. She knew that she would be killed and she would also have to witness her mother's and sister's killing. So she went to another room where she didn't know anyone. Everyone hiding in all the rooms including hers was brutally killed but somehow they weren't able to find her as she was hiding in a very narrow place. She even had to witness an infant being slaughtered. She is haunted by the memories every time she closes her eyes.

Vignette 15

A 45 -year old man developed feelings of sadness and betrayal, paranoia and had trouble sleeping. He was hiding in his house along with his family and friends. The men of the house fought but were exhausted and defeated. They caught him and smashed his hand and threw him to one side. He was badly hurt but he managed to hide in the bushes. He then witnessed them killing many people, even pregnant women. He also witnessed them smashing children to the walls and killing them. He feels betrayed as the people who were killing were his neighbours and colleagues. He is constantly on the lookout as he feels that his neighbours may strike again. And because of this he hasn't been able to sleep ever since.

REFERENCES

1947 Partition Archive. 2013. http://www.1947partitionarchive.org/ (accessed on 18 May 2014).

Achberger, M., M. Linden and O. Benkert. 1999. 'Psychological Distress and Psychiatric Disorders in Primary Health Care Patients in East and

West Germany 1 Year after the Fall of the Berlin Wall', *Social Psychiatry Psychiatric Epidemiology*, 34(4): 195–201.

American Psychiatric Association. 2013. *Diagnostic and Statistical Manual of Mental Disorders* (5th edition, revised). Washington, DC: Americam Psychiatric Publishing.

Bayntun C. 2005. 'What Are We Capable Of? The Motivations of Perpetrators in South Africa during the Apartheid Era', *Medicine Conflict and Survival*, 21(1): 3–18.

Brass, Paul R. 2003. 'The Partition of India and Retributive Genocide in the Punjab 1946–47: Means, Methods and Purposes', *Journal of Genocide Research*, 5(1): 71–101.

Butalia, U. 1998. *The Other Side of Silence: Voices from the Partition of India.* London: Penguin Books.

Catani, C., N. Jacob, E. Schauer, M. Kohila and F. Neuner. 2008. 'Family Violence, War, and Natural Disasters: A Study of the Effect of Extreme Stress on Children's Mental Health in Sri Lanka', *BioMed Central Psychiatry*, 8: 33.

Cultures of Resistance. 2011. 'The Courage of Neighbors: Stories from the Rwandan Genocide'. http://www.youtube.com/watch?v=VaX7vQxNAOk (accessed on 18 May 2014).

Eisenman, D.P., L. Gelberg, H. Liu and M.F. Shapiro. 2003. 'Mental Health and Health-Related Quality of Life among Adult Latino Primary Care Patients Living in the United States with Previous Exposure to Political Violence', *Journal of American Medical Association*, 290(5): 627–34.

Jain, S. and A. Sarin. 2000. 'Some Reflections on the Development of Psychiatry in India', *National Medical Journal of India*, 13(6): 329–30.

Kamtekar, I. 1995. 'The Military Ingredient of Communal Violence in Punjab, 1947'. Paper presented at the 56th Indian History Congress, *Proceedings of the Indian History Congress*, pp.568–72, [Date], [Place].

Kecmanović, D. 2002. *Ethnic Times: Exploring Ethno Nationalism in the Former Yugoslavia.* Westport, CT: Praeger.

Khwaja, A., A. Mian and P. Bharadwaj. 2008. 'The Big March: Migratory Flows after the Partition of India', *Economic and Political Weekly*, 43(35): 39–49.

Kraemer, B., L. Wittmann, J. Jenewein and U. Schnyder. 2009. '2004 Tsunami: Long-Term Psychological Consequences for Swiss Tourists in the Area at the Time of the Disaster', *Australia and New Zealand Journal of Psychiatry*, 43(5): 420–25.

Kunitz, S.J. 2004. 'The Making and Breaking of Yugoslavia and Its Impact on Health', *American Journal of Public Health*, 94(11): 1894–1904.

Maercker, A., C.R. Brewin, R.A. Bryant, M. Cloitre and M. Van Ommeren, L.M. Jones, A. Humayan, A. Kagee, A.E. Llosa, C. Rousseau, D.J. Somasundaram, Ŕ. Souza, Y. Suzuki, I. Weissbecker, S.C. Wessely, M.B. First and G.M. Reed. 2013. 'Diagnosis and Classification of Disorders Specifically Associated with Stress: Proposals for ICD-11', *World Psychiatry*, 12(3): 198–206.

Norris, F.H. 2009. 'The Impact of Disasters and Political Violence on Mental Health in Latin America', *PTSD Research Quarterly*, 20(4): 1050–1835.

Portney, C. 2003. 'Intergenerational Transmission of Trauma: An Introduction for the Clinician', *Psychiatric Times*, 20(4): 1–3.

Rwandan Stories. 2013. 'Genocide'. http://www.rwandanstories.org/genocide.html (accessed 18 May 2014).

Sabin, M., L. Cardozo B., L. Nackerud, R. Kaiser and L.Varese. 2003. 'Factors Associated with poor Mental Health among Guatemalan Refugees Living in Mexico 20 Years after Civil Conflict', *Journal of American Medical Association*, 290(5): 635–42.

Schick, M., N. Morina, R. Klaghofer, U. Schnyder and J. Müller. 2013. 'Trauma, Mental Health, and Intergenerational Associations in Kosovar Families 11 Years after the War', *European Journal of Psychotraumatology*. http://www.ejpt.net/index.php/ejpt/article/view/21060 (accessed on 18 May 2014).

Sharon, A., I. Levav, J. Brodsky, A.A. Shemesh and R Kohn. 2009. 'Psychiatric Disorders and Other Health Dimensions among Holocaust Survivors 6 Decades Later', *British Journal of Psychiatry*, 195(4): 331–35.

Shone, Terence. 1947. Letter to Secretary of State for Commonwealth Relations, 14 October 1947 (DO 142/259). http://www.nationalarchives.gov.uk/education/topics/evaluating-partition.htm (accessed on 18 May 2014).

Varshney, A. 2001. 'Ethnic Conflict and Civil Society India and Beyond', *World Politics*, 53: 362–98.

Weine, S.M. 1999. *When History Is a Nightmare: Lives and Memoires of Ethnic Cleansing in Bosnia-Herzegovina*. Piscataway, NJ: Rutgers University Press.

World Health Organization. 2007. *The ICD-10 Classification of Mental and Behavioural Disorders* (Indian edition). Delhi: AITBS.

Notes on Contributors

SIDDIQ WAHID has been Vice Chancellor of the Islamic University of Science and Technology in Jammu and Kashmir and Maharaja Gulab Singh Chair Professor at the University of Jammu. He has taught at Harvard University in the department of Inner Asian and Altaic Studies. His fields of interest include contemporary Islam, political philosophy and Central Asian history. Wahid is also Director of J&K Muslim Waqf Board and is on the governing board (senate) of the National Institute of Technology, Srinagar. He is a founding member of India Forum and a member of the board of directors of Panos India. A political activist involved in the process of resolution of the Jammu and Kashmir question, he is the author of *Ladakh Between Earth and Sky* and has been published widely in anthologies on literature, politics and history. He is currently working on a translation of the epic of *Kesar*.

RITA KOTHARI is an author, translator and academic. Her research and pedagogy span across literature, sociology and cultural studies. Her books include *Memories and Movements: Borders and Communities in Banni, Kutch, Gujarat* (2013); *The Burden of Refuge: Sindhi Hindus of Gujarat* (2007); and *Translating India: The Cultural Politics of English* (2003). She has translated *Angaliyat: The Stepchild* (2004); *Unbordered Memories: Partition Stories from Sindh* (2009); *Speech and Silence: Literary Journeys by Gujarati Women* (2006) and is the co-translator of *Modern Gujarati Poetry: A Selection* (1998) and *Coral Island: The Poetry of Niranjan Bhagat* (2003). She has co-edited *Decentering Translation Studies: India and Beyond* (2009), and *Chutnefying English: The Phenomenon of Hinglish*

(2011). Several of her essays on issues of linguistic identity, identity politics in Gujarat, hybridity in language, and translation studies have been published in books and refereed journals. Professor Kothari is with the Humanities and Social Sciences department, Indian Institute of Technology, Gandhinagar.

KAVITA PANJABI is Professor of Comparative Literature and Co-ordinator of the Centre for Studies in Latin American Literatures and Cultures at Jadavpur University. She has edited *Poetics and Politics of Sufism and Bhakti in South Asia: Love, Loss and Liberation* (2011); co-edited *Women Contesting Culture: Changing Frames of Gender Politics in India* (2012), and *Cartographies of Affect: Across Borders in South Asia and the Americas* (2011). She is also the editor of *Jadavpur Journal of Comparative Literature.* Active in the women's movement for over two decades, she has been a member of the Pakistan India People's Forum for Peace and Democracy since 1997and authored *A Pakistan Diary, Old Maps and New: Legacies of the Partition* (2005). Her oral history of the Tebhaga Women's Movement in Bengal is forthcoming with Zubaan.

VISHWAJYOTI GHOSH diligently pursues his interest in comics, illustrations, art and films. His comics are regularly published in various journals and anthologies, both in India and abroad. His most recently published work includes contributions in two international anthologies, When *Kulbhushan Met Stockli* and *Ctrl.Alt.Shift Unmasks Corruption.* Vishwajyoti was also the author of 'Backlog', a comics column in *The Little Magazine*, and currently writes a column, 'Acid Test', in *Down to Earth.* His first graphic novel *Delhi Calm* received much critical acclaim. He has recently curated a collection of graphic stories about Partition entitled *This Side, That Side* (2013).

AMIYA SEN is a Bengali novelist and short story writer whose works have been published in various Bengali journals, including *Desh, Jugantar* and *Basumati.* She engaged with the world of migrants and refugees through most of her writings. Apart from her non-fiction books, *Aranyalipi* and *New Delhi-r Nepathye*, she also wrote *Shonai Shono Rupkatha*, a children's book and a memoir of her childhood engagement with the Indian freedom movement.

Sanjib Baruah is Professor of Political Studies at Bard College, Annandale-on-Hudson, New York, where he teaches comparative politics and international relations. He is also Honorary Research Professor, Centre for Policy Research, New Delhi. Baruah was born in Shillong in northeast India and was educated in Cotton College in Guwahati, Assam, the University of Delhi and the University of Chicago.

Jhuma Sen is Assistant Professor and Assistant Director of Centre for Human Rights Studies at Jindal Global Law School. She obtained her undergraduate degree in law from Symbiosis Law School, Pune, and her Masters of Law (LL.M concentrating on international law and human rights and jurisprudence and legal theory) from Boalt Hall (School of Law), University of California at Berkeley. The American Association of University Women granted her their international fellowship to read for an LL.M degree at Berkeley. Sen has worked as a legal researcher with Amnesty International, India, and as a consultant with Lawyers Collective (Women's Rights Initiative) before joining the Office of the Additional Solicitor General of India, Ms. Indira Jaising, as an associate. She has also been a Central Government Panel Counsel in the Supreme Court of India appearing on behalf of various government departments and representing the Union of India in several matters. She has also been associated in the chambers of senior advocate Dr Rajeev Dhavan. Sen has several years of experience in conducting legal literacy workshops and trainings on gender and law. Her primary areas of scholarship and research are constitutional law theory, gender and law, Third World approach to international law, and postcolonial theory and law. She has been Visiting Fellow at the Faculty of Law, National University of Singapore and Erik Castrén Institute of International Law and Human Rights, Faculty of Law, University of Helsinki.

Andrew Whitehead is the author of *A Mission in Kashmir* (2007), an account of the initial stages of the Kashmir conflict in 1947 based primarily on the testimonies of those who lived through the events of that year. His wider archive of interviews with several hundred people across South Asia about their experiences of Partition is deposited at the School of Oriental and African Studies at the University of London. Whitehead is an editor of *History Workshop Journal* and works as a news journalist. His personal website is at http://www.andrewwhitehead.net/

SUKESHI KAMRA teaches courses in South Asian literatures and cultures in the English department at Carleton University, Ottawa, Canada. In recent years, she has developed an interest in the culture of proscription that emerged in British India in the late-nineteenth and early-twentieth centuries, a subject on which she has published a monograph entitled 'The Indian Periodical Press and the Production of Nationalist Rhetoric'(2011). She has written several articles and also published a book on the 1947 partition of India.

TARUN K. SAINT is Associate Professor and teaches English literature at Hindu College, Delhi University. His research interest is in the area of the literature of Partition. He has edited *Bruised Memories: Communal Violence and the Writer* (2002), co-edited *Translating Partition* (with Ravikant, 2001) and authored *Witnessing Partition: Memory, History, Fiction* (2010).

PRAJNA PARAMITA PARASHER is a filmmaker/scholar and multimedia artist practising at the shifting intersection of classical thought and new technologies. Born in the foothills of the Himalayas, she began her education as a filmmaker in Paris and went on to earn a Ph.D at Northwestern University. Currently she holds the posts of Professor of Art, Film and Cultural Studies, Chair of the Arts, Design and Communication department and Program Director of the Film and Digital Technology program at Chatham University. Her personal focus on postcolonial studies comes to realization in several forms –films, 2-D art, installations and scholarly writing. Her creative work is experimental and has been shown across the country in venues from small towns to the Smithsonian Institution; Carnegie Museum; Brooklyn Museum; The Nehru Center, London; The Tagore Center, Berlin; and the San Francisco Cinematheque. Already part of the canon at major American universities, her films are used in ethnic, diaspora, cultural and women's studies. She has received recognition via multiple fellowships, awards and grants in postcolonial and critical theory, film history and theory, new media and gaming.

JYOTIRMAYA SHARMA is Professor of Political Science at the University of Hyderabad. He has been Fellow at Swedish Collegium for Advanced Study and Lichtenberg-Kolleg at Georg-August-Universität in Göttingen, Germany. He is also a member of the Scientific Advisory Council of the French Network of Institutes for Advanced Study, RFIEA, since 2013. His recent publications include *Cosmic Love and Human Apathy: Swami Vivekananda and the Restatement of Religion* (2013), *A Restatement of Religion: Swami Vivekananda and the Making of Hindu Nationalism* (2013), *Hindutva: Exploring the Idea of Hindu Nationalism* (2003/2011)(also translated into three other Indian languages), *Terrifying Vision: M.S. Golwalkar, the RSS and India* (2007) (also translated into Malayalam), and a co-edited volume *Grounding Morality: Freedom, Knowledge and the Plurality of Cultures* (2010). He has been a fellow at the Centre for the Study of Developing Societies and Indian Institute of Advanced Study, and has lectured at the universities of Baroda, Hull, Oxford, and St. Stephens College, Delhi. He was Visiting Professor in democratic theory at the South Asia Institute at Ruprecht-Karls University at Heidelberg in 2005, and Asia Leadership Fellow with the International House of Japan. Sharma also held senior editorial positions at the *Times of India* and *The Hindu* between 1998-2006, and continues to write columns for *Hindustan Times* and *Outlook*.

ALOK SARIN, M.B.B.S, & M.D. (Psychiatry), is a practising clinical psychiatrist with an active interest in medicine, psychiatry, ethics, society, history and literature. He practises at the Sitaram Bhartia Institute of Science and Research, New Delhi, and is a former Senior Fellow of the Nehru Memorial Museum and Library, New Delhi.

SANJEEV JAIN is a professor of psychiatry at the National Institute of Mental Health and Neurosciences, Bangalore, and an adjunct faculty at National Centre for Biological Sciences (TIFR). His research interests include exploring the genetic and cellular basis of psychiatric and neurological diseases. His current work includes modeling brain disorders (dementia, psychoses) in cell-based systems, as also epigenetics in addictions and psychoses. His historical and social research involves documenting the history of mental health services in India, from the colonial to the contemporary period, with a focus on the diagnoses, asylum practice, community responses and socio-political influences on ideas about individuals and society in order to understand the interface between science, medicine and social responses to mental illness in India.

SARAH GHANI is an M.Sc in Clinical Psychology, and is currently working on a Ph.D in the history of Psychiatry at the National Institute of Mental Health and Neurosciences, Bangalore. Her research interests include documenting socio-demographic data and studying the pattern of clinical services at NIMHANS in the late nineteenth century and the twentieth century.